Education:
Straitjacket or Opportunity?

Education:
Straitjacket or Opportunity?

Edited by

James Benét

Arlene Kaplan Daniels

Transaction Books
New Brunswick, New Jersey

Library of Congress Catalog Number: 79:65129
ISBN: 0-87855-298-7 (cloth)
Printed in the United States of America

Library of Congress Cataloging in Publication Data

Main entry under title:

Education, opportunity or straitjacket?

    Reprinted from Social problems, vol. 24, no. 2, 1976.
    Bibliography: p.
    1. Educational equalization. 2. Home and school. 3. Education, Bilingual. I. Benet, James. II. Daniels, Arlene Kaplan, 1930-
LC213.E38   1979   370.19   79-65129
ISBN: 0-87855-298-7

CONTENTS

SCHOOL DESEGREGATION

Education: Straitjacket or Opportunity?

INTRODUCTION*

JAMES BENÉT
University of California
Berkeley

and

ARLENE KAPLAN DANIELS
Northwestern University

A new and major theme is emerging in current discussion of education. From Jencks' *Inequality* to Coleman's recent and controversial pronouncements on desegregation orders and "white flight" from central cities, we hear the theme, put bluntly, whether educational reform can work. The papers in this book all consider this theme. The recent work providing the most insights into the nature of contemporary education comes from radical theorists exploring new areas for research previously undiscussed. Levin is a leader in this movement; his paper, in the first section, extends analysis formerly confined to the United States to discussion of Western Europe school systems. Patterson elaborates on this discussion in her analysis of higher education in France. Squires presents data from the U.S. supporting the general pattern found by Levin and Patterson in their papers on education and class in Western Europe: the spread of educational opportunities has not created the degree of social mobility predicted earlier—neither abroad nor in the United States.

The second set of papers takes us from considering the overall system into the classroom, and the perceptions of individuals—students, teachers, families. The Schwendingers argue, like Levin, that the structure of our economic system produces not only socialized workers and citizens but also a group of marginals corresponding to the marginal group in the labor force. The following two papers show how this production of marginal workers—and the production or workers for lower class and middle class jobs as well—can actually proceed. The authors of these papers explain the processes of social control and channeling of students at the individual school and classroom level. Through

---

*We should like to express our thanks to the National Institute of Education which, through auspices of the Education Equity Group under contract number P-76-0101 made this special issue of *Social Problems* possible. We are particularly grateful to Dr. Ray Rist who, in his capacity as former Associate Director at N.I.E. negotiated this special issue for us. As is always the case with a special issue, we have been dependent upon our regular associate editors and the wider range of referees who always give so generously of their time and effort. In this case we are especially grateful to the following outside advisors-referees-consultants who helped find potential contributors as well as choose the final selections from this pool:

Herbert Aurbach
Sarane Boocock
Remi Clignet
Peter Conrad
Ronald Corwin
Paul DiMaggio
Kevin Dougherty
Elizabeth Eddy
Sethard Fisher
Edgar Z. Friedenberg

Peter Garabedian
Paula Goldsmid
Peter Hall
Joseph Kirschner
Edith Kurzweil
Sarah Lawrence Lightfoot
Helen Miller
Michael Otten
Caroline Persell
Wilson Record

Stephen Richer
Philip Ross
George Rothbart
Lillian Rubin
William Spady
Ralph Turner
Michael Useem
Murray Wax
Robert Wegmann
David T. Wellman

observation and interview, Wittig shows how school authorities manipulate students and their parents to prevent external interference with bureaucratic judgments about pupil processing, Wilcox and Moriarity show how daily teacher-pupil interactions are sensitively tuned to the task of socializing middle and working class children for different stations in adult life. Finally, Swidler's paper describes the result of a recent effort at reform, the free school, to mitigate the stratifying and oppressive effects of the traditional classroom.

But the contemporary structure of school systems is not their only problem. One that increasingly besets the school is that of large numbers of children whose native language is not English. Our third set of papers, then, focuses on bilingualism, even though most current efforts to cope with it hardly merit the label of a full-grown concern with a social problem. Verdet shows, through her careful observation of Haitian children in New England, how complex and difficult the problem is, even for people of good will. Lopez reports a pioneering study of Spanish-speaking children, showing that the social stigma imposed by use of a second language stems from its association with the poorest and least educated group in the system.

Although the foregoing writers believe that profound structural changes in society are needed before school reform can succeed, for more than a decade the federal government has tried to improve American education with financial aid to desired programs. In our fourth set of papers, Donicht and Everhart show how federal aid can be subverted to the needs of a local school system. Fry and Miller show the unfortunate consequences of this subversion for program, school and students. Nevertheless, hope for school reform is not entirely extinguished. Havighurst proposes how, in contrast to past federal programs, problems of inner city schools might be solved by adopting a different pedagogical strategy based on advocacy of equal outcomes.

The resistance of educational structures to deep reform is illuminated in our final section by the paper of Platt et al., arguing that faculty teaching goals are unchanged since 1968 despite the educational uproar and consequent professions of determination to make important reforms. Lewis and Ryan, analyzing the concerns expressed over the years by the leaders of the principal professional association, suggest that members of the professoriate don't really put the actual process of education at the forefront of their interests anyway. These last papers raise the question of whether even the structural changes in society advocated by others in this volume could change the nature of the faculty.

The potential for change is discussed by Rhodes. He evaluates future possibilities of faculty organization on the basis of current trends in collective bargaining agreements. These trends suggest how duties and conditions of employment will change, how professors will be evaluated and how the effects of evaluation will structure teaching and research.

In our final section we present one more study engendered by the controversy over court-ordered desegregation and busing. That controversy has already generated so much discussion and analysis that we felt we should limit its attention here. In the final section, Levine and Meyer add yet another log to the fire fuelled by the "white flight" controversy in their analysis of Missouri public school data. These authors show the social policy implications for their description of how white enrollment declines when black students appear in large numbers.

While economists and others in social planning and policy have been concerned about the crisis of financial support and its significance for the public schools, sociologists have not really begun to study what might well fall within their purview: What does this crisis tell us about the relation of public school systems to their communities? What will people pay to educate the proletariat? Political scientists like Carnoy and Levin (1976) have shown that all efforts to reduce inequalities through special programs generally benefit the "haves" far more than the "have nots." Yet even these minor and relatively unsuccessful efforts at reform are resisted in the general trend toward cutbacks in education. Idealists who believe in the viability of the American dream would call this trend a temporary aberration of a conservative administration. They think that with better times—and progressive, liberal leaders—we will get back on the track with the best education. The Carnegie Commission (1973) concluded that in the future higher education will demonstrate its former willingness to accept continuing reform and perhaps play an even greater part than formerly in helping shape society. But sociologists might profitably focus on elementary and secondary schools where problems are clearly community-oriented. There are few studies to build upon (or even match) Rubin's (1972) analysis of the relation of the community to the school system. Why (or when) does a community permit schools to close or deteriorate? For the not uncommon practice of shutting down school systems upon failure of school tax measures is becoming a national public crisis. Lawyers have done the most research on this issue to date. Coons et al (1970) have argued that wide disparities in school revenues arising from the local property tax system are unconstitutional and this argument was adopted by the California Supreme Court in *Serrano vs. Priest*. But certainly sociologists should bring their perspective to bear on the problem. They should analyse what has gone wrong in the implicit contract between the electorate and the school system. For example, they might investigate the public acceptance of "hidden" tax breaks for business while resisting school taxes—out in the open—and subject to public decision.

What interest groups and community leaders participate in the discussion leading to these consequences? In what kinds of communities can strong support for the public school system still be found? How are attitudes formed and strengthened within various segments of the community, whatever the outcome? Is there a trend toward mass media support of the most conservative community elements against adequate taxes for the school systems? How can we explain the change from 30 to 40 years ago when we built schools to show our pride in them, emphasizing their symbolic meaning by constructing them like temples or palaces? Now the trend is toward temporary relocatable buildings. What has caused the shift? What has changed from the time Lincoln signed the act creating land grant colleges to now, when a California governer peevishly compares professors with mandarins?

The growth of explicit conflict between teachers and administration (representing bureaucratic controls) has been one element contributing to the furor in public education and, possibly, to the disaffection of the public. Sociologists should seriously examine the complaint from teachers that even in the face of tax cuts and shrinking budgets big city bureaucracies continue to increase administrative staff while burdening teachers with increasing class size and wiping out special programs—with special teachers. How do middle-sized cities manage? Are they more successful at solving these problems and evading conflict? If so, what is it about the big systems that stimulate bureacratic proliferation, and can it be altered and controlled?

One attempt to circumvent various antagonisms to the public school system has been to try decentralization of the educational bureaucracy. The paradox of this popular reform is that increasing involvement and authority for community spokespersons can only be attained at the price of threatening teachers' competence and control of the educational turf. Some educators have believed that greater decision-making powers and more on-site authority for principals to share with parents might resolve problems with the schools. But we have no systematic evidence about what consequences this process can have. In California, the possibility of reforming schools by state laws has been discussed at the governor's level (Reeves, 1975). Yet a solid body of evidence to support a social policy for moving authority away from the superintendent to the individual school is lacking.

Teachers, in their efforts to protect their "turf" from the incursions of parents and administrators while fighting for wage and fringe benefits, have increasingly turned to trade unionism. This issue has been a great concern for educators, union officials, and lawyers. Most concern has been directed to the case of New York City. And, of course, the question of unionization also attracts the attention of sociologists of work. But the relation of unionization to the substance of education has received relatively little serious attention (discounting the ideologues for and against unionization who make the plight of the student their rallying cry). Obviously, teachers will be less biddable to administrators with their own axes to grind. (Teachers will, for example, no longer have to tolerate principals who use communication system hook ups into individual classrooms to blast out messages about schedule changes or lunch room tickets at any time during the teaching period without concern for the inevitable disruption of the lesson.) Yet it is undeniable that a content analysis of union demands and grievances throughout this country would find more attention to traditional "pork chop" issues than to improving the substance and process of education. Any systematic analysis of the political and social effects of teacher unionization, then, should examine the consequences of the particular "mix" of educational and professional aggrandizement issues for the educational process.

The concerns of radical theorists, which dominate in this book, focus on the relation of the education system to society. This interest seems to be displacing an earlier focus on the content of teaching—the substance of what is taught and its relationship to the society's explicit norms. In this issue, only Havighurst focuses on issues of pedagogy—illustrating, we believe, a concern that has become unfashionable. But it is not for that reason unimportant.

Another "unfashionable" issue—or at least one given little atteniton by sociologists—involves achievement tests and scores. Psychologists and educationists have developed measures and argued about their validity and reliability. Currently, the meaning of test scores is hotly debated by those who find hidden racism or sexism in the construction and in evaluation of results, and by others who contend they show education is in decline. Yet, our discipline has not yet undertaken much systematic study of what achievement tests mean, what they measure; nor have sociologists given enough attention to the more significant questions of what do people *think* these tests measure or *want* them to measure. These questions must be considered within the context of changing attitudes toward sex- and ethnic-related differences, changing attitudes about the relation between aptitudes and learned abilities. And all of these questions must be examined within the larger social problems issue of whether American schooling is declining or improving, whether test results could or should be used in reviewing this issue.

These issues are important for sociologists to consider because the data collected about them are clearly important for the construction of social policies in education. However, since the issues have already bee discussed—and argued over—by specialists (in education, anthropology, psychology) and idealogues (racists and social determinists of various persuasions; civil libertarians and militant egalitarians, cultural pluralists and militant feminists and spokespersons for various minority and ethnic groups), it is difficult to review and assess all the past argument without losing focus on the context suggested here. Fortunately, there are new areas for study as well. As the federal government has continued to make educational social policy through administrative rulings in addition to laws, sociologists always have new opportunities to study how new enactments actually affect the fabric of social life. In education, for example, the Title IX regulations (making discrimination by sex or age illegal in all federally supported eduation systems) have the potentiality for changing the style and content of education at all levels and for all ages of students. Sociologists should study how patterns of athletics and organized sports change—as well as how they resist changes—in response to this regulation requiring equality of opportunity and facilities in sports for boys and girls, men and women. What will happen to the educational curriculum after systematic efforts to expunge racism and sexism for all its aspects? How will the behavior (even more important than expressed attitudes) of students change, or will it? Can changes in individual and group behavior patterns be initiated by school endeavors? Or, as the radical theorists would insist, will significant changes only arise after drastic reorganization of all other social institutions?

A more general concern involves a systematic study of the curriculum. What Benson Snyder (1971) has called the "emotional and social surround of the formal curriculum" should be studied to help us grasp what is in fact happening in our schools. For example, how are students prepared for citizenship by the way their schools are administered? How does the behavior of teachers and principals accord with what the textbooks say about American history and government? And how do textbook descriptions tally with the student's own experience in the big high schools of any central city? Psychiatrists like Robert Coles (1967, 1972 a,b) have considered this question in interviews of younger children—both black and white, privileged and deprived, rural and urban, southern and northern. Where are the sociological studies to add to our knowledge of the "fit" between formal education and informal education (or experience in the world)?

For sociologists to answer such questions, they will have to take a "social system" approach seriously. Neither micro nor macro analyses will provide answers to such questions independently of one another. Nor can specialists in the study of the community power structure manage without information from observers of the educational department bureaucracy and researchers on the politics of professional organizations and unions in teaching and administration. It may even be necessary for sociologists to look beyond their own professional turf, in work with economists, educationists, journalists, political scientists, psychologists and social policy analysts in order to understand the play between individual aspirations and interconnecting social systems and institutions in the development of the growing exasperation with (or indifference to) the schooling question. But only such understanding, we would suggest, can enable our colleagues at last to answer our thematic question, whether educational reform can work.

REFERENCES

Carnegie Commission on Higher Education
   1973 "The purposes and the performance of higher education in the United States." Berkeley: Carnegie Commission.
Carnoy, Martin and Henry M. Levin
   1976 The Limits of Education Reform. New York: David McKay Co., Inc.

Coles, Robert
    1972a Children of Crisis. Vol. 3: The South Goes North. Boston: Atlantic, Little, Brown.
    1972b Children of Crisis. Vol. 2: Migrants, Mountaineers and Sharecroppers. Boston: Atlantic, Little, Brown.
    1967 Children of Crisis. Vol. 1: A Study of Fear and Courage. Boston: Atlantic, Little, Brown.
Coons, John E., William H. Clune, III, Stephen D. Sugarman
    1970 Private Wealth and Public Education. Cambridge: Harvard University Press.
Reeves, Richard
    1975 "How does the governor of California differ from a shoemaker? New York Times Magazine August 24, 1975.
Rubin, Lillian
    1972 Busing and Backlash. University of California Press.
Snyder, Benson
    1971 The Hidden Curriculum. New York: Alfred A. Knopf, Inc.

EDUCATIONAL OPPORTUNITY AND SOCIAL INEQUALITY IN WESTERN EUROPE *

HENRY M. LEVIN
Stanford Univeristy
and
Center for Economic Studies

The existence of equality of educational opportunity is assessed according to four standards: (1) equality of educational access; (2) equality of educational participation; (3) equality of educational results; and (4) equality of educational effects on life chances. By all of these criteria it appears that the educational systems of Western Europe fail to provide a significant equalizing influence, and that to a large degree the educational treatments and results for western European youth tend to mirror their initial social class origins and sex differences in favoring students from more advantaged families and males. It is argued that the interpretation of this pattern can best be understood by considering the dual role of schooling in preparing wage-labor for the systems of monopoly-capitalist and state work enterprise as well as in representing a vehicle for social mobility and sustaining an ideology that such mobility is possible. The combination of prodigious educational expansion in conjunction with a reduction in the postwar rate of economic growth has created a crisis of an educated and underemployed proletariat. The magnitude of this crisis is engendering interventions by both the state and capitalist employers to mediate the contradiction by altering both educational and work patterns. The effectiveness or failure of these interventions to resolve the contradiction will have a profound impact on the nature and magnitude of inequality within both the schools and the larger society in Western Europe.

I—INTRODUCTION

The role of education in creating a just and productive society is very much a topic of controversy today. On the one side are those who see the educational system as that institution of modern society which develops, sorts, and selects persons according to their productive proficiencies to fill the hierarchical positions of modern, large-scale bureaucratic organizations in a rational and meritocratic manner (Inkeles, 1975; Bell, 1973). These spokesmen also believe that the schools are the most important socialization influence in preparing people for modern institutions, generally (Inkeles and Smith, 1974). On the other side are those who see the schools as agencies for reproducing the social relations of production for monopoly capitalism and its supportive state structures (Bowles and Gintis, 1976; Althusser, 1971:127-186). In their view the schools serve the role of preparing wage-labor for capitalist enterprise with its attendant needs for docile and disciplined workers who are socialized and certified for particular places in the work hierarchy with an awareness only of their individual relations to the enterprise rather than of solidarity with other workers as a class.

Both groups probably agree with the description by Bowles (1973:352):

*This paper is a shortened version of "Equal Educational Opportunity in Western Europe: A Contradictory Relation," presented at the Annual Meetings of the American Political Science Association, Chicago, September 1976. The author is presently a Fellow at the Center for Advanced Study in the Behavioral Sciences. Research support for his work in Western Europe was received from the Spencer Foundation under its grant to Stanford University on "Education and the Distribution of Income" and from the National Institute of Education under its grant to the Center for Economic Studies on "The Educational Requirements for Industrial Democracy."

> The school is a bureaucratic order with hierarchical authority, rule-orientation, stratification of 'ability' (tracking) as well as by age, role differentiation by sex (physical education, home economics, shop) and a system of external incentives (marks, promise of promotion and threat of failure) much like pay and status in the sphere of work.

But the former group interpret this function of the schools as necessary for preparing the young for modern, large-scale production and its technological relations, while the latter group views this preparation as an essential ingredient for the domination of capitalist enterprise over a fragmented work force socialized to work in behalf of profits and capital accumulation for a ruling class while remaining unaware of the inherent exploitation as well as its own potential class power in overthrowing the process (Bowles and Gintis, 1976). While other important versions of the role of the school exist (Jencks, 1972; Illich, 1970), the poles of the present debate are represented by the functionalists who see schooling as the essential institution for preparing competent members of a modern, rational, efficient, and meritocratic society and the Marxists who see schooling as one of the most important instruments of the state for supporting the capitalist hegemony over the worker.

It is very clear that the popular rhetoric and ideology of modern governments in the United States, Western Europe, and much of the rest of the world is predominantly sympathetic with the meritocratic vision. Throughout the world constitutions, laws, and declarations of human rights declare a national commitment to equality of opportunity, and invariably this notion is further reduced to equality of educational opportunity. To the degree that philosophers are cited on the relation between education and equal opportunity, they are the ubiquitous and optimistic quotes of persons such as Horace Mann (Cremin, 1957) and John Dewey (1916) rather than those who saw education as a means of creating a modern, industrially based set of inequalities to replace the traditional unequal, social structure. Typically, a discussion of equality of opportunity begins with the quote by Mann: "Education . . . prevents being poor (A. Mann, 1968:13)". But just to remind us that not all visions of the role of schools were ones of equality, it is useful to cite T. Malthus and his argument for a national system of schooling (in his famous essay On Population, written in 1798) that would explain to the poor their condition:

> Among the poor themselves, its effects would be still more important. That the principal and most permanent cause of poverty has little or no *direct* relation to forms of government, or the unequal division of property; and that, as the rich do not in reality possess the *power* of finding employment and maintenance for the poor, the poor cannot, in the nature of things, possess the *right* to demand them; are important truths flowing from the principle of population, which, when properly explained, would by no means be above the most ordinary comprehensions. And it is evident that every man in the lower classes of society who became acquainted with these truths, would be disposed to bear the distresses in which he might be involved with more patience; would feel less discontent and irritation at the government and the higher classes of society, on account of his poverty; and would be on all occasions less disposed to insubordination and turbulence; and if he received assistance, either from any public institution or from the hand of private charity, he would receive it with more thankfulness, and more justly appreciate its value (emphasis in original, T. R. Malthus, 1960: 590-592).

That the words of Malthus on the purposes for advocating a national system of education have all but been forgotten and those of Horace Mann and John Dewey are cited again and again might very well be a "wish-fulfillment" on our part for it is certainly more comforting for us to think of schools as the agents of justice and development of human potential than as agents for preparing the young for the inequalities of the productive structure and of life itself. In this paper I review the equality of educational opportunity perspective for Western Europe. In principle, this is a formidable task which should occupy several volumes. First, the meaning of the term equality of educational opportunity requires both philosophical and operational analysis. Second, the collection and analysis of data for some twenty countries is a herculean undertaking in itself. Finally, the interpretation of data necessitates an extensive discussion of competing hypotheses on the relations between the distribution of educational attainments and the distributions of income and other outcomes as well as an effective integration of this discussion with the data analysis.

The goals of this paper are far more modest. First, I suggest some standards for considering equality of educational opportunity. Second, I assess what existing data tell us about the attainment of these standards. Finally, I summarize the findings and their consequences. Although summarizing a complex phenomenon for a large number of countries rather than concentrating on a single nation in much greater detail presents difficulties, we are also aided by the extensive work on this subject of T. Husen (1972, 1974 and 1975), Boudon (1973), Anderson (1961), Bourdieu (1966), Glass (1954), and Miller (1960 and 1975) as well as the very substantial data resources of the Organization for European Cooperation and Development (OECD) and its recent two volume work on *Education, Inequality and Life Chances* (1975b).

II–STANDARDS AND MEASURES FOR ASSESSING EQUALITY OF EDUCATIONAL OPPORTUNITY

One of the major reasons for so much disagreement and misunderstanding about whether equality of educational opportunity exists or is improving or deteriorating is the fact that many different tacit standards are imposed on the use of this equality criterion.[1] In general, there have been four classes of criteria that have been used to examine this issue: (1) equal access to the educational system; (2) equal participation in the educational system; (3) equal educational results; and (4) equal educational effects on life chances. Coleman (1968) has argued that the different interpretations have risen as a result of historical evolution where initially the focus was only on the preparation of persons to have opportunities in the expanding industrial or modern sector of the society; but the failure of this standard to provide more equal results by race and social class has created a progressive legal and social transformation of the standard toward equality of life outcomes.

An important assumption underlies all these criteria. They presume that relatively large inequalities in capitalist societies are inevitable by the nature of production with its emphasis on the hierarchical division of labor as well as by the requirements for attracting scarce talent into their most socially productive endeavors. As one of the leading spokesmen for the so-called economic liberal view has asserted: " . . . a capitalist system involving payment in accordance with product can be, and in practice is, characterized by considerable inequality of income and wealth (Friedman 1962:168). The issue of equality of educational opportunity is then based upon how far the educational system can develop and identify talents to be allocated to the productive hierarchy through a system of labor markets where workers will receive a reward commensurate with their contribution to output. Of course, this view rests upon a nineteenth century version of laissez-faire capitalism where the competition of the marketplace prevails, and it ignores the historic tendency towards monopoly capitalism where relatively few economic entities dominate the markets for products, services, and

---

[1] Of course, even when the same standards and data are used, there appear to be strong ideological factors dominating the interpretation of whether there is a high or low degree of equality of opportunity and what is the appropriate method of analysis. Compare, for example, the commentaries of S.M. Lipset (1972) and S.M. Miller (1975) on the former issue and R. Hauser (1976) and R. Boudon (1976) on the latter one.

purchase of factors of production with the tacit or explicit support of the State (Baran and Sweezy, 1966; Edwards, Reich, and Weisskopf, 1972; Poulantzas, 1973).

So, equality of educational opportunity is viewed essentially as a version of social mobility where the educational system will keep access open to positions in the productive hierarchy by assuring that all talent will be developed, identified, and allocated according to merit rather than criteria of social origin, sex, race, or other "irrational" bases. As a result, none of the different definitions of equality of educational opportunity are premised on eliminating inequalities, although some suggest a reduction in inequalities as the productivities of persons at the lower end of the spectrum are raised more than those at the upper. Instead the concept of equality of educational opportunity in a capitalist society refers to reducing or eliminating the connection between the social circumstances of birth and those of adulthood by making access to the existing inequalities a strict function of merit rather than social status or family ties (Miller, 1975). Of course, such a goal must necessarily assume that merit is not intrinsically a function of class or social origin as suggested by some of the recent literature on the "hereditary meritocracy," of IQ (Young, 1958; Jensen, 1969; Hernnstein, 1963). In this context, both the heritability and productive significance of such measures as IQ have been strongly challenged (Kamin, 1974; Bowles and Gintis, 1976: Chap. 4). But, virtually all views have presumed that equality of educational opportunity is attained when representative members of different races, sexes, and social origins have the same choice of occupational positions, work roles, incomes, and other adult alternatives.

(1) *Equal Access to the Educational System*

The simplest standard of equal educational opportunity involves equality of access to the educational system. Coleman (1968:11) has suggested this notion rests on:

> providing a free education up to a given level which constituted the principal entry point to the labor force; providing a common curriculum for all children, regardless of background; and providing that children from diverse backgrounds attend the *same school*.

Presumably, the principal of equal access is satisfied through the provision of similar educational facilities for all students at least up to the age of labor market entry. At that age further participation would depend on previous performance as well as occupational intent. Thus, even if the higher levels of education were more restrictive, they could still be equally accessible to students with similar academic performances and intentions. Of course, such a standard presumes no social class-related factors to inhibit the performance of students from lower-class origins or prevent such children from taking advantage of educational offerings.

In examining the standard of equal access to education, it is important to note the structure of Western European education. Bearing in mind the dangers in generalizing for some twenty countries, it is still accurate to describe virtually all of the countries operating what Husen (1975:109-112) has called a "dual system" consisting of a public and free system of primary education for all children up to age 12-14 or so and a selective system of secondary schools to prepare students who continued for lower level careers among vocational schools or for entrance to the university for the academic ones (gymnasium or lycee). Of course, a large number of students have not continued beyond the compulsory schooling period. In recent years there have been attempts to provide comprehensive secondary schools that would encompass both vocational and academic studies as well as to increase the mandatory period of attendance to provide some secondary schooling for all youngsters.

For most countries in Western Europe the compulsory schooling period begins at the age of 6 or 7 and extends until the age of 14-16 (OECD, 1974c: 12 & 28). Within these age ranges virtually all countries have been successful in enrolling most of their youth with enroll-ment rates that are 94 percent or higher (OECD, 1974c: 12 & 28). The only exceptions seem to be the Mediterranean countries of Spain, Greece, Italy, Turkey, and Yugoslavia—in the 76-90 percent category. Yet schooling opportunities are not identical for all children. The national systems differ from the highly centralized French educational system to the much more decentralized ones of West Germany and the United Kingdom. But even in a highly centralized system such as France, there are likely to be differences in the types of teachers attracted to Paris and the major cities on the one hand and to the rural provinces on the other—as well as in the social class orientations of schools (Rist, 1970). Accordingly, the high enrollments at the lowest educational levels do not guarantee that all children receive the same education or the same opportunities to continue beyond the post-compulsory period.[2]

Until recently, movement into the secondary phase required passing an examination or fulfilling some other type of selection procedure in most Western European countries.[3] Thus, a very early examination, sometimes as early as at 10 years of age, would determine the educational future, and by implication, the occupational future of each child. Various structural reforms in countries like England, France, Belgium, Germany, Sweden, and other nations have modified this pattern by establishing comprehensive secondary schools where—in theory—students would have a choice of curricula with the ultimate selection of specializa-tion based upon actual attainments in the secondary school. Such reforms were believed to offer youngsters a longer period and greater choices for developing their talents as well as eliminating the social stratification that is so obvious in the early selection and separation of the academic versus nonacademic student. Whether these reforms are successful in achieving these goals is problematic, and it is probably too early to know since in many cases the transi-tion to comprehensive schools is proceeding slowly. Husen (1973) has found that the top students in countries with comprehensive educational systems perform about as well as comparable student populations in countries with very selective ones.[4]

Clearly there are drastic reductions in the proportions of children in Western European countries who continue to attend school beyond the compulsory period. Among the coun-tries of the OECD the fulltime rates among youth 15-18 years of age around 1970 varied from about 25 percent in such countries as Spain and Portugal to almost 70 percent in Sweden and Norway (OECD, 1974c: 29). Relatively few of the countries showed even half of their 15-18 year olds enrolled fulltime (OECD, 1974c: 29). Of course, this funding is not necessarily inconsistent with the equality of access standard if the reductions in participation are based purely on "merit" rather than on factors of social class, sex, or race.

Again, the policies for admission to post-secondary educational opportunities vary from country to country. But, in general, they operate as follows. Graduates of the academic secondary schools or general secondary schools are admitted directly to the university, al-

---

[2] It is generally accepted that the schools of working-class youngsters tend to be much less supportive than those of students from higher class origins. An insider's view of such class orientations is reflected in *Letter to a Teacher* written by a handful of Italian youth from peasant families in the region of Tuscany. "You won't remember me or my name. You have flunked so many of us. On the other hand I have often had thoughts about you, and the other teachers, and about that institution which you call school and about the kids that you flunk. You flunk us right out into the fields and factories and there you forget us" (Schoolboys of Barbiana, 1971: 3).

[3] Some detail on the structure and changing nature of secondary education in Western Europe is found in OECD, 1969).

[4] This finding supports the view that inequalities within the educational system reflect the inequalities of the societies where education occurs more than the formal characteristics of the educational system such as whether it is selective or comprehensive in participation. Compare this finding with the predic-tions of Boudon (1973), Bowles and Gintis (1976) and Carnoy and Levin (1976).

though some countries require entrance examinations as well (Pellegrin, 1974). Examinations are required for the most selective institutions and/or the most selective careers of study within universities. Graduates of the nongeneral or academic secondary schools have traditionally been eligible only for entrance to so-called "short-cycle" higher education oriented towards preparation for a specific career (Pellegrin, 1974). In recent years these distinctions have begun to erode with the admission of the latter to the university by special examination or by other procedures, but the change in procedures seems more theoretical than actual (Pellegrin, 1974:89). Particularly, since the student movements of 1968, pressure for expanding university enrollments in the European universities to encompass a larger variety of backgrounds has been somewhat successful.

According to the estimates compiled by OECD, almost all the Western European countries show less than one-quarter of the appropriate age group entered higher educational institutions of all types in 1970 (OECD, 1974c: 40). Sweden showed a significantly higher entrance rate of about 38 percent of the eligible population, but rates in the 15-20 percent range were more typical (OECD, 1974c: 40).

As noted, the educational systems of Western Europe are characterized by almost complete enrollments of youngsters during the compulsory schooling period; about half of the appropriate age group during the noncompulsory secondary schooling phase; and about one-quarter of the relevant age group entering the post-secondary educational cycle. Of course, there are large variances from country-to-country. The data do not show whether this pattern is consistent with the equal access standard, but there is good reason to believe that children from lower social class origins are less able to take advantage of "equal accessibility" provisions than are children from higher social class backgrounds. Differences in family income, class culture, social reinforcement, and other factors are likely to differ so substantially, that Tawney has viewed such a conception of equality of educational opportunity as a "fraud" much like " . . . the impertinent courtesy of an invitation offered to unwelcome guests, in the certainty that circumstances will prevent them from accepting" (Cited in Husen, 1975: 38). In fact, the class-related inequalities in educational experiences and outcomes have suggested that the examination of *ex-post* results rather than *ex-ante* provisions are a more useful approach to examining equality of educational opportunity (Coleman, 1968).

(2) *Equality of Educational Participation*

One measure of educational results is that of the actual educational participation among groups drawn from different social origins, while another is the equality of educational results in terms of what is accomplished in the educational system. Equal educational participation is viewed as the equal probability of representative persons from different social origins achieving the same amount of educational participation in both a qualitative and quantitative sense. This standard is reviewed here, while the concept of equality of educational results is considered subsequently.

There are two types of barriers operating to reduce the educational participation of children from lower-class origins relative to those from higher ones. These are (1) barriers external to the school and (2) those within the school structure. The former include such factors as family expectations and limited income where the lower-class family may have lower expectations for its children with respect to education; and limited income restricts the provision of funds for books, clothing, tuition charges for special courses or for examination preparation as well as making it more necessary for youngsters to provide financial support for the family. In addition, the intellectual stimulation that reinforces the schooling experience is less likely to be present in the family from lower social origins than in their more highly educated and wealthier counterparts. These factors have been reviewed elsewhere (Husen, 1975: Chap. 6; Levin, 1973), and they represent a prime base for Tawney's (1931: 142) skepticism: "As though opportunities for talent to rise could be equalized in a society where the circumstances surrounding it from birth are themselves unequal."

The second type of barrier is that created by the structure and operations of the educational system itself. In an excellent discussion of these obstacles, Husen (1975: 119) divides them into four classes:

(1)   In the selection of students for academic secondary education or for institutions of higher learning.

(2)   In the screening in terms of grade-repeating and drop-out that takes place during a given stage.

(3)   In grouping practices, such as "streaming" or "tracking" that tend to bias against students with a particular background.

(4)   In curriculum practices that prevent the promotion of certain types of talent or students with certain backgrounds.

To these one might add the systematic differences in educational resources one might find between schools enrolling students of different social classes such that better teachers, facilities, and other educational resources are available to children from higher social class origins. Since Husen (1975: Chap. 5) reviews such barriers in both a theoretical and empirical context, it is enough to say that both educational structures and social class influences external to the school systematically induce higher educational participation among persons of higher social classes.

Reviews of studies of educational participation for Britain, West Germany, France, Holland, Denmark, and Sweden show a direct relation between such measures of social class origin as father's occupation and the amount of and type of education that a student receives (Husen, 1975: Chap. 4). Extensive recent studies on the subject for Britain (Halsey, 1975), Spain (Diez, et al., 1975), Germany (Pfaff and Fuchs, 1975), and France (Boudon, 1973; Eicher and Mingat, 1975) Sweden (Fägerlind, 1975) and Holland (Peschar, 1975) are consistent with these reviews as well as with such earlier studies as those of Glass (1954) and Floud (1956). All of these investigations suggest that the advantages bestowed upon a person by social class origin or sex are important determinants of how much education as well as the type of education received. Moreover, even when one removes the effect of measured intellectual differences—themselves partly a result of social class influences—the participation rates of persons with similar academic ratings are lower for persons from working-class families than from middle-class or upper-class ones.

A summary of inequalities in participation is found in Table One showing estimates of relative chances of students from different social class origins in gaining access to higher education. The lack of availability of a uniform data set among countries suggests caution in making precise inter-country comparisons, although large differences among countries are probably indicative of large underlying differences in access. On the basis of these estimates it was about five times as likely for an upper-class youth as a lower-class one to enter the higher educational segment in relatively egalitarian Yugoslavia in 1960, while in Portugal the likelihood was 125:1. Between these two extremes are a wide range of ratios, but the overall interpretation is that a child of a professional or manager had an overwhelmingly greater probability of reaching the higher educational level than the child of a worker, even in countries known for their attempts at improving educational equity such as Sweden —with a 26:1 ratio in favor of the more advantaged youth.

Table One shows more recent data on these ratios for the countries and years where infor-

TABLE 1

Estimates of Ratio of Chances of Access to Higher Education for Child From Professional or Managerial Background[1] Relative to One From Working Class Background

	About 1960	Year	Later Period
Austria	51:1		n.a.
Belgium	7:1	1966	8:1
Denmark	9:1		n.a.
Finland	n.a.	1969	7:1
France	83:1	1968	18:1
Germany	41:1	1970	15:1
Greece	8:1	1970	3:1
Ireland	21:1		n.a.
Italy	36:1	1967	18:1
Luxembourg	72:1	1972	28:1
Netherlands	56:1	1970	27:1
Norway	7:1	1970	7:1
Portugal	125:1		n.a.
Spain	66:1	1970	25:1
Sweden	26:1		n.a.
Switzerland	20:1		n.a.
U.K.	8:1	1971	2:1
Yugoslavia	5:1	1969	3:1
U.S.	8:1	1969	3:1

Source: OECD, *Education, Inequality, and Life Chances* (Paris: OECD, 1975b: 168).
[1]The lack of comparability among data available for different countries suggests great caution in inter-country comparisons. Reader should not cite these results without reviewing Source:,pp. 176–181 for definitions and methodology.

mation was available. In most cases the probability of access of youth from lower social origins has improved in comparison with their more advantaged counterparts, and in some cases the improvements are rather drastic. Of course, the relative disadvantage of the lower-class person in gaining access to higher education is still rather large according to these later data, and the "true" disadvanatage is likely to be greater if one consider the qualitative differences in opportunities.

Just as the United States has expanded its higher educational offerings primarily through the lower cost community colleges (Karabel, 1972; Bowles & Gintis, Chap. 8; Clark, 1960), the countries of Western Europe have opened new institutions of a relatively less rigorous nature to absorb the increases of secondary school graduates seeking participation in higher education. Such expansion occured in new institutes as well as in correspondence and television universities such as the Open University in Great Britain. Even the expansion of such traditional universities as the University of Paris or Madrid in the post-1968 period has been characterized by enrollment increases far exceeding resource increases, with a resultant depreciation of the higher educational opportunities offered. That is, while a large portion of the children from upper-class backgrounds are attending the most prestigious institutions and the most prestigious schools within those institutions, the absorption of the lower-class student has occurred primarily through low cost expansion of traditional institutions or the establishment of lower cost, non-traditional alternatives (Pellegrin, 1974: 80-81).

In addition to the summary data on participation in higher education by social class, information is also available on the relative participation of women. Table Two shows female enrollments in higher education as a percentage of total enrollment in higher education as well as the most prestigious component, university enrollments. Comparisons are shown for

TABLE 2

Female Enrollment in Higher Education as Percentage of
Total Enrollment in Higher Education

	Total			University		
	1960	1965	1970	1960	1965	1970
Austria	23.9	24.3	28.6	23.1	23.9	24.8
Belgium	26.3	34.0	n.a.	19.2	25.7	n.a.
Denmark	30.5	34.0	36.4	24.3	30.2	31.9
Finland	46.5	50.7	48.6	46.9	49.0	47.6
France	37.1	40.3	n.a.	39.7	41.4	n.a.
Germany	17.1	18.0	24.1	20.8	22.5	29.6
Greece	25.3	31.8	30.4	23.0	30.5	31.4
Ireland	n.a.	29.5	n.a.	n.a.	28.1	n.a.
Italy	26.8	32.9	38.5	26.2	32.5	38.3
Luxembourg	9.1	20.0	(30.3)	12.5	20.0	(30.5)
Netherlands	24.9	25.2	27.5	17.9	18.0	19.6
Norway	n.a.	39.2	37.6	n.a.	23.8	28.6
Portugal	29.5	37.5	44.7	31.0	40.2	47.9
Spain	n.a.	28.1	28.8	n.a.	21.1	26.4
Sweden	n.a.	n.a.	n.a.	33.5	n.a.	37.2
Turkey	19.9	22.0	19.7	17.4	22.8	19.9
U.K.	n.a.	30.2	34.0	n.a.	25.6	27.3
Yugoslavia	28.8	33.4	39.5	n.a.	29.5	37.0

Source: OECD, *Educational Statistics Yearbook,* Vol. 1 (1974C:24).

both categories for 1960, 1965, and 1970. With the exception of Finland, Portugal, and perhaps France, only about one-fifth to one-third of the students at this level are female. While some countries have made important gains toward a more equal level of participation between the sexes, others show a surprisingly static pattern with little or only a very modest improvement.

In summary, using the standard of equality of educational participation, all of the evidence suggests massive differences in equity favoring youth drawn from higher social origins and males. While these differences seem to be diminishing over time, they are still substantial. Moreover, much of the improvement in the educational attainments of youth from the lower social classes is deceptive in that it is qualitatively inferior to that of students from more advantaged backgrounds.

(3) Equality of Educational Results

A third standard that might be used to assess equality of educational opportunity is that representative members of each sex and social class obtain similar educational results from their educational development for each year of schooling and for their overall educational career. This standard suggests that it is not just the amount of education that is important, but its level of effectiveness in providing those skills, behaviors, and attitudes contributing to a productive adulthood. This concept informed the well-known Coleman Report in the U.S. (Coleman *et al.*, 1966; Coleman, 1967), and by 1968 Coleman (18-19) asserted that " . . . *effects* of inputs have come to constitute the basis for assessment of school quality (and thus equality of opportunity) . . ."

Of course, the relation between the measure of educational effects and the measure of participation should be remembered. Since many of the selection devices for both secondary and post-secondary education in Western Europe are predicated heavily upon academic achievement, the student who shows better educational results is more likely to have the options to proceed further and to the most prestigious branches of the educational system. Thus, equality of participation and equality of educational results are closely intertwined.

While there may be many characteristics of educational development affecting adult productivity, the only ones assessed among countries are those of achievement test scores. The International Education Association (IEA) under the leadership of Torsten Husen of the University of Stockholm has undertaken international studies of the determinants of achievement in mathematics, science, reading comprehension, civics, literature, and foreign languages (Husen 1967, Vols. I & II; Walker, 1976; Passow *et al.*, 1976; Purves, 1973; Thorndike, 1973; Comber and Keeves, 1973). Several of the Western European countries were sampled for each of the subjects, and the pattern of results for social class and achievement is fairly uniform.

In general, differences in the socio-economic background of the students as reflected by father's occupation and education, mother's education, books in the home, and family size were the most important factors statistically associated with achievement for all countries (Thorndike, 1975). This pattern was similar for the Western European countries included in the sample, although there was variance from country to country (Thorndike, 1975: 96).

An analysis of mathematics achievement for six Western European countries (Belgium, England, France, West Germany, Netherlands, Scotland, and Sweden) was made to learn how mathematics performance varied according to the social class origins of students as reflected by their fathers' occupations (Husen, 1967: 207). Specifically a comparison was made between the mathematics test scores of students whose fathers were in the highest occupational grouping (professionals, executives, high technical workers, and administrators) and those in the lowest one (manual workers except farming, fishing, and forestry). Among these countries the students from the higher social backgrounds showed average mathematics scores from one half of a standard deviation higher in Sweden to two standard deviations higher in England than their average counterpart from a working-class background. Most of the differences were about eight-tenths of a standard deviation. Remember that a difference of even a half of a standard deviation implies that the average student from the higher social class background had a higher test score than seventy percent of the persons of lower class origin. A difference of one standard deviation implies that the average advantaged child in these samples were performing at or above eight-four percent of the working-class students.

Moreover, the more recent results for science, literature, reading, and civics cognitive achievement suggest also that the best predictor of test scores among Western European countries is the family and home background of the child (Walker, 1975). This generalization is true not only across subjects, but among the age groups that were sampled: 10 year olds, 14 year olds, and students in the final year of secondary school. As one might expect, the statistical relation between achievement and family background is smaller among the students in the final year of secondary school where:

> Most of those from the lower socioeconomic groups have dropped out unless they were especially competent. Thus, the selection has operated both to reduce the range of socio-economic status and to leave in school a nonrepresentative fraction of children from the lower socioeconomic strata (Thorndike, 1975: 98).

In the relation between sex and achievement, women performed more poorly in science (Walker, 1976: 98-100) and in mathematics (Husen, 1967, Vol. II: 233-250), and in cognitive civic achievement (Walker, 1975: 229). But, females appeared to be consistently stronger than males in literature achievement and slightly superior in reading comprehension (Walker, 1975: 299). This mixed pattern suggests a different relationship between educational participation between the sexes than among representatives of different social classes where persons from lower social origins show both lower achievement and a lower likelihood of reaching secondary school or the post-secondary level.

(4) *Equality of Educational Effects on Life Chances*

The fourth standard that might be used to assess equality of educational opportunity is its effect on the life chances of persons from different social origins. The most complete application of this standard would be that it exists when the educational system intervenes in the social system so that there is no systematic relation between a person's social origins (or sex) and his or her ultimate social attainments. That is, the educational system would compensate for differences in parental wealth, income, education, political power, social connections, culture, and so on so that these factors would not influence the chances of attaining a particular level of wealth, income, education, political power, and social connections for adult offspring. Rawls (1971: 100-101) calls this the principle redress for "undeserved" inequalities such that:

> . . . in order to treat all persons equally to provide genuine equality of opportunity, society must give more attention to those with fewer native assets and to those born into the less favorable social positions. The idea is to redress the bias of contingencies in the direction of equality.

Of course, education could have an equalizing effect on life outcomes without complete randomization between the social origins of parents and the adult attainments of offspring. If the existence of the educational system were to reduce the link between the status of parents and the ultimate attainments of their children, the equalization effect would be present; although its ability to overcome the other sources of unequal opportunity would obviously depend upon its strength rather than its mere existence. Finally, education might serve to reinforce or even to reproduce the class structure from parent to child. In this case, education would not only fail to offset the inequalities of birth, but it would function on the basis of those inequalities along with other agencies of class transmission such as the family (Kohn, 1969; Bowles and Gintis, 1976; Althusser, 1971: 127-186).

On the basis of what information we do have, the overall thrust of the educational systems in Western Europe is not to break the tie between birth and life chances. The evidence for this is that on the average persons from lower social class backgrounds receive fewer years of schooling; schooling of lower quality; and poorer educational results for each year of schooling that is undertaken. Moreover, they are likely to be studying in less prestigious and remunerative careers, if they reach the higher educational level, and they lack the social and political connections to obtain the better jobs in a set of countries where the problem of unemployment and underemployment of graduates is becoming more and more serious as a result of the prodigious expansion of secondary and higher education. Let us consider each of these in turn.

As shown earlier, children from more advantaged families are more likely to complete secondary and enter the higher educational level. In some cases the differential probabilities between children from workers' families and those from professional families reaching higher educational attainments is greater than 25:1, and it is probably not less than 3:1, even considering improvements. In fact, it may be that more nearly current data will not change the picture. For example, a recent Swedish statistical report that analyzes the participation of students in higher education according to the occupation of fathers has found that the proportion of children from workers' families in Swedish higher education rose only until 1969-70 with virtually no change through 1972-1973, the last year for which data were reported (Ministry of Education, Sweden 1976:24).

Second, much of the expansion of higher education absorbing the student from lower social class origins has been short-cycle higher education partially comparable to the community college of the U.S. (OECD, 1973b).[5] Both admission procedures and other factors will likely continue to promote this course of studies as the version of higher education allotted to the lower-class student for giving him or her a "chance" at the higher level (Pellegrin, 1974; 80-81; Bowles, 1974; Karabel, 1972; Clark, 1960). This is a much cheaper solution to the problem of providing education for lower social class youth, for not only would they undertake fewer years of study in the short-cycle, but the public cost is about one-third to one-half as much as the University for each student-year (OECD, 1973b: 403).

Even when lower social class youth are able to gain access to the universities, they are likely to be in the less selective institutions and in the less selective and prestigious fields of studies (Pellegrin, 1974: 81).[6] For example, while about 25 percent of male students in Swedish higher education in 1972-73 came from workers' families and 15 percent came from families where the father had an academic degree, the percentage of working class males studying law and medicine were 4.4 percent and 1.5 percent respectively with comparable figures for the higher social class group of 7.7 percent and 7.3 percent, respectively (Ministry of Education, Sweden, 1976: 24 & 39). Remember that Sweden appears to have the most egalitarian educational system in Western Europe, so that data for other countries would probably show considerably more disparate participation by social class.

While much can be said about the interesting and innovative approaches represented by such non-traditional alternatives as "new" universities to serve working-class youth like the Open University in Great Britain, it is also clear that their clientele would not be selected or could not participate in the more prestigious universities. Moreover, their principle advantage is said to be relatively low cost per unit of instruction, a factor apparently important only for institutions serving lower-class university enrollees rather than Oxford, Cambridge, and some of the red-bricks serving a much more advantaged clientele (Lumsden and Ritchie, 1975).

Further, there exists uncontested evidence of poorer measured cognitive achievement for each year of study for children from lower social class origins, and this factor also has operated to prevent such students from enrolling in the more prestigious institutions or courses of study (Pellegrin, 1974). Finally, in labor markets that are becoming flooded with secondary and university graduates as a result of the recent expansions, youth from more disadvantaged backgrounds are severely handicapped in finding employment comparable with their more advantaged counterparts. Average annual growth rates of enrollment in higher education have been in the 5-12 percent range in Western Europe, while economic growth rates have been less than half of these (OECD, 1974c: 32).

The present reforms in secondary education guarantee a continued expansion of higher education that will vastly exceed the economic growth rates for the foreseeable future. While good data are lacking on this problem for recent years, unemployment and underemployment of educated persons is a serious problem that will probably become even more aggravated in the future (International Labour Organisation, 1976: 50-52).

Unfortunately, good information on this phenomenon are not yet available because the

---

[5] Short-cycle higher education differs from vocationally-oriented curricula in the community colleges of the U.S. in one very important respect. It does not prepare a student to transfer to the University after two years of studies as does the Community College. However, there has been discussion of moving towards the Community College model more fully by using it for a course of basic academic studies as well as applied career-studies (OECD, 1973b).

[6] Evidence of differences in pecuniary returns to schooling of different quality is found for the United States in a number of studies (Alwin, 1976; Solmon and Wachtel, 1975; and G. Psacharopoulos, 1975: Chap. 4). Differences in returns to type of education and to education within occupation for a Swedish sample of men are found in I. Fägerlind (1975: 70-76).

educational expansion is recent and perhaps because governments have little zeal for revealing the details of a rather somber situation, although some data are beginning to emerge (ILO, 1976: 50-52; Levy-Garboua, 1975; Esnault and Le Pas, 1974). But what is important is that in the race for jobs, the graduates from the lower social classes are likely to do even more poorly than the average graduate. Not only are such students likely to be less-well prepared, to be found in less prestigious fields, and to receive their training in less prestigious institutions, but they also will have fewer family resources and connections to obtain good jobs. This situation is increasingly common in the United States as well (Thurow, 1975), where it has been argued that persons from lower social classes systematically lack access to those labor markets that provide the higher paying and prestigious jobs (Gordon, 1972; Gordon, Reich and Edwards, 1973; Carnoy and Carter, 1974). Finally, the advent of higher educational participation for the less advantaged youth is coming at a rather late stage historically in the system of educational development where the increasing masses of graduates have tended to bid down the return to higher education relative to what it had been in its more elite period (R.B. Freeman, 1976; Carnoy, 1971).

Summary of the Four Standards

Whether we use the standard of equality of educational access, educational participation, educational results, or educationally-induced life chances, the operation of the educational systems of Western Europe fails to meet them. The educational treatments and results for western European youth mirror the initial differences in their social class origins as well as sex differences. But, even if education has not seemed to alter the relative positions of persons within the educational, occupational, and income distributions, perhaps the distributions themselves are now more nearly equal as a result of the educational system? That is, have differences between the two groups diminished, *even* if the offspring of working class families are not as well off as those from professional families?

There is little doubt that the distribution of education has become more nearly equal throughout Western Europe. Analysis of the distribution of education, by age cohort, shows a universal trend towards increasing equality for virtually all countries (Kotwal, 1975). But, there seems little relation between the increasing equality of educational attainments (in nominal years of schooling) and the distribution of income. Comparative studies of the distribution of income in Western Europe have found evidence of rising inequalities or relative stability of the income distribution with no tendency towards greater equality (Jain, 1975). This relation holds whether one uses such summary measures of the income distribution as the gini coefficient or whether one examines the share of income received by the richest and poorest segments of the population under similar sampling approaches.[7] And the same results have been found for the United States (Thurow, 1975).

III. INTERPRETATION AND CONSEQUENCES

There are at least two explanations why, despite the existence of official policies of equal educational opportunity by western European nations, the actual results are quite the opposite. One explanation is that the governments and educators have simply not found the appropriate reforms or given them enough time. This typical optimistic response comes from the educators and their liberal supporters as well as most government spokesmen. It is a call for more reforms, more educators, more social science evaluators, and an under-

---

[7] A good overview of problems in the measurement and analysis of the distribution of income is found in A.B. Atkinson (1975) and A.K. Sen (1973).

lying ideology that the problem of obtaining equal educational opportunity and greater social mobility is essentially a technical problem.

In contrast, it might be argued that the extent of social mobility and inequality are conditions that derive from the basic functioning of economic, political, and social institutions in capitalist or socialist societies and particularly from the relations of production, and that all institutions of socialization tend to reproduce the requirements for maintaining these institutions. In this case, it would be functional for the schools to reproduce the inequalities of the larger society according to the initial class origins of its members. Indeed, from this perspective it is absurd to think of the state as a neutral observer countering the power of the dominant groups in society to maintain their own positions, for the state is in itself a creature of that society and its ruling classes (Miliband, 1969; Poulantzas, 1973). It is in this latter context I think we can best view the functions of schooling in Europe (Baudelot and Establet, 1971; Lenhardt, 1974; Hallak, 1974) as it is increasingly viewed in the United States as well (Bowles and Gintis, 1976; Carnoy and Levin, 1976). The basic problem is that the schools serve to reproduce labor for the unequal relations of capitalist production, and there is a basic contradiction between this function and that of increasing social mobility or equality. While this explanation is detailed in recent works (Althusser, 1971; Boudelot and Establet, 1971; Bowles and Gintis, 1976; Carnoy and Levin, 1976; Levin, 1974; Carnoy, 1974; Lenhardt, 1974; and Levin et al., forthcoming) only a brief description can be presented here.

The advent of universal schooling had its origins in the early phases of industrialism that spread across the U.S. and most of Western Europe at the beginning of the nineteenth century (Bowles and Gintis, 1976). Prior to industrialism, most production occured in the home, the small workshop, or the farm, and preparation for work involved clerkships, apprenticeships and other learning-by-doing activities.

But, the impersonal and bureaucratic nature of large-scale production represented by the emerging factory system required a new type of worker. Essentially, such a worker had to know how to behave in a de-personalized hierarchy where he or she was governed completely by the rules, regulations, organization, and external reward structures established by the capitalist owners and managers (Weber, 1958). The school arose in a fashion much like the factory with its emphasis on rules, hierarchical relationships, system of extrinsic rewards, high degree of discipline, to prepare wage labor for the expanding system of large-scale capitalist production and its need for a growing and socialized work force with appropriate work behaviors.

The quest for profits and unending capital accumulation required an expanding work force of docile, disciplined, and structurally alienated workers, and the initiation of state-sponsored schools emerged to satisfy these needs. As a result, the social relations of "production" in schooling served to reproduce the social relations of work.

> It takes little imagination to see the correspondence between grades for school performance and wages for work performance; to see the alienation and boredom of the assembly line mirror the stifling environment and boredom of the educational assembly line; to see the competition among students for grades parallel the competition among workers for advancement; to see the teacher in the classroom impose his arbitrary values on his underlings just as does the boss on the job (neither legitimacy of authority resulting from a democratic election) (Levin, 1974).

But, the schools represented not only a principal agency of socialization for reproducing the social division of labor for capitalist production. They also began to represent the vehicle for social mobility from traditional to industrial society, from rural to urban society, from the farm to the factory as exposure to schooling opened new opportunities for persons otherwise relegated to marginal agriculture. This aspect was especially promoted by the state in assisting the capitalists to obtain an expanding and appropriately trained work force through the initiation of state-sponsored schooling and the advent of compulsory attendance laws to assure the provision of a growing pool of surplus labor with its depressing effect on wage costs. Indeed, as already noted, the public promotion of schooling has always been advertised as being associated with its role in fostering social mobility as well as the ideology that mobility is possible through the schooling system.

Accordingly, two of the principal roles played by the educational systems of Western Europe are (1) the preparation of an expanding, disciplined and docile work force for filling the needs of capitalist and particularly, monopoly-capitalist enterprises for wage-labor and (2) the vehicle for providing social mobility as well as for inculcating the ideology that social mobility is possible through diligence in educational endeavor. But, there is a basic contradiction between these two roles since capitalist production is based upon the existence of a work force consisting of a pyramidal hierarchy of positions that differ substantially in income, prestige, and power. The vast majority of positions are at the bottom of the productive enterprise, and there is only limited mobility among the many "mini-ladders" of occupational positions that compose the larger hierarchy from the many alienated workers at the bottom ot the relatively few and independent capitalist managers and owners at the top (Braverman, 1974; Marglin, 1974). Moreover, the schools, family, and other agencies of socialization for work tend to reproduce the work structure on the basis of the initial class structure of the previous generation (Kohn, 1959; 1969; Kohn and Schooler, 1969; Bowles and Gintis, 1976; Carnoy and Levin, 1976).

Thus the only way social mobility is compatible with class reproduction is when there is a constant expansion of higher level occupational positions in the productive structure. More specifically, the social mobility of educated workers depends crucially on the expansion and growth of enterprises in order to provide more and better positions for educated workers. That is the key to reconciling both the preparation of workers for highly unequal positions in the productive work structure and its associated class hierarchy and the provision of social mobility is a pattern of economic growth able to provide increasing numbers of higher and higher occupational positions for larger and larger numbers of educated workers produced by the schools.

In short, there is a rather delicate relationship between the ability to prepare persons for the existing hierarchical relations of capitalist production and to provide occupational positions commensurate with their levels of education, and the correspondence is only established when the expansion of the productive hierarchy is at least large enough to absorb the numbers of educated persons created at each educational level. In periods of very rapid economic growth, no contradiction arises even if the occupational expansion exceeds the educational increases, because firms will have an incentive to train and upgrade existing workers and labor-market entrants to fill needed positions. But, when the level of economic growth is not adequate to absorb the increases in educated workers at appropriate occupational levels, an obvious contradiction arises between the expectations of educated workers for social mobility and the needs of the work place.

In general, the Western European countries experienced high levels of economic growth during the post-World War II period to absorb rising enrollments. But, since the early seventies the rates of economic growth have slowed, while post-secondary educational expansion has remained high, although varying considerably from country to country (Cerych *et al.*, 1974: 18-23). Even with relative declines in the size of the eligible population groups:

> . . . there is little to indicate that the expansion will be less than 4-6% per annum, which means a further doubling of enrollments within the next 12 to 18 years, . . ., and it must be remembered . . . that practically all past projections have represented under-estimations . . . (21).

It is highly dubious that rates of economic growth will keep pace, as a number of factors in the early seventies have contributed to what appears to be a long run reduction in the historic post-war growth rate.[8] As Gorz (1976:1) has noted, the low growth rates are due largely to an over-accumulation of capital and a resulting decline in the rate of profit that results from the existing saturation of home markets as well as the lack of basic technological breakthroughs to stimulate the writing off of past investment and the replacement of existing capital.

> Such a type of crisis of overaccumulation has been overcome in the past only by either destruction of capital, mainly through war, or technical revolutions which, most of the time, were also a side effect of war (2).

But, he adds to this dilemma a new physical limitation on growth, the exhaustion of cheap mineral and energy resources as well as the traditionally "free" resources as air and water.

> In the last decade the cost of economic growth, both direct and indirect, has skyrocketed for physical, environmental reasons which were totally unpredicted and unpredictable by neo-classical economists. Amongst other things, industrial growth has run up against a shortage of hitherto unlimited resources such as space, water, and air, and the willingness of people to accept the requirements of work in industry. To take a rather striking example—in Europe, the chemical industry in the Rhine Valley, which as you know, is made up of three very large German chemical corporations, has experienced the impossibility of further local growth unless it first built new cities to house new workers which would require the buying of very expensive agricultural land; and, second, unless it took drastic measures to control air and water pollution since the Rhine water is already in such a state that it can no longer be made drinkable in its lower portion which compels the Netherlands to import much of their drinking water by boat, from Norway (2).

In addition to these factors, investment of European capital is likely to move increasingly to Asia, Latin America, and Africa where those governments can still provide expanding labor supplies at subsistence wages. In such countries as South Korea, Taiwan, the Philippines, and Brazil, the state has created a cheap and exploitable labor supply to attract foreign investment. Free trade unions are forbidden, and protective minimum wages, social security benefits, and occupational safety standards substantially do not exist as they are by-passed by various types of "non-coverage" provisions or "gifts" to the appropriate governmental officials. There are few restrictions against despoliation of natural resources by foreign capital as well. Finally, the safety of these investments is guaranteed by totalitarian governments with strong internal repression by the military and police, so that investment risk is low while profits are extraordinarily high.

Thus, there are limits on the future economic growth of the Western European countries that will result in lower secular growth rates for the foreseeable future. But, at the same time the educational expanion generated by the reforms of secondary education in the sixties has spawned a high rate of growth and level of enrollments among the universities so that the economic system has not and will not be able to expand rapidly enough to absorb the increasing supply of educated workers. Already, the relative and absolute unemployment rates of university graduates are rising as such persons are increasingly unable to find suitable

---

[8] Of course, even if the post-secondary expansion does not exceed the growth of GNP, the disparity between the nature of jobs and job entrants remains as long as there are initial compositional differences between the two. For example, if in 1970 a Western European country had an occupational distribution that required university graduates for fifteen percent of its jobs, but twenty-five percent of the labor force were university graduates, then the disparity between jobs and education will continue to exist even if GNP and the number of college graduates grow at the same rate. I am arguing that not only is there an initial excess of educated persons relative to appropriate jobs, but that for many countries in Western Europe the increases in educated persons will also exceed the increases in the development of appropriate jobs.

placements. For example, as late as 1971 French university graduates faced unemployment rates only half as great as those faced by holders of a terminal Baccalauréat, 3.9 percent and 8.3 percent, respectively (Levy Garboua, 1975:9). But, in 1972 the unemployment rate rose to 9 percent and 8.7 percent, respectively, and in 1974 the rate of unemployment for those with university degrees actually exceeded slightly that of persons with the Baccalauréat, 8.5 percent to 8.7 percent, respectively (*Ibid.*).[9]

The contradiction between the educational expansion with its rising expectations of an increasingly educated labor force for jobs commensurate with their educational attainments and the inability of Western European monopoly capitalism and its supportive state bureaucracies to meet those expectations will provide the basis for change in both the educational and the work setting. For as more young educated workers find their job expectations unfulfilled, they will not be integrated into work structures as readily or submissively as were their predecessors. Higher education tends to inculcate skills, values, and attitudes that correspond to the most prestigious jobs in the work hierarchy as well as creating expectations of having the high status, income, independence and mobility that such jobs afford. In contrast, young university graduates will find themselves competing with relatively less-educated workers for jobs of lower prestige and income allowing only limited mobility and characterized by a much greater tendency towards routinized work.

The symptoms of this contradiction between the schools and the work place will be the increasing disaffection of youth toward both work and society and rampant social instability as the expectations created by the system of socialization are dashed by the cold reality. Ensuing frustrations and dissatisfaction will increasingly create disruptions of production and lower productivity. Further consequences may well be further deterioration in the quality of workmanship so that quality control will become a more serious problem. In addition, we are likely to see rising incidences of absenteeism, employee turnover, and alcohol and drug usage on the job as well as increasing work stoppages created by wildcat strikes and employee sabotage. These problems are already evident in Western Europe (David Jenkins, 1974; 1974a) and they have become significant enough in the U.S. that the national government has issued its own report on the subject (U.S. Department of Health, Education, and Welfare, 1973: Chaps. 2 and 3).

---

[9] In the United States the unemployment rate for college graduates is lower than for secondary school graduates as the former have tended increasingly to replace the latter in the occupational structure (Berg, 1970; Milner, 1972; Thurow, 1975; Freeman 1976). But in Western Europe a university graduate has a social position to maintain that does not permit easy acceptance of a job as a clerk, waiter, or operative. Indeed, to obtain such a job may jeopardize future options for appropriate positions at the university graduate level. Accordingly, the European university graduate without a "proper" position is more likely to sit in the cafe while engaged in political and intellectual discussions than to wait on tables in the cafe as do many American counterparts.

One important assumption is that the present disjuncture between the number of graduates and jobs is not a cyclical phenomenon, but a secular one. This assumption is based partly upon my projection of lower economic growth rates for the foreseeable future and partly upon my presumption that growth rates in European post-secondary enrollments will continue in spite of high levels of unemployment and increasing underemployment of graduates. The latter presumption is based upon the relatively high social prestige of higher education in Europe as well as the emergence of job competition where those with more education will increasingly accept positions that require less education and displace the lower educated. Under such a "job-queue" phenomenon, the private rates of return to investment in higher education may remain high or increase as the opportunity cost represented by the returns to a secondary school diploma diminish in relative terms (Thurow, 1975).

Freeman (1975) argues that the "overeducation" phenomenon in the United States is also a secular phenomenon that will improve somewhat in the nineteen eighties but will never return to the situation experienced in the sixties. Finally, while demographic trends and recession certainly explain part of the recent excess of educated labor in Western Europe and conditions may improve in the short-run, I see a secular and structural problem rather than one created only by cyclical phenomena.

In short, the increasing disjuncture between the values and expectations of the educated worker and the realities of the work place will create what Gintis (1975) has called a new working class of revolutionary youth, an educated proletariat. Moreover, the magnitude of the contradiction and its effects is likely to move beyond the work place to the schools and possibly the streets and other institutions in the form of a sequel to the strikes of 1968, at least in countries like France and Germany where the contradictions will be most exacerbated. The timing and extent of the crisis will depend on the ability of the state and capitalist employers to mediate the contradiction by altering both education and work to bring them once again into correspondence. A number of efforts to mediate these contradictions have already been proposed or are in the process of implementation. These alterations include attempts to change the normal patterns of educational development and to reduce expectations of high occupational status and mobility for educated workers by altering the organization of work. Specific reforms or proposed reforms that are developing under the auspices of the state and capitalist enterprise include the following:

(1) *Increasing the Selectivity of Universities*—There has been a progressive introduction of restricted entrance into the universities in such countries as Germany, France and the Scandinavian nations where the most prestigious fields of study are restricted to students who meet specific study or examination requirements (Pellegrin, 1974: 86). These types of admission structures may well discourage students from applying as well as reduce the numbers otherwise eligible to attend. In addition, we are likely to see increases in drop-out or wastage rates as pressures rise for university faculties to "cool-out" higher numbers of enrollees. This phenomenon has been historically associated with those institutions of higher education that are less selective at entry (OECD, 1971a: Chap. VI).

(2) *Absorbing Increases Through Alternative Higher Education*—There will be an increasing move towards absorbing the enrollments of the "new entrants" through lower cost and less prestigious alternatives such as Open Universities that use correspondence, radio, and television courses; a renewed emphasis on the short-cycle higher education course and development of community college types of institutions as they exist in the U.S. and U.K.; and expansion of the relatively non-prestigious fields of study. These developments will further develop a system of social stratification within higher education to identify the marketability of students according to a refined credentialism. Since the lower status student will more likely appear in the lower cost and lower status alternatives (Pellegrin, 1974a: 32), this development will enable employers to discriminate in favor of students from higher socio-economic origins on the basis of an educational credential with the tacit defense that the credential is related to productivity (Arrow, 1973; Spence, 1973; Karabel, 1972; Bowles, 1974). Thus educated unemployment and underemployment will be more severe among graduates from lower social class origins than from higher ones.

(3) *Developing an Alternative Educational Pattern*—There will be strong attempts to change the traditional educational pattern by developing systems of recurrent education where students will be encouraged to leave secondary schooling or higher education to return at some future time as they develop new educational needs (Mushkin, 1974: E. Faure, *et al.*, 1972). This effort will be aimed at reducing the present high social demand for education by breaking the traditional educational cycle. Of course, the relative lack of productive work for young persons who leave the educational system will militate against taking the recurrent educational approach seriously. However, persons in the labor force who undertake recurrent education to obtain new skills may create positions for job entrants during the schooling period. In conjunction with this latter possibility, there is increasing provision in Western

Europe for educational sabbaticals that would permit workers to leave for a specified period of time to study at government expense—generally through the support of a payroll tax (H. A. Levine, 1974). This device would also emphasize recurrent education while increasing labor market opportunities for new entrants.

(4) *Emphasizing Career Education*—As in the United States there is an emerging trend to consider the educational system in the context of "career education," an attempt to integrate schooling more closely with the workplace (Grubb and Lazerson, 1975; Esnault and Le Pas, 1974: 165-169). Such an approach tries to integrate the worlds of education and work by increasing career guidance on the nature and attributes of existing job positions; increasing the career content of curricula; interspersing periods of work and schooling as part of the regular educational cycle; and providing a more "realistic" understanding of the nature of work and available opportunities. Obviously, an important aspect of this approach is to reduce the "unrealistically high" expectations for high-level careers and to guide students into preparing for the more attainable lower-prestige ones. Already, the French government has announced a university reform to increase the influence of the business community on the curriculum and policy of the university in order to improve its career preparation (Patterson, 1976).

All four of these educational reforms may reduce the pressure on the workplace for better jobs, while further stratifying the students in higher education in order to improve the credentialism of the higher educational system according to social class. A variety of reforms in the workplace are also being initiated in order to mediate the contradiction between education and work. The three general categories include:

(1) *Changing the Organization of Work*—Throughout Europe there are increasing attempts to decrease worker turnover, absenteeism, and product quality problems that are emerging, by altering the organization of the work place. In general, these changes emphasize an increasing role for worker participation at either the level of the governing board (Mitbestimmung) or at the shop floor (OECD, 1976; OECD, 1975e; Jenkins, 1974). Reforms are expected to increase the loyalty of workers to the firm by expanding their direct participation or representation in decision making as well as by emphasizing their allegiance to fellow workers through the use of work teams (Blumberg, 1968). There is also an increasing orientation towards horizontal rather than vertical mobility within the firm. Thus, the educational sabbatical approach already noted does not necessarily prepare persons for higher positions, but it can be interpreted as a job benefit in itself that gives workers time away from the work place to pursue their own interests. In the long run we will see increasing attempts to flatten the work hierarchy with emphasis on horizontal differences in work roles and work rotation. Of course, the success of such changes will depend on the ability of the enterprises to maintain worker discipline and production when the possibilities of upward mobility are reduced in favor of horizontal mobility (Marglin, 1974).

(2) *Increasing the Prestige of Blue-Collar Work*—A second alteration on the work-side of the relationship is the attempt to reduce the social emphasis on white-collar positions and to raise the social prestige of blue-collar work. If successful, many students who might otherwise have sought university educations may be content with secondary completion and short-cycle higher education or will even leave secondary school with vocational preparation. Already in France there is a public media campaign to raise the status of the blue-collar workers by emphasizing that they have a craft and produce "real" things that are important to society rather than just pushing papers.

(3) *Providing Public Jobs*—Finally, attempts to provide more jobs in the public sector for the educated-unemployed may be made. This strategy has worked historically as much of the increase in educated labor was absorbed by the public bureaucracies. But, the approach depends upon rapid economic growth to obtain the public tax revenues for support of such government expansion. With slow economic growth the increases in revenues of the important value-added tax as well as other sales and excise taxes will not provide rapidly increasing yields. It will also be difficult to raise taxes from other sources such as income to finance the expansion of social services necessary to provide the additional jobs. Accordingly, the expansion of the public sector to absorb the increases in educated persons will also face intrinsic barriers.

The success of these changes in education and work to mediate the basic contradiction between the two major functions of the schools in Western Europe—to provide a trained work force for capitalist production as well as a means of social mobility—are difficult to ascertain. Even if they are partially successful, they are not likely to avoid rising class consciousness within the expanding educated proletariat, a factor which will have its own consequences. But, above all, it is clear there are limits to the use of the educational system to provide social mobility and equality, and these limits are embedded in the structures of the societies rather than in the lack of educational reforms (Carnoy and Levin, 1976). Without a movement toward greater equality in the economic sphere and its related political and social arenas, we are not likely to see an improvement in social mobility or equality in Western Europe.

BIBLIOGRAPHY

Althusser, Louis
    1971   Lenin and Philosophy and Other Essays. New York: Monthly Review Press.

Alwin, Duane F.
    1976   "Socioeconomic background, colleges, and post collegiate achievements," in W.H. Sewell, R. Hauser, and D. Featherman (eds.) Schooling and Achievement in American Society. New York: Academic Press, Inc.:343-372.

Anderson, C. Arnold
    1961   "A skeptical note on education and mobility," in A. M. Halsey, et al., (eds) Education, Economy, and Society. New York: Macmillan and Co.:164-179.

Arrow, Kenneth
    1973   "Higher education as a filter," Journal of Public Economics, 2, No. 3(July):193-216.

Atkinson, A.B.
    1975   The Economics of Inequality. Oxford: Clarendon Press.

Baran, Paul and Paul Sweezy
    1966   Monopoly Capital. New York: Monthly Review Press.

Baudelot, Christian and Roger Establet
    1975   L'Ecole Capitaliste en France. Paris: Librairie Francois Maspero. Available in Spanish as La Escuela Capitalista. Madrid: Siglo Veintiuno Editores.

Bell, Daniel
    1973   Coming of Post-Industrial Society: A Venture in Social Forecasting. New York: Basic Books.

Bendix, R. and S.M. Lipset (eds)
    1966   Class, Status, and Power: Social Stratification in Comparative Perspective. New York: The Free Press.

Bengtsson, Jarl, et al.
    1975   Does Education Have a Future? The Political Economy of Social and Educational Inequalities in European Society. Plan Europe 2000, Project 1, Educating Man for the 21st Century, 10, The Hague: Martinus Nijhoff.

Berg, Ivar
    1970   Education and Jobs: The Great Training Robbert. New York: Praeger.

Blumberg, Paul
    1968   Industrial Democracy: The Sociology of Participation. New York: Schocken Books.

Boudon, Raymond
    1973   Equality, Opportunity, and Sociel Inequality. New York: John Wiley and Sons, Inc.

1976   "Comment on Hauser's review of education, opportunity, and social inequality," American Journal of Sociology 81, No. 5(March):1175-1186.
Bourdieu, Pierre
1966   "Condition de classe et position de classe," Archives Européennes de Sociologie 7:201-223.
Bowles, Samuel
1974   "The integration of higher education in the wage labor system," Review of Radical Political Economy 6, No. 1:100-133.
1973   "Understanding unequal educational opportunity," American Economic Review 63(May):346-356.
Bowles, Samuel and Herbert Gintis
1976   Schooling in Capitalist America. New York: Basic Books, Inc.
Braverman, Harry
1974   Labor and monopoly Capital. New York: Monthly Review Press.
Busch, Georg
1975   "Inequality of educational opportunity by social origin in higher education." in Education, Inequality and Life Chances, 1, Paris: OECD:159-181.
Carnoy, Martin
1971   "Class analysis and investment in human resources: A dynamic model." The Review of Radical Political Economics 3, No. 4(Fall/Winter):56-81.
1974   Education as Cultural Imperialism. New York: David McKay Co., Inc.
Carnoy, Martin and Henry M. Levin
1976   The Limits of Educational Reform. New York: David McKay and Co., Inc.
Carroll, J.B.
1975   The Teaching of French as a Foreign Language in Eight Countries. New York: John Wiley and Sons.
Cerych, Ladislav, Dorotea Furth, and George S. Papadopoulos
1974   "Overall issues in the development of future structures of post-secondary education." in Policies for Higher Education. Paris: OECD:15-51.
Clark, Burton
1960   "The 'cooling out' function in higher education." The American Journal of Sociology 65, No. 6(May):569-577.
Coleman, James S.
1968   "The concept of equality of educational opportunity." Harvard Educational Review 38, No. 1:7-22.
Coleman, James S., et al.
1966   Equality of Educational Opportunity. U.S. Office of Education, Washington, D.C.: U.S. Government Printing Office.
Coleman, James S.
1967   "Towards open schools." The Public Interest 6(Fall):20-27.
Comber, L.C. and J.P. Keeves
1973   Science Education in Nineteen Countries. New York: John Wiley and Sons.
Cremin, Lawrence A. (ed.)
1957   The Republic and the School: Horace Mann on the Education of Free Man. Washington, D.C.: National Education Association.
Dewey, John
1916   Democracy and Education. New York: The Macmillan Co.
1966   Democracy and Education. New York The Free Press (paperback edition).
Diez, Nicholas J., U. Martinez Lazaro, and J.M. Porro Monondo
1975   "Education and social mobility in Spain." in Education, Inequality and Life Chances, 1. Paris: OECD:563-612.
Edwards, Richard, C., Michael Reich, and Thomas E. Weisskopf (eds.)
1972   The Capitalist System. Englewood Cliffs, N.J.: Prentice Hall, Inc.
Eicher, Jean Claude and Alain Mingat
1975   "Education et egalite en France." in Education, Inequality and Life Chances, 1. Paris: OECD:202-292.
Esnault, Eric and Jean Le Pas
1974   "New relations between post-secondary education and employment." Towards Mass Higher Education. Paris: OECD:105-169.
Fäegerline, Ingemar
1975   Formal Education and Adult Earnings. Acta Universitatis Stockholmiensis, Stockholm Studies in Educational Psychology 21. Stockholm: Almquist and Wiksell.
Faure, Edgar, et al.
1972   Learning to Be: The World of Education Today and Tommorrow. Paris: UNESCO/Harrap.
Floud, J.E.
1956   Social Class and Educational Opportunity. London: William Heinemann Ltd.

Federal Republic of Germany
  1976a   Arbeiterkinder im Bildungssystem. Bonn: Druckhaus Bayreuth.
  1976b   Der Bundesminister fur Bildung und Wissenschaft, Bildungspolitische Zwischenbilanz. Bonn: Bonner Universitats-Buchdruckerei.
Freeman, Richard B.
  1976   The Over-Educated America. New York: Academic Press.
Friedman, Milton
  1962   Capitalism and Freedom. Chicago: University of Chicago Press.
Gintis, Herbert
  1975   "The new working class and revolutionary youth." in M. Carnoy (ed.), Schooling in a Corporate Society, Second Ed. New York: David McKay and Co., Inc.:293-309.
Glass David
  1954   Social Mobility in Britain. London: Routledge and Kegan.
Gordon, David M.
  1972   Theories of Poverty and Underemployment. Lexington, Mass.: Lexington Books.
Gordon, David, Michael Reich, and Richard Edwards
  1973   "A theory of labor market segmentation." American Economic Review 63, No. 2(May):359-365.
Gorz, Andre
  1973   Socialism and Revolution. Garden City, N.Y.: Anchor Books, Doubleday and Co., Inc.
  1976   "Untitled." Paper presented at Faculty Seminar on Social Thought and Social Institutions, Stanford University (February 6), copies available from Henry M. Levin.
Grubb, W. Norton, and Marvin Lazerson
  1975   "Rally round the workplace: Continuities and fallacies in career education." Harvard Educational Review 45, No. 4(November):451-474.
Hallack, Jacques
  1974   A Que Profite L'Ecole? Paris: Presses Universitaires de France.
Halsey, Albert H.
  1975   "Education and social mobility in Britain since World War II." in Education, Inequality and Life Chances, 1. Paris: OECD:501-559.
Hauser, R.M.
  1976   "On Boudon's model of social mobility." American Journal of Sociology 81, No. 4(January):911-928.
Herrnstein, Richard
  1973   IQ in the Meritocracy. Boston: Atlantic Monthly Press.
Husen, Torsten (ed.)
  1967   International Study of Achievement in Mathematics, I and II. New York: John Wiley and Sons.
Husen, Torsten
  1972   Social Background and Educational Career. Centre for Educational Research and Innovation. Paris: OECD.
  1974   Talent, Equality and Meritocracy. Europe 2000, Project 1, 9. The Hague: Martinus Nijhoff.
  1975   Social Influences on Educational Attainment. Centre for Educational Research and Innovation. Paris: OECD. "The Standard of the Elite: Some Findings from the IEA International Survey in Mathematics and Science." Acta Sociologica, 16, No. 6:305-323.
Illich, Ivan
  1971   Deschooling Society. New York: Harper and Row.
Inkeles, Alex
  1975   "The emerging social structure of the world." World Politics 27, No. 4(July):467-495.
Inkeles, Alex and David H. Smith
  1974   Becoming Modern. Cambridge, Mass.: Harvard University Press.
International Labour Organisation
  1976   World Employment Programme: Research in Retrospect and Prospect. Geneva: ILO.
Jain, Shail
  1975   Size Distribution of Income. Washington, D.C.: The World Bank.
Jenkins, David
  1974   Industrial Democracy in Europe. Geneva: Business International, S.A.
  1974a   Job Power. Baltimore: Penguin Books Inc.
Jencks, C., et al.
  1972   Inequality. New York: Basic Books.
Jensen, A.R.
  1969   "How much can we boost IQ and scholastic achievement?" Harvard Educational Review 39:1-123.
Kamin, Leon
  1974   The Science and Politics of IQ. Potomac, Md.: Erlbaum Associates.

Karabel, Jerome
   1972   "Community colleges and social stratification." Harvard Educational Review 42, No. 4(November):521-562.
Kohn, Melvin L.
   1969   Class Conformity: A Study in Values. Homewood, Ill.: Dorsey Press.
   1959   "Social class and parental values." American Journal of sociology 64:337-351.
Kohn, Melvin L. and Carmi Schooler
   1969   "Class, occupation, and orientation." American Sociological Review 34:659-678.
Kotwal, Marilyn
   1975   "Inequalities in the distribution of education between countries, sexes, generations, and individuals." in Education, Inequality and Life Chances, 1. Paris: OECD:31-108.
Lenhardt, Gero
   1974   Berufliche Weiterbildung und Arbeitsteilung in der Industrieproduktion. Frankfurt: Suhrkamp Verlag, 1974.
Levin, Henry M.
   1973   "Equal educational opportunity and the distribution of educational expenditures." Education and Urban Society (February):149-176.
Levin, Henry M., et al.
           Education and Work: The Development of a Radical Hypothesis. Palo Alto, California: Center for Economic Studies (forthcoming).
Levin, Henry M.
   1976   "Equal educational opportunity in Western Europe: A contradictory relation." Paper presented at the Annual Meetings of the American Political Science Association, Chicago, September 4, 1976.
   1974   "Educational reform and social change." The Journal of Applied Behavioral Science 10, No. 3(August).
Levine, Herbert A.
   1974   "Strategies for the application of foreign legislation of paid educational leave to the United States scene." Paper prepared for the Career Education Program, National Institute of Education, NIE-G-74-0107, processed.
Levy-Garboua, L.
   1975   "The development of mass university education in France and the student dilemma." Paris: CREDOC and University of Paris-Nord, (December) processed.
Lewis, G.E. and C.E. Massad
   1975   The Teaching of English as a Foreign Language in Ten Countries. New York: John Wiley and Sons.
Lipset, S.M.
   1972   "Social mobility and equal opportunity." Public Interest 29(Fall):90-108.
Lipset, S.M. and R. Bendix
   1959   Social Mobility in Industrial Society. Berkeley: University of California Press.
Lumsden, Keith G. and Charles Ritchie
   1975   "The open university: A survey and economic analysis." Instructional Science 4, No. 3/4(October):237-292.
Maddison, Angus
   1975   "Education, inequality and life chances: The major policy issues." in Education, Inequality and Life Chances, 1. Paris: OECD:12-30.
Malthus, Thomas R.
   1960   On Population Modern Library Edition. New York: Random House, Inc.
Mann, Arthur
   1968   "A historical overview: The lumpenproletariat, education, and compensatory action." in the Quality of Inequality: Urban and Suburban Public Schools, Charles U. Daley (ed.). Chicago: University of Chicago Press:9-26.
Marglin, Steve
   1974   "What do bosses do?" Review of Radical Political Economics (Summer):60-112.
Miliband, Ralph
   1969   The State in Capitalist Society. London: Weidenfeld and Nicholson.
Miller, S.M.
   1975   "Social mobility and equality." in Education, Inequality and Life Chances, 1. Paris: OECD:394-433.
   1960   "Comparative social mobility." Current Sociology IX:1-89.
Milner, Murray
   1972   The Illusion of Equality. San Francisco: Jossey-Bass.
Ministry of Education, Sweden
   1976   Högskolestatistik II.
Mushkin, Slema J. (ed.)

1974   Recurrent Education, National Institute of Education, U.S. Department of Health, Education, and Welfare. Washington, D.C.: U.S. Government Printing Office.

OECD
1972a   Classification of Educational Systems. Paris: OECD.
1971a   Development of Higher Education. 1950-1967 Analytic Report. Paris: OECD.
1970   Development of Higher Education, 1950-1967 Statistical Survey. Paris: OECD.
1969   Development of Secondary Education, Trends and Implications. Paris: OECD.
1975b   Education, Inequality and Life Chances, 2 Volumes. Paris: OECD.
1974a   Education in OECD Developing Countries, Trends and Perspectives. Paris: OECD.
1975c   Education and Working Life in Modern Society. Paris: OECD.
1975a   Educational Development Strategy in England and Wales. Paris: OECD.
1974b   The Educational Situation in OECD Countries. Paris: OECD.
1974c   Educational Statistics Yearbook, 1, International Tables. Paris: OECD.
1972b   Educational Policy and Planning: France. Paris: OECD.
1975d   Educational Statistics Yearbook, II, Country Tables. Paris: OECD.
1973a   Long-Range Policy Planning In Education. Paris: OECD
1967   Methods and Statistical Needs for Educational Planning. Paris: OECD.
1965   Manpower Forecasting in Educational Planning. Paris: OECD.
1974d   OECD Policies for Higher Education. Paris: OECD.
1974c   Participatory Planning in Education. Paris: OECD.
1971b   Reviews of National Policies for Education. Paris: OECD.
1973b   Short-Cycle Higher Education. Paris: OECD.
1974f   Towards Mass Higher Education. Paris: OECD.
1975c   Work in a Changing Industrial Society. Paris: OECD.
1976   Workers' Participation. Paris: OECD.
Passow, A.H., H.J. Noah, M.A. Eckstein, and J.R. Mallea
1976   The National Case Study: An Empirical Comparative Study of Twenty-One Educational Systems. New York: John Wiley and Sons.
Patterson, Michelle
1976   "Governmental policy and equality in higher education: The junior collegization of the French university." Social Problems (this issue).
Pellegrin, Jean-Pierre
1974a   "Quantitative trends in post-secondary education." In Towards Mass Higher Education: Issues and Dilemmas. Paris: OECD: 9-62
1974   "Admission policies in post-secondary education." in Towards Mass Higher Education: Issues and Dilemmas. Paris: OECD.
Peschar, Jules
1975   Equal Opportunity in the Netherlands: The Influence of Social Class on Education and Occupation: An Ex-Post-Facto Study 1958-73," Sociologia Neerlandia, XI, No. 1:60-75.
Pfaff, Martin and Gerhard Fuchs with the assistance of Peter Koppl
1975   "Education, inequality and life income: A report on the Federal Republic of Germany." in Education, Inequality and Life Chances, 2. Paris: OECD:7-128.
Poulantzas, Nicos
1973   Political Power and Social Classes. London: NLB.
Psacharopoulos, George
1975   Earnings and Education in OECD Countries. Paris: OECD.
1973   Returns to Education: An International Comparison. San Francisco: Jossey-Bass, Inc.
Purves, A.C.
1973   Literature Education in Ten Countries. New York: John Wiley and Sons.
Purves, Alan C. and Daniel U. Levine (eds.)
1975   Educational Policy and International Assessment. Berkeley, Cal.: McCutchan Publishing Co.
Rawls, John
1971   A Theory of Justice. Cambridge, Mass.: The Belknap Press.
Rist, Ray C.
1970   "Student social class and teacher expectations: The self-fulfilling prophecy in ghetto education." Harvard Educational Review (August).
Schoolboys of Barbiana
1971   Letter to a Teacher. New York: Vintage Books.
Sen, Amartya
1973   On Economic Inequality. Oxford: Clarendon Press.
Sewell, William H. and Robert M. Hauser.
1976   "Causes and consequences of higer education: Models of the status attainment process." in W.H. Sewell, R. Hauser, and D. Featherman (eds.), Schooling and Achievement in American Society. New York: Academic Press, Inc.:9-28.
Solomon, Lewis, C. and Paul Wachtel

1975   "The effects on income of type of college attended." Sociology of education 48(Winter).
Tawney, R.H.
1931   Inequality. London: George Allen and Unwin Ltd.
Thorndike, R.L.
1976   Reading Comprehension Education in Fifteen Countries. New York: John Wiley and Sons.
1975   "The relation of school achievement to differences in the backgrounds of children." in A. Purves and D. Levine (eds.), Educational Policy and International Assessment. Berkeley, Cal.: McCutchan Publishing Co.: Chap. 4.
Thurow, Lester
1975   Generating Inequality. New York: Basic Books.
Tinbergen, Jan
1975   "Education, inequality and life chances: A report on the Netherlands." in Education, Inequality and Life Chances, 2. Paris: OECD: 404-426.
Torney, J.V., A.N. Oppenheim and F.F. Farnen
1976   Civic Education in Ten Countries. New York: John Wiley and Sons.
Trow, Martin
1974   "Problems in the transition from elite to mass higher education." Paris: OECD:51-101.
U.S. Department of Health, Education, and Welfare
1973   Work in America. Cambridge, Mass.: The MIT Press.
Walker, David A.
1976   The IEA Six Subject Survey: An Empirical Study of Education in Twenty-One Countries. New York: John Wiley and Sons.
Weber, Max
1958   "On bureaucracy," in Hans Gerth and C. Wright Mills, From Max Weber: Essays in Sociology. New York.
Young, Michael
1958   The Rise of the Meritocracy. London: Thames and Hudson.

GOVERNMENTAL POLICY AND EQUALITY IN HIGHER EDUCATION: THE JUNIOR COLLEGIZATION OF THE FRENCH UNIVERSITY*

MICHELLE PATTERSON
University of California
Santa Barbara

This article examines the implementation of the ideology of equality of educational opportunity in governmental policy by examining the 1976 French higher education reform. It argues that the reform was designed to suppress growing class conflict in the higher education system. It further argues that France, like the United States, has a dual system of higher education and that class dominance of this system has been assured by governmental policy using the ideology of equality of opportunity to legitimate that dominance. The 1976 reform represents an attempt by the government to preserve the dual system of higher education and to preserve class dominance of that system. This attempt is accomplished by junior collegizing and devaluing the French University, and thus reserving the elite institutions with entrée to the highest occupations to the highest social class.

In both the United States and France the decade of the 1960's was a time of belief in a never-ending spiral of higher education leading to higher jobs. Spurred by the ideology of equality of opportunity as well as expanding economies, demand for higher education rose and enrollments swelled on both sides of the Atlantic. Amid the growth, a few voices, such as that of Ivar Berg (1971), warned that an "educational inflation" was occurring where higher credentials, bearing no relationship to needed job skills, were required by employers simply to take advantage of and to absorb the supply of graduates. Such voices were not heeded and the boom of the 60's rapidly gave way to the bust of the 70's.

In the United States governmental belt-tightening contributed to the bust by reducing a major source of the demand for highly educated labor. Aside from paying lip service to the concept of "career education," the American government largely permitted the decentralized and diversified public and private higher education institutions to cope with the problem. In France, however, where higher education is a centralized service of the state whose policy is set by the government in power and administered by a national bureaucracy, the government's response to such a problem constitutes an immediate political issue. The government of French President Giscard d'Estaing stepped into the breach in January 1976 with a reform ostensibly aimed at improving the students' economic plight by aligning university studies with job opportunities.

While economic hard times seem to have made American students more docile, French students again took to the streets to protest this situation and the Giscardian policy to manage it. Demonstrations begun in February at the urging of leftist teacher and student unions peaked in April when 40,000 students marched in Paris and clashed with French riot police. By that time there were more than 100,000 students involved and nearly two-thirds of the universities were on strike.

*The research reported was supported in part by a grant from the General Research Fund, University of California, Santa Barbara, and in part by a Summer Faculty Fellowship, University of California, Santa Barbara.

The author is greatly indebted to many more people in France, who gave generously of their time, knowledge and insights, than can possibly be named. Raymond Boudon, Jean-Claude Casanova, Michel Crozier and Bertrand Girod de l'Ain in France and Burton R. Clark in the United States merit special thanks for their assistance at various stages of this French research.

32

Why did French students protest against a reform enthusiastically hailed by the Prime Minister as "destined to allow the adaptation of education to the realities of life, to give students more chances to acquire knowledge that will permit them actually to emerge into an occupational life" and to find "that which it is proper to term employment today?" This article argues that the reform was designed not so much to aid the students as to suppress growing class conflict in the higher education system. France, like the United States, has a dual system of higher education and class dominance of this system has been assured by governmental policy using the ideology of equality of opportunity to legitimate that dominance. The 1976 reform represents use of governmental policy to preserve class dominance of the higher education system by junior collegizing the French University.[1]

Equality and Democracy: The Dual System of Higher Education

In France, as in most other countries, class dominance of the educational system has been assured through the years by governmental policy. The Giscardian government, even more than the Pompidolian and Gaullist ones before it, is a government of landowners, industrialists and the bourgeoisie. The policy of this government, as of virtually all French governments since Napoleon, has fostered and maintained a dual system of higher education—one for the elite, the other for the mass. This dual system has reserved the best education, leading to the highest positions in government and private enterprise for the children of the upper and upper-middle class, and this process has been justified in the name of equality of educational opportunity.

Despite its universal flavor, the phrase "equality of educational opportunity" is sufficiently vague that it accommodates substantially different meanings in different societies and at different times within the same society, and thus is malleable to many political purposes. The construction of "equality" most commonly adopted defines equality of educational opportunity as equality of access to education. "Equality of access" itself, however, is subject to substantially different meanings and attendant applications as the two polar cases make clear. These are the selective and open-door systems. In the former, entry to higher education is limited by pre-enrollment selection on the basis of academic ability as attested to by grades, competitions, tests or other "objective" criteria. In such a system socioeconomic status is purportedly eliminated as a barrier by free higher education, scholarships and subsidies, expected to equalize the material opportunity to attend college and thus to provide equal access to all "qualified" students. In the open-door system, on the other hand, entry to higher education is guaranteed to all who want it with, at most, nominal pre-enrollment selection, such as the requirement of a high school diploma or *baccalauréat*.[2]

Not unexpectedly, the implementation of these two equal access systems operates quite differently. The selective system openly chooses those who shall enter higher education. In the open-door system, on the other hand, sorting becomes a major internal consideration

---

[1] After Napoleon the entire national system of academic secondary and higher education institutions in France was referred to as *l'Université de France*. In 1850 the official designation was abolished but the informal usage has continued. Since this article is devoted to higher education, the author has used the term "university" in the American sense. The "University" or "French University" with a capital "U" is used to refer to the entire state system of universities and related establishments. The word "university" with a lower case "u" refers to one of the branch universities in the University system.

[2] Another possible conception of equality in higher education defines equality in terms of results, experience or possibility of success. This formulation rests on the fact, noted by a Ford Foundation Task Force on Higher Education, that "access alone does not automatically lead to a successful education. It measures only the exposure of a particular age group to whatever educational institutions there are, and not the equality of the experience they are likely to find there" (U.S. Department of Health, Education, and Welfare, 1971:1). No system of higher education of which I am aware is committed to the goal of equal educational results.

and selection of students is made after entry, often covertly. The two major selection-after-entry mechanisms are failing out and "cooling out" students. The "cooling out" mechanism is frequently used in American junior colleges where students are eased out of four-year academic transfer programs and into two-year terminal vocational programs (Clark, 1960a; 1960b).

The French Constitution, embodying the revolutionary ideal of *egalité,* places upon the state the duty to organize "state-provided, free, secular education at all levels." Consequently, the French system of higher education consists of very few private institutions and governmental education policy, in fullfilling its charge to provide free and equal higher education, has adopted the definition of "equality" as equality of access. This equal access system is divided into two main components, one selective and the other following an open-door policy.

The selective segment is comprised of the *grandes écoles* ("great schools") operated by the Ministry of National Education and certain other ministries. Although they are said to offer a more technically-oriented education than the universities, the *grandes écoles* educate the true elite in French society and are well attuned to the needs of the French bureaucratic and social system. Entry into the *grandes écoles* is controlled by a double system of selection: the student must, upon graduation from the *lycée,* first be accepted into the preparatory classes for the *grandes écoles* (CPGE), an extremely competitive process heavily dependent upon letters of recommendation, and then two years later must pass another highly competitive entrance examination. Graduation from the *grandes écoles* assures a prestigious and high-paying position in public service or private enterprise. The open-door segment consists primarily of the French University, a highly centralized system of approximately 70 individual universities, which admits anyone with a *baccalauréat.*

These two segments of French higher education constitute a dual system of higher education, with the selective segment virtually the exclusive province of the very highest social classes. At the start of the decade of the 1960's the balance between the selective and open-door segments of French higher education was such that nearly one-fourth of all students were in the CPGE and the *grandes écoles* (Ministère de l'Education, 1975). The French postwar baby boom and the increasing social demand for higher education combined to cause higher education enrollments to sky-rocket, more than doubling between the start of the decade and the May-June 1968 student demonstrations (Patterson, 1972). The tremendous growth in numbers was not felt evenly throughout the system, however: the number of students in the CPGE and the *grandes écoles* increased by less than one-third, while the University population grew by a factor of nearly two and one-half.

The University As Safety Valve

Governmental policy implementing the ideology of equality of educational opportunity continued to reserve the *grandes écoles* to the dominant class by not expanding their enrollments to meet the growing demand for higher education. Instead, the open-door University acted as a safety valve, absorbing the growing number of students and, at the same time, defusing any demands for access to the elite segment of French higher education. The net result of the boom of the 1960's, therefore, was that in a very significant sense French higher education became less open than before. By the end of the decade, the chances of a French student entering the selective segment of higher education were lower than ever.

Figure 1 shows the growth in first-year enrollments in all higher education and in the CPGE from 1960-61 to 1972-73. It also shows the proportion of first-year students entering the elite, selective CPGE. The figure graphically demonstrates that the chances of a French student entering the CPGE after leaving the *lycée* in 1972-73 were less than one in ten (9.1

FIGURE 1
First-Year Enrollments in French Higher Education

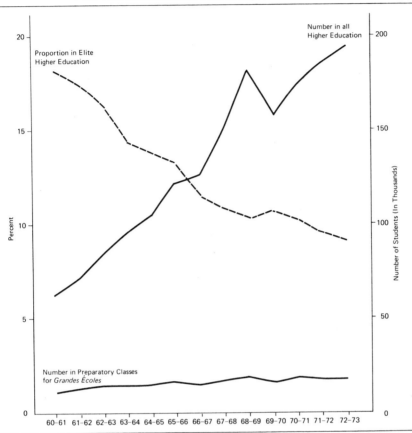

SOURCE: Constructed from statistics in Ministère de l'Education (1975:20).

percent), only one-half those of students receiving their *baccalauréat* about a decade earlier. This compares to a 15.4 percent chance of an American freshman entering an elite institution in 1973 (Astin, et al., 1973).[3]

Thus France, like the United States, witnessed a tremendous growth in higher education in the 60's, but at a lower level than previously. In the United States the expansion was into the junior colleges (see Karabel, 1972; Bowles, 1971; Gintis, 1971), in France it was into the University. Governmental policy implemented the ideology of equality of educational opportunity, not by opening all of higher education equally, but by directing students away from the bastions of the dominant class and into non-elite open-door institutions. The expansion of the 60's, by emphasizing (over-emphasizing, according to some like Berg [1971]) the importance of higher education, may actually have widened the gap between

---

[3] The *baccalauréat* is the degree awarded upon completion of the French *lycée* and passage of an examination. As such it is roughly the equivalent of the American high school diploma. However, in France it is awarded to a far smaller proportion of the age cohort and is also considered the first degree of higher education.

the relatively fewer in the elite segment of French higher education and the mass in the open-door segment. If the boom did not create equality between the elite and mass institutions, did it at least lead to greater democratization of the student body?

The higher education system in France, including the University, has always had a strong social class bias (see Bourdieu, 1966; Bourdieu & Passeron, 1964, 1968, 1970; Bisseret, 1968a, 1968b). From formal and informal processes of pre- and post-entry selection, the French University developed a class character which belied its establishment as an equal access, open-door institution. The proportion of students from the upper class (approximately one-third of the student population) is more than three and one-half times the proportion in the overall population. The working class, with only about 10 percent of the University students, is represented less than one-third as much in the University as in the general population. The percentage of University students from each social class, moreover, remained virtually unchanged from 1961-62 through 1971-72 (Patterson, 1975; Ministère de l'Education, 1975).

Although there was little change in social class composition, the overall growth in numbers during the decade of the 60's meant that there were more students from the middle class and below attending the University (Patterson, 1975). Proportionately, the greatest numerical increase took place among students from a working-class background. Their ranks grew by more than one and one-half times the overall rate, with those whose fathers were manual workers growing at more than twice the University-wide rate.

For the grandes écoles the situation is even more aggravated than in the University. The French government does not publish any official statistics on the socioeconomic status of students at the grandes écoles comparable to those published for the University, a practice helping to mask the class dominance of the dual system of higher education. However, a special study group appointed by the Prime Minister in the early 1960's to examine the general state of the grandes écoles included in its published report its own findings on the socioeconomic status of students in these schools. These data showed that almost half of the students in all the grandes écoles were from upper-class backgrounds, nearly six times their proportion in the general population. Another quarter were from the middle class (Groupe d'Etudes, 1964). Only 13 percent were from the working class. Although the proportion of working-class students was double that in the University at the time, the explanation lies in the fact that the grandes écoles include several institutions devoted to agriculture where the proportion of working-class students varied from a low of 17 percent to a high of 33 percent. The gross statistics are misleading in another respect. They do not disclose that the proportion from the upper class is highest in the most prestigious grandes écoles. For example, the Ecole Polytechnique, the top grande école, is comprised of 70 percent upper-class students and another 23 percent middle-class students. No one believes these figures have changed much in the last fifteen years.

The dual system of higher education in France thus functions to reserve the elite institutions with their entrée into the highest occupational positions primarily to upper and upper-middle-class students. The expansion of opportunity in higher education for working- and middle-class students in the 60's took place at the lower level of the dual system of higher education—the University—and it was there that the pressure of the events of May-June 1968 was felt (Patterson, 1972; 1975). It was, as we shall see, these increasing numbers of working- and middle-class students who painfully discovered they had been cheated by the University and that the higher education they thought constituted their route to social mobility was but a brief passage through a cultural center, leaving them with only disparate knowledge and mediocre jobs.

Higher Education and Jobs: The Missing Link?

The safety valve function of the open-door University could only be performed so long as the students channelled away from the *grandes écoles* and into the University were also channelled into jobs upon the completion of their studies. But, for a number of years prior to the explosive events of May-June 1968, the lack of training given by the French University had been widely criticized. The economic growth and industrial evolution of French society created increasing pressure for a redefinition of the goals of the University that would prepare students to assume roles in a technological environment. These pressures came from surprisingly diverse sources and often for conflicting reasons. The *Federation Nationale des Etudiants de France*, a right-of-center student union, urged the vocational training of students. On the other side of the spectrum, the French Communist Party demanded that the University not only give to the population—and especially workers—a "culture of a high level" but that it also ease the flow of students into the economic life of the country.

Such criticisms had much validity. Vocationally, the French University, unlike its American counterparts (and unlike the *grandes écoles*), had systematically isolated itself from the needs of the nation. The Langevin-Wallon report, a major educational reform proposal which preceded May-June 1968 by 20 years, had recommended breaking down the isolation between all levels of French schools and the life of the nation, but nothing was done. Bourdieu and Passeron (1964) criticized the French University for treating its students as if they were all to be future professors, an emphasis bound to frustrate the vast majority. Discussing the effect of the University's separation from the economy, they highlighted the vocational aimlessness of students at entry, the absence of any perceived relevance of the courses studied, and the general lack of connection of University studies with career possibilities. They concluded that the University was responsive to neither the immediate interests nor the future activities of its students. Aron (1969:149) noted:

> Until recently most graduates went into the teaching profession. There was a kind of vicious circle in which teachers educated students, the best of whom progressed when the time was ripe to join the dignified ranks of their mentors.

The growth of University student numbers, however, forced a break with this noble tradition. There were not enough teaching jobs in the *lycées* and the universities. One study (Vermot-Gauchy, 1965) predicted that in 1975 nearly two-thirds of the *licenciés* (holders of the *licence,* the basic teacher's degree) produced by the University would not find a job at the level of their training. That year the University was expected to award 65,000 *licences* and there would be 45,000 jobs theoretically requiring this level of competence. But 20,000 of these jobs would be filled by *licenciés* graduated from the *grandes écoles,* leaving 40,000 University *licenciés* unemployed or under-employed. In psychology it was estimated that only 20 percent of the students could reasonably hope to be employed in their discipline (Oléron, 1967). Thus, beginning in the late 60's and early 70's, most French University graduates would have to find jobs outside the teaching profession, but they had recived an education that prepared them for nothing else. At the same time, projections of French personpower requirements showed there would be a shortage of trained personnel at all levels—except for teachers (Patterson, 1975).

When the University students were surveyed on their views of the reasons for the events of May-June 1968, nearly three-fifths said that "anxiety about the probability of finding a job related to one's studies" was the most important reason (Institut Français d'Opinion Publique, 1968). Another one-third chose "unresponsiveness of the University to the needs of a modern society" as the most important factor. Thus, fully 90 percent of all University students were vitally concerned about the isolation of the University.

If the students' anxiety about jobs was high in 1968, it must have been even higher in 1976 when they again demonstrated against the government's newest reform of the University. Indeed, the statistics on joblessness presented an increasingly gloomy picture. The overall French unemployment rate had increased by one-fourth, from 1.7 percent in 1968 to 2.1 percent in 1974 (OECD, 1975).[4] The increase among workers in the less than 25 year-old bracket accounted for a substantial portion of the overall increase. Unemployment among this age group went from 3.3 percent to 4.9 percent, double the overall rate of increase and three times that for the fifty and over group. A University diploma provided no protection and university graduates shared in the increased unemployment. Four years after graduation more than one-sixth of the 1966 recipients of the *licence* in arts, political science, economics and law were still looking for work (Vrain, 1973). Of these, three-fourths still hoped to find a job in teaching at one level or another.

Even those students who do find jobs are not finding them in fields directly related to their University studies. A study of science students who entered the University between 1968 and 1970 found that 70 percent of those leaving during or at the end of the first cycle of higher education (more than half of those entering the University) responded that some training other than the University's was decisive in their professional lives (Dufrasne, 1975).[5] Less than one in ten said that their University studies were essential. For students who continued beyond the first cycle, the prospects of finding a job related to their studies were still dim. Slightly more than half of those who completed the second cycle and received a *licence* credited their University training as important, but fully one-fourth said that some training other than that received in the University was the key to their professional careers. Among those who completed the third and highest cycle (doctorates), not unexpectedly, the proportion whose jobs were related to and determined by their education jumped to 76 percent. However, more than one-fifth still reported that the decisive element was some training other than that received in the University.

Immediate and future prospects are even more grim. Preliminary estimates are that 100,000 of the 160,000 University graduates last year are presently unemployed. Between 1975 and 1980 150,000 new jobs per year are expected, but 260,000 new workers per year will appear, more than half of them coming from the University (Lefournier, 1975). By 1980 the overall unemployment rate is predicted at between 3 and 6 percent.

The missing link between higher education and jobs may signal the breakdown of higher education as a mechanism either for social mobility or even for the maintenance of present social status (Boudon, 1969). Here the situation in France is not dissimilar from that in the United States. Berg (1971) discovered that nearly 80 percent of American college graduates were taking jobs previously filled by workers with lower educational credentials. O'Toole (1975a; 1975b) analyzed the American situation and concluded that we have a "reserve army" of "underemployed" persons who hold jobs needing less education than they have. Most recently, economist Richard Freeman (1976) concluded that the bust in the college-educated job market is evidence that our society is "overeducated" and that college education offers only limited opportunities for economic and social advancement, with increased education leading to rapidly declining relative incomes for graduates (see also Freeman & Holloman, 1975).

---

[4] The "elite" American institutions are those 4-year colleges and universities which the American Council on Education characterized as being of "high" or "very high" selectivity.

[5] To Americans these figures seem insignificantly *low* and it is hard to imagine anyone complaining about what we would consider "full employment." However, France, like most of Europe in recent years, has not experienced or tolerated more than token unemployment. The increase, therefore, is perhaps equivalent to a change in the umemployment rate in the United States from 4 to 6 or 7 percent.

The missing link between University education and jobs not only threatens higher education as a route to social mobility, it also threatens the safety valve in the dual system of higher education. If University students are not able to find employment, more and more demands will be heard for greater access to the *grandes écoles,* assuring employment at a very high level for their graduates. This in turn would bring submerged class conflict over the higher education system to the surface.

The Junior Collegization of the French University

The object of the 1976 reform of higher education was to replace the missing link between education and jobs. Alice Saunier-Seïté, Secretary of State for Universities, declared: "These reforms will permit graduates to find jobs. They correspond exactly to what students have been demanding for years." The protests of the spring of 1976 belied Mrs. Saunier-Seïté's assertion; the reform was not "exactly" what a large proportion of the students were demanding. It attempts to change the second cycle of French higher education by shortening the time required to earn certain degrees and by directing the seventy-odd French universities to modify certain degree programs to make them more vocationally oriented. The modified second cycle programs must be submitted by the universities to the Secretary by the end of 1976 and the Secretary will decide by next spring which ones are to receive the sanction of national degrees.

The 1976 reform was not the first attempt in recent years to adapt French higher education to the job market and simultaneously to deal with the numerical pressure of mass enrollment. The 1966 Fouchet reform aimed at the same problems by creating new institutions, the *Instituts Universitaires de Technologie* (University Institutes of Technology or IUTs), the basic equivalent of American junior colleges. The IUTs, awarding a new degree and, unlike the University, open to students without a *baccalauréat,* "are to provide a two-year course of training for higher technicians in industry and the services, who will be responsible for putting formal knowledge and theoretical research results to practical use. These graduates should therefore have a more specific and more thorough practical technical training . . . and a broader overall training than technicians" (Directorate for Scientific Affairs, OECD, 1972: 14).

The reaction to the creation of IUTs was not entirely enthusiastic. Cappelle (1966) pointed out that the University had rejected pre-entry selection in favor of maintaining its open door policy, but that it wanted to channel the poorer students into the IUTs. The effect of the Fouchet reform was thus to create a new higher education hierarchy with the IUTs on the bottom.

This fact is reflected most vividly in the disappointing (from the standpoint of the French Fifth Plan) enrollment statistics for the IUTs. The IUTs were initially established in 12 provincial universities and Paris; by 1967-68 there were IUTs in 18 universities and by 1968-69 all 23 then-existing universities had IUTs. The Fifth Plan projected that by 1972 there would be 750,000 students in all branches of French higher education (a fairly accurate estimate) and, in a burst of optimism, predicted that one-fourth—nearly 190,000—of them would be in IUTs. The actual attraction of IUTs for students was far less than the formulators of the Fifth Plan guessed. In the academic year 1970-71 there were 45,000 places in the IUTs, but only about half that number (24,000) of students; there were more students enrolled in the preparatory classes for the *grandes écoles* in that year (36,000 students) than in the IUTs. It was not until the 1974-75 academic year that the IUTs reached even the 40,000 student level.

The Fouchet reform thus failed either to divert a significant number of students from regular University studies or to improve noticeably the poor job prospects of University students. It accordingly did little to suppress the growing class conflict over the distribution of rewards from higher education. Seven years later the Pompidolian government made its own effort to make University studies subservient to the economy. The Ministry of National Education instituted a reform of the first cycle of the University designed both to reduce the number of students continuing to the second cycle and to channel those not going on into lower level jobs.[6] This reform created a new and terminal degree, the *diplôme de "études universitaires générales* (DEUG): these studies were intended better to suit students for employment. The intent underlying the reform was, as declared by the Minister in announcing the new policy:

> There exists a quantity of employment demanding a formation more extensive than the *baccalauréat* [the high school diploma], but less than the *licence* [like the B.A.] as it is organized. That's why I wonder whether it's not necessary to foresee, for the students who abandon or fail before the end of the second cycle, a first cycle permitting them to acquire a training that is sufficient in itself.

Like the establishment of the IUTs before it, the creation of the DEUG as a terminal degree failed to provide an attractive alternative to the traditional and longer college degree (the *licence*). The proportion of students continuing their studies into the second cycle is as high now as before its existence.

Both of these earlier reforms represented attempts to "cool out" students from the higher studies of the University, where they were trained for teaching and other jobs that only existed in small numbers, and into other channels with surer outlets to lower level jobs. The failure of the previous reforms to "cool out" significant numbers of students into technical junior colleges (in the case of the IUTs) or into first cycle terminal programs (in the case of the DEUG) created the necessity for further action with a new reform in 1976.

Although the stated rationale for the governmental policy in each instance was that the University was poorly adapted to a modern, technological world, the real purpose was to preserve the dual system of higher education and thereby insure the domination of the elite *grandes écoles.* This purpose was to be accomplished by reestablishing the link between higher education and any jobs, even jobs at a lower level. This link allows the government to appear to meet the dual demands for higher education and social advancement by assuring students and their families that the training they receive in the open-door University will lead to employment. Since this employment will be at a level previously requiring no higher education, the net result is a devaluation of higher education for the masses.

The claims of the 1976 reform's supporters that it will lead to jobs for University graduates masks the fact that the reform amounts to a downgrading or junior collegization of the University. The reform constitutes a junior collegization of the University because, if successful, its end result will be to tie university studies more closely to the needs of French employers for trained personnel of a lower level. University graduates may find it easier to get jobs as a result of the reform; indeed, IUT graduates are very successful in finding jobs, but they are usually dead-end ones (Murcier, 1975). For students from the working and lower-middle class the danger of this educational devaluation lies in the fact that social mobility slips further and further away. For middle-class students educational devaluation brings about the anxious realization that attaining the same education and degrees as their parents will not bring them the same jobs; in fact, they see the social status received from their families slipping from their grasp.

---

[6] French higher education is organized into "cycles" of two years each. The first cycle leads to a general diploma of doubtful value. More than one-half the students do not progress beyond the first cycle. The second sycle leads to the *licence,* roughly the equivalent of an American B.A. and the basic teacher's degree.

It remains to be seen how the individual universities respond to the governmental imperative to modify their second cycle programs. If they act in accordance with the reform's intent, the reform will succeed in preserving, at least temporarily, the dual system of higher education in France. By "cooling out" students into lower jobs it will resupply the missing link between higher education and jobs, a link essential for the University to act as the safety valve of the system. In this way it will help avert pressure for greater access to the elite *grandes écoles* and, simultaneously, continue to reserve the highest occupational positions to the children of the highest social classes. The price of this strategy will be to widen the gap in quality between the *grandes écoles* and the University, but this is a price the Giscardian government clearly seems willing to pay.

REFERENCES

Aron, Raymond
1969   The Elusive Revolution. New York: Praeger Publishers.
Astin, Alexander W., et al.
1973   The American Freshman: National Norms for Fall 1973. Los Angeles: Cooperative Institutional Research Program.
Berg, Ivar
1971   Education and Jobs: The Great Training Robbery. Boston: Beacon Press.
Bisseret, Noëlle
1968a   "La 'Naissance' et le diplôme: Les Processus de sélection au début des études universitaires." Revue française de sociologie, 9 (numéro spécial): 184-207.
1968b   "La Sélection a l'université et sa signification pour l'étude des rapports de dominance." Revue française de sociologie, 9 (October-December):463-496.
Boudon, Raymond
1969   "La Crise universitaire francaise: Essai de diagnostic sociologique." Annales: Economies Societés, Civilisations, 24 (May-June): 738-764.
Bourdieu, Pierre
1966   "L'Ecole conservatrice: Les Inégalités devant l'école et devant la culture." Revue française de sociologie, 7 (July-September): 325-347.
Bourdieu, Pierre and Jean-Claude Passeron
1964   Les Heritiers: Les Etudiants et la culture. Paris: Editions de Minuit.
1968   "L'Examen d'une illusion." Revue française de sociologie, 9 (numéro spécial): 227-253.
1970   La Reproduction. Paris: Editions de Minuit.
Bowles, Samuel
1971   "Unequal education and the reproduction of the social division of labor." Review of Radical Political Economics, 3 (Fall): 1-30.
Capelle, Jean
1966   L'Ecole de demain reste à faire. Paris: Presses Universitaires de France.
Clark, Burton R.
1960a   "The 'cooling-out' function in higher education." American Journal of Sociology, 65 (May): 569-576.
1960b   The Open Door College. New York: McGraw-Hill.
Directorate for Scientific Affairs, OECD
1972   Educational Policy and Planning: France. Paris: Organisation for Economic Co-operation and Development.
Dufrasne, Claude
1975   Le Devenir professionnel des étudiants en sciences. Paris: Université Paris VII.
Freeman, Richard B.
1976   The Over-Educated American. New York: Academic Press.
Freeman, Richard and J. Herbert Holloman
1975   "The declining value of college going." Change 7 (September): 24-31, 62.
Gintis, H.
1971   "Education, technology, and the characteristics of worker productivity." American Economic Review (May): 266-279.
Groupe d'Etudes
1964   Les Conditions de développement, de recruitement, de fonctionnement et de localisation des grandes écoles en France: Rapport de Groupe d'Etudes au Premier Ministre, 26 Septembre 1963. Paris: La Documentation Française.
Institute Français d'Opinion Publique
1968   "Sondage étudiants, Septembre 1968." Réalités, No. 254 (November).

Karabel, Jerome
    1972   "Community colleges and social stratification." Harvard Educational Review, 42 (November): 521-562.
Lefournier, Philippe
    1975   "Une nouvelle pénurie: l'emploi." L'Expansion, 85 (May): 80-89.
Ministère de l'Education, Secretariat d'Etat aux Universités
    1975   Données statistiques sur le developpement des effectifs de l'enseignement supérieur en France, depuis 1960. Paris: Service d'Informations Economiques et Statistiques.
Murcier, Alain
    1975   "Les Pionniers des I.U.T." L'Expansion, 88 (September): 138-141.
OECD
    1975   OECD Economic Surveys: France. Paris: Organisation for Economic Co-operation and Development.
Oléron, Pierre
    1967   "Données statistiques sur un échantillon d'étudiants en psychologie." Bulletin de Psychologie, 21 (October): 1-4.
O'Toole, James
    1975a   "The reserve army of the underemployed—part i." Change, 7 (May): 26-33, 63.
    1975b   "The reserve army of the underemployed—part ii." Change, 7 (June): 26-33, 60-63.
Patterson, Michelle
    1972   "French university reform: renaissance or restoration?" Comparative Education Review, 16 (June): 281-302.
    1975   Conflict, Power and Structure: Crisis and Reform in the French University. Unpublished manuscript.
    1976   "Organizational adaptation and conflict: exit and voice in the french university." Paper presented at the annual meetings of the American Sociological Association.
Vermot-Gauchy, Michel
    1965   L'Education nationale dans la France de demain. Monaco: Editions du Rocher.
Vrain, Philippe
    1973   Les Débouchés professionnels des étudiants. Paris: Presses Universitaires de France.

EDUCATION, JOBS, AND INEQUALITY: FUNCTIONAL AND CONFLICT MODELS OF SOCIAL STRATIFICATION IN THE UNITED STATES*

GREGORY D. SQUIRES
Michigan State University

This study examines two competing interpretations of the relation between formal education and the occupational structure, and the dynamics of social stratification in the United States. The techno-democratic model points to the rising requirements of technical skill for jobs and the pursuit of greater economic equality to explain the expansion of formal education. The class conflict model maintains that formal education has expanded in order to maintain the stability of work organizations and the class structure by imparting noncognitive characteristics encouraging existing social relationships. The findings suggest that: (1) The expansion of education cannot be explained by changing technical skill requirements of work. (2) While inequality in educational attainment has been reduced for the population as a whole and between whites and nonwhites, this has not led to a reduction of economic inequality. (3) The noncognitive attributes inculcated by schooling are rewarded in the occupational structure; this reflects employers' concern for social control within organizations. The major implication of this study is that the relationship between education, jobs, and social inequality can be better understood in terms of class structure rather than assumed differences in the characteristics (marginal productivity) of individuals who interact within the constraints of that structure. If a reduction of economic inequality is a policy objective, the focus of social policy should be on the structural determinants of inequality rather than on the education, training, or some other characteristic of individuals.

. . . industry places a high value on the college degree, not because it is convinced that the four years of schooling insure that individuals acquire maturity and technical competence, but rather because it provides an initial starting point of division between those more trained and those less trained; those better motivated and those less motivated; those with more social experience and those with less[1] (Gordon and Howell, 1959: 121).

Formal education has expanded throughout the history of the United States, particularly since World War II. With each passing generation more people are attending school, staying in school longer, and spending more on formal education. The school year is longer and students attend a higher percentage of their classes (U.S. National Center for Education Statistics, 1975: 34-35). One of the major attractions of formal education is the higher level of

---

*Some of this material will appear in a forthcoming book by the author, *Education and Jobs: The Imbalancing of the Social Machinery*, Transaction Books.

[1] Labor Department estimates for 4000 jobs in 1949 were reported in *Estimates of Worker Trait Requirements for 4000 jobs as Defined in the 1949 Dictionary of Occupational Titles*, 1957. A revision entitled *Selected Characteristics of Occupations, (Physical Demands, Working Conditions, Training Time) 1966—A Supplement to the Dictionary of Occupational Titles* provided similar information for 14,000 jobs in 1965. These estimates were based on job descriptions provided in the second and third edition of the *Dictionary of Occupational Titles*. In order to compare functional requirements with educational attainment, GED scores in the *Dictionary* must be translated into years of schooling, a problem compounded by the fact that the seven point GED scale used in the second edition was collapsed into a six point scale in the third edition. For a description of how these estimates were made see *Estimates,* p. iv-ix and 110-158 and Berg, 1971, p. 43-45.

economic reward available to the better educated. Yet there is debate over what constitutes the link between education and jobs, and the dynamics of social stratification.

Several explanations exist for the expansion of education, the relation between educational attainment and occupational status, and the nature of social inequality in the United States, but most follow two basic models. One, the techno-democratic model, maintains that education has expanded in response to the rising technical skill requirements of jobs (Cubberley, 1909: 18-19; Kerr, et. al., 1974: 70-77; Killingsworth, 1966: 106-116) and to create greater equality, or at least equality of opportunity (President's Commission on Higher Education, 1947: Vol. I & II; Commager, 1950; Lipset and Bendix, 1959: 101; Cremin, 1961: VII-IX, 3-22; Schultz, 1961: 16; U.S. Commission on Civil Rights, 1974: 87), and social mobility for all segments of the population (Blau and Duncan, 1971: Hechinger, 1976). Rooted primarily in functional sociological theory and human capital economic theory, this model emphasizes the differences in the cognitive abilities (marginal productivity) of individuals in accounting for inequality, and points to the nation's schools as the key for providing people with the skills required to compete in American society.

This perspective has been challenged in recent years, mainly from the perspective of a class conflict model. In this view, formal education expanded to meet the rising social control problems generated by industrialization and urbanization in the United States by imparting noncognitive traits of obedience, desciplining, and respect for authority in students rather than by responding to the changing technical skill requirements of jobs, or desires to reduce inequality or increase mobility (Katz, 1971; Greer, 1972; Spring, 1972). The primary function of education is to socialize workers into the socio-economic status of their parents and perpetuate the class structure. (Bowles and Gintis, 1976; Karier, 1972; Friedenberg, 1965; Goodman, 1964; Illich, 1971). Educational credentials are used to rank workers rather than measure a level of skills (Thurow, 1975); to allocate workers to existing, unequal slots within the occupational structure (Jencks, et. al., 1973); and to restrict access to more desirable jobs (Collins, 1971; Stiglitz, 1975; Griliches and Mason, 1972; Taubman and Wales, 1974). Inequality is rooted in the dynamics of the class structure and inherent in a capitalist mode of production, rather than in the characteristics of individuals. Education has served to legitimize class relationships in a capitalist economy. Until those relationships are dealt with directly, educational expansion or reform is unlikely to alter the distribution of rewards.

This study examines a variety of empirical data to determine which model more adequately reflects the education-jobs nexus and the dynamics of social stratification. Evidence will be examined for answers to the following questions:

1. Can the expansion of formal education in the United States be explained in terms of technological advances or changes in the technical skill requirements of jobs?

2. Has the expansion of formal education resulted in a reduction of economic inequality?

3. While education has long been associated with income and occupational status, is it the noncognitive characteristics or the technical skills inculcated by formal schooling which are rewarded in the occupational structure?

TECHNOLOGY AND EDUCATION

Whether advancing technology has been a primary determinant of educational expansion will be assessed by looking at the following: (1) the relation between changes in the technical skill requirements of jobs and changes in the educational attainment and job performance; (2) the kinds of training workers use in learning the skill requirements of their jobs; and; (3) a simulated longitudinal analysis of the educational attainment of workers within selected occupations.

Technical Skill Requirements of Jobs and Educational Attainment of Workers

U.S. Department of Labor estimates of changes in the amount of formal education dictated by changes in the technical skill requirements of jobs, and U.S. Census Bureau reports on the increasing educational attainment of workers, show that attainment has far surpassed the level which functional requirements could explain. Berg found that as of 1950, 1.1 million jobs required a college degree while 4.1 million workers were college graduates. In 1960, 1.4 million jobs required a degree while 6.0 million workers were graduates. This methodology was used in other studies, yielding similar results (Rawlins and Ulman, 1974; Miller, 1971).

That educational attainment has risen faster than technical skill requirements, and that functional requirements cannot explain the expansion of formal education, is further indicated by an increase in the educational attainment of workers in all occupational groups, not just in the highly skilled professions. For example, between 1948 and 1973, the median number of school years attained by farmers and farm laborers increased from 8.0 to 10.7, for service workers the increase was from 8.7 to 12.0, for all blue-collar workers the comparable figures are 9.0 and 12.1, while for professional and managerial workers the increase was from 12.8 to 15.6 (U.S. Department of Labor, 1974a: 303).

The Impact of Technological Change on the Skill Requirements of Jobs

A review of over five hundred bibliographic titles, published between the early 1950's and mid 1960's on the effects of technological change on job skill requirements yielded the following conclusion:

> From the current literature one cannot generalize about the effects of automation and technological change upon job content and skill requirements, except to say that they differ (Horowitz and Herrnstadt, 1966: 230).

In perhaps the most exhaustive case studies of the effects of mechanization and automation on job skills, Bright concluded:

> the net effect of automation in almost every plant I studied was still to reduce—or at least not to increase—the demand for skills and abilities of the direct labor force (1966: 214).

One finds that when the technical skill requirements of jobs are affected by technological change, workers learn whatever additional skills are required informally on the job, and rarely participate in a formal training program (Bright, 1958; Collins, 1969; Fine, 1964; Jaffee and Froomkin, 1968; Mueller, 1969).

Recent historical analyses of the labor process and the bureaucratization of work have illustrated how, in part as a result of the advent of Taylor's principles of scientific management, skilled occupations have been fragmented into several unskilled jobs, thus reducing the skill requirements for many clerical, service, craft, sales, and some professional and technical occupations (Aronowitz, 1973: 291-322; Braverman, 1974: 155-248, 292-409; Marglin, 1974; Stone, 1974). Shifts in the occupational structure from farm laborer to operative or from blue-collar to white-collar occupations are often misinterpreted as representing an upgrading of skill requirements. This interpretation rests on conventional assumptions about the nature of U.S. Census Bureau occupational classifications, when the skills required on jobs actually have been reduced (Braverman, 1974: 424-449). An assembly line worker may use more sophisticated machinery than the small family farmer, but operatives are not therefore more highly skilled workers. While the proportion of white collar jobs has been expanding, the largest growth has been in clerical occupations (U.S. Census Bureau, 1960:

74; U.S. Census Bureau, 1974a: 350), not clearly distinguishable from many blue-collar occupations, which often pay more. (U.S. Census Bureau, 1973c: Tables 227 & 228).

No doubt jobs have been created as a result of technological changes requiring newer and higher levels of skill. But the available evidence indicates that skill requirements of jobs throughout the occupational structure have not undergone massive upgrading. When changes have occurred, they have not resulted in a demand for extensive formal retraining or educational programs.

The Effects of Formal Education on Job Performance

While employers have been steadily increasing educational requirements of jobs, few attempt to validate this selection criterion (Berg, 1971: 15) and even fewer are willing to make public the results of studies which are conducted in an attempt to determine whether or not better educated workers are more productive. I wrote to sixty companies asking for such information.[2] Of the twenty-nine which responded, nine said it was company policy not to provide such information for the public, three said they had done some analysis along these lines in the past, and seventeen said they never conducted this kind of research. Available information suggests why employers are not anxious to cooperate.

Berg (1971: 85-176) found that in terms of productivity, turnover, absenteeism, supervisors' ratings, and rates of promotion, education was frequently inversely related to job performance for jobs throughout the occupational structure. In a study of entry level jobs Diamond and Bedrosian (1970: 6) concluded, "little or no difference in job performance could be attributed to differences in education." A study of tool and die makers (Horowitz and Herrnstadt, 1969) concluded that the relation between type of training (ranging from formal schooling to "just picked it up on the job") and competence was not statistically significant.

Employers are aware of such findings, but they do not appear to affect hiring practices. A Bank of America Vice-President argued, "The banking business isn't so mysterious that an employer need hold more than one degree" (*Business Week,* 1972a: 51). However, the proportion of male bank officers and financial managers with five or more years of college ranges from 9.6% of those between the ages of 55 and 64 to 15.4% of those between 25 and 34 (U.S. Census Bureau, 1973b: 54). There apparently is a trend towards hiring workers with more than one degree.

In a study of the promotion rates of the 1600 employees in one division of one of the major automobile manufacturers, workers with bachelor's degrees progressed at a faster rate than those with master's and Ph.d.'s and, based on current trends, would surpass the income levels of those with advanced degrees after fifteen years (Forum on Graduate Student Employment, 1974). A company representative informed me, however, that the firm had no intention of dropping the master's degree requirement.

Standard Oil of California is one company which acknowledged an attempt to validate its educational requirements. In a letter from a professional employment coordinator I was told:

> . . . some years ago we did a study to determine if there was any correlation between achievement in college and performance on the job (GPA vs. highest rank achieved). Unfortunately after several months of study and much data gathering for 6,000 unclassified (professional) employees we found there was *no* correlation at all!

---

[2] These companies were selected from a list of those recruiting at Michigan State University. Those companies most likely to maintain this kind of information, according to Jack Shingleton, Director of Placement Services at Michigan State University, were chosen.

Although evidence is fragmentary, the relationship between educational attainment and occupational status cannot be explained by superior levels of performance by better educated workers. When educational requirements are established they serve to disqualify people from those positions, but such requirements do not determine workers in terms of their abilities to perform on the job.

How Are Job Skills Learned?

If modern technology is an important determinant of the expansion of formal education, one would expect that formal education is an important means for workers to learn their jobs. This is not the case. In 1963 the Labor Department conducted the only nationwide survey of how workers learned their jobs (U.S. Department of Labor, 1964). Only 30.2% of those with less than three years of college (over 85% of the civilian labor force) said they used formal training, compared to 56% who cited on-the-job training and 45% who cited other informal methods. Those with three or more years of college were asked a different set of questions, so no comparable findings could be reported for this group of workers. Even if one assumes that all of the better educated workers relied on formal training, this leaves almost 60% of the civilian labor force not using formal training to learn skills required on their jobs.

No doubt professional workers depend more on their formal training than do others, but available evidence on how much even highly skilled workers rely on formal and informal training suggests they, too, use skills learned informally as often as those learned in the classroom (Pierson, 1959: 127-140; Rawlins and Ulman, 1974: 208-211; Bird, 1975: 96-105).

Age and Education of Similarly Employed Workers: A Simulated Longitudinal Analysis

One way to test the relative merits of the techno-democratic and class conflict models is to examine the age and educational attainment of workers within specific occupations. If technical skill requirements dictate educational requirements and attainment, there should be little variation by age in the education of workers within a given job. If education is used to allocate workers to unequal slots within the occupational structure and to restrict access to jobs, one would expect younger workers to have higher levels of educational attainment than older workers in the same job, for employers will raise requirements when better educated workers are available.

When the age and educational attainment of workers in specific occupations is examined, it is clear that educational attainment has increased. Of the seventy-three professional, managerial, sales, and clerical occupations for which age and education are reported in *Earnings by Occupation and Education: 1970 Census of Population* those between the ages of twenty-five and thirty-four were better educated than those between fifty-five and sixty-four in sixty-five (89%) of them (U.S. Census Bureau, 1973b: Table 1). The average difference in the percentage of each group with four or more years of college in these sixty-five occupations was fourteen percentage points.

The difference between specific jobs could be suppressed in an analysis of census occupations. Younger workers may simply hold the more highly skilled jobs within these occupations. In order to examine this relationship among workers holding the same job, performing the same duties within the same organization, data were obtained for 1701 workers in thirty-nine entry level positions currently requiring a college degree, in five private firms.[3]

---

[3] The organizations include: (1) a retail clothing chain; (2) a beer manufacturer; (3) a meat processor; (4) a pharmaceutical drug manufacturer; and (5) a communications equipment manufacturer. For a more complete description of the data see (Squires, 1976: Appendices B and C).

In thirty-three (84.6%) of the thirty-nine jobs the percentage of those under thirty-five with a bachelor's degree was higher than the percentage of those thirty-five or older who held a degree. The average difference in the percentage of each group with a degree was 33.8 percentage points.

The data in Table 1 were provided by an office machine manufacturer for the entry level position of manufacturer sales representative (copier duplicator), a position currently requiring a degree.

Assuming that the younger, more recent entrants into the job market are those most recently receiving their degree, it is again clear that educational requirements have increased, above the level of some veteran workers, for reasons other than technical skill requirements. Recruiters from two of the six firms told me that educational requirements have been raised simply as a response to the available supply of better educated workers.

That changes in the technical skill requirements of jobs cannot explain the educational expansion that has taken place is further demonstrated by the growing phenomenon of underemployment, particularly among college graduates. Several labor market experts have noted that the problem of underemployment for graduates is increasing every year (Shingleton, 1972: 1; Johnston, 1973; O'Toole, 1975; Rosenthal, 1973). In 1973 the Carnegie Commission on Higher Education estimated that at least 10% of those graduating from college in the 1970's would be underemployed (Carnegie Commission on Higher Education, 1973: 4). And the gap between the supply and demand for college graduates in jobs traditionally held by graduates is expected to increase in the 1980's (Rosenthal, 1973).

As college graduates dip further down in the job market, those with less education will have even fewer opportunities (Rosenthal, 1973: 24-25; Johnston, 1973: 28). For example, the percentage of high school graduates entering professional and managerial jobs declined from 8.6% of 1966 graduates to 2.3% of 1972 graduates (U.S. Department of Labor, 1973: A-12; U.S. Department of Labor, 1969: A-8). Better educated workers do earn more and do obtain more attractive jobs, but it is evident that it is the amount of schooling rather than the content of a particular amount of education or the skill requirements of jobs which accounts for the relationship between educational attainment and occupational status. What is the role of formal education in determining the distribution of rewards in society in general? Has the expansion of formal education led to a reduction of economic inequality?

EDUCATION AND ECONOMIC INEQUALITY

A brief review of changes occurring in the distribution of educational resources and the ensuing changes (or lack of change) in the distribution of economic resources indicate that, at least in the post-war years, the equalization predicted by the techno-democratic perspective has not occurred.

TABLE 1

Degrees Earned and Average Number of Years Since Graduation For
Office Machine Manufacturer Sales Representatives (Copier/Duplicator)

Degree	Number of People Holding Degree	Average Number of Years Since Graduation
Ph. D	1	2
Master's	110	4
Bachelor's	958	5
Associate	43	8

TABLE 2

*Percentage of Total Family Income Received by Each Fifth and by Top
Five Percent of Families, Selected Years Between 1947 and 1974*

Families	1947	1955	1969	1972	1974
Lowest Fifth	5.1	4.8	5.6	5.4	5.4
Second Fifth	11.8	12.2	12.3	11.9	12.0
Middle Fifth	16.7	17.7	17.7	17.5	17.6
Fourth Fifth	23.2	23.4	23.7	23.9	24.1
Highest Fifth	43.3	41.8	40.6	41.4	41.0
Top 5 Percent	17.5	16.8	15.6	15.9	15.3

Sources: *Statistical Abstract of the United States 1974*, Bureau of the Census, U.S. Department of Commerce (Washington, D.C.: U.S. Government Printing Office, 1974), No. 619, p. 384. "Money Income and Poverty Status of Families and Persons in the United States: 1974," Current Population Reports, Series P-60, No. 99, Bureau of the Census, U.S. Department of Commerce (Washington, D.C.: U.S. Government Printing Office, 1974), Table 4, p. 8.

An Overview

Not only have people come to spend more time in school over the years, but educational attainment, in terms of the number of school years completed, has also become more equal (Jencks, et. al., 1973: 20). But this expansion and equalization has not been translated into economic equality, as Table 2 illustrates.

While the percentage of total family income accruing to each quintile has changed little, the absolute income gaps have increased. For example, the difference in the mean income of families in the top and bottom quintiles increased from $12,339 in 1947 to $21,312 in 1971, an increase of $8,973 (1971 constant dollars, U.S. Office of Management and Budget, 1973: 179). Table 3 shows that the distribution of income has not been reduced (in fact it has increased) despite a reduction in educational inequality for white males.

Wealth is much more highly concentrated than income, and, as in the case of the distribution of income, inequality in the distribution of wealth has not been reduced in the postwar years. According to Lampman's (1962: 24) estimates, one percent of the adult population owned 23.3% of all wealth in 1945 and 26.0% in 1956. Smith estimated that one percent owned 28% in 1962 and 25% in 1972 (*Business Week*, 1972b).

The correlation between unemployment and low levels of educational attainment is frequently cited as a justification for expanding education (Becker, 1964: 2; Killingsworth,

TABLE 3

% Share of Education and Income For Each Quintile of Adult White Males, 1950-1970

	% Share of Years of Educational Attainment		% Share of Total Adult White Male Income	
	1950	1970	1949	1969
Lowest Fifth	8.6	10.7	3.2	2.6
Second Fifth	16.4	16.4	10.9	9.4
Middle Fifth	19.0	21.3	17.5	16.7
Fourth Fifth	24.9	22.3	23.7	25.0
Highest Fifth	31.1	29.3	44.8	46.3

Source: Lester C. Thurow, "Education and Economic Equality," *The Public Interest*, Summer, 1972, p. 70.

1966: 108-115). But not only has unemployment gradually increased from 3.9% in 1947, to 4.9% in 1973 (U.S. Department of Labor, 1974a: 271) and to 8.5% in 1975 (Wool, 1976: 28), but long term unemployment (those out of work fifteen weeks or longer) as a percentage of total unemployment has gradually increased from 15.1 in 1967 to 30.7 for the first six months of 1975 (National Urban League Research Department, 1975: 6). Since 1969, job losers have constituted an increasing proportion of the unemployed (U.S. Department of Labor, 1974b: A-12; National Urban League Research Department, 1975: 6). More people are out of work, and are out of work longer; and it is those who are seeking work rather than the voluntarily unemployed who are inflating the unemployment rate.

Racial Economic Inequality

Substantial progress has been made since World War II in reducing the educational gap between whites and nonwhites, at least in terms of educational attainment and degrees earned. The median number of school years attained by whites 25 years of age or older increased from 9.7 in 1950 to 12.3 in 1972 compared to 6.9 and 10.5 for nonwhites. The ratio of the nonwhite/white median number of school years completed rose, therefore, from .71 to .90. The nonwhite/white ratio of the percentage of each group with four or more years of high school increased from .38 to .70 and the comparable figure for those with four or more years of college increased from .34 to .57.[4] (Comparable figures for the 25-29 age group reveal an even greater reduction in educational inequality. U.S. National Center for Education Statistics, 1975: 14.) These figures do not consider the quality of education for such factors bearing on educational equality as school organization (Blau, 1973; Goodman, 1959; Mollenkopf and Melville, 1956), the social context of schooling (Coleman, 1966; Pettigrew, 1974; Sewell and Shah, 1968), or the social climate (Brookover, 1973; McDill and Rigsby, 1973; Rist, 1970; Rosenthal and Jacobson, 1968). And the reward for a given level of education, even when quality is controlled, is greater for whites (Weiss, 1970; Harrison, 1972). But the educational attainment data do show that the education gap between whites and nonwhites has been reduced. No comparable economic progress, however, has been made.

While the nonwhite/white median family income ratio has increased from .54 in 1947 to .62 in 1974, after peaking at .64 in 1970 (U.S. Census Bureau, 1975: 3; U.S. Census Bureau, 1974b: 25; U.S. Census Bureau, 1973a: 329), the absolute gap between median white and median black family income increased by $1,174, from $2,784 to $3,958 (1971 constant dollars, U.S. Census Bureau, 1973a: 329). And virtually no progress has been made in reducing the income gap between white and nonwhite males. The male nonwhite/white median income ratio was .53 in 1945 and .55 in 1969 although it reached .61 in 1946, 1950, and 1968 (Franklin and Resnik, 1973: 38).

Nonwhites have suffered an increasing proportion of the unemployment burden in recent years as the nonwhite/white ratio of the percentage of each group that is unemployed has risen from 1.69 in 1948 to 2.1 in 1973 (U.S. Department of Labor, 1974a: 271). If discouraged part-time workers seeking full-time work are added to the official unemployment rate, the nonwhite/white ratio would be even larger (National Urban League Research Department, 1975: 5). Among 20-24 year old workers, those with the greatest educational gains, the male nonwhite/white unemployment ratio increased from 1.83 in 1948 to 1.94

---

[4] Attending an institution for four years is not synonymous with graduation. But even if a higher percentage of nonwhites completed four years of high school or college and did not receive a diploma, these figures do reflect a trend in the direction of a reduction of inequality between percentages of whites and nonwhites earning degrees.

in 1973 (U.S. Department of Labor, 1974a: 273). Among teenagers this ratio increased from 1.8 to 2.4 between 1964 and 1974 (U.S. Census Bureau, 1974b: 65).

While the percentage of people officially defined as poor was cut in half between 1959 and 1974 (U.S. Census Bureau, 1974c: 18) the proportion of nonwhites among the nation's poor has increased over time. The nonwhite/white ratio of the percentage of each group defined as poor increased from 3.10 to 3.31 between 1959 and 1974 (U.S. Census Bureau, 1974c: 18). The comparable ratio for families living on incomes between 100% and 125% of the official poverty level increased from 1.23 to 1.95 between 1959 and 1972 (U.S. Census Bureau, 1974a: 390).

Much has been made of the rising black middle class. Nonwhites recently have moved into white-collar jobs at a more rapid rate than whites. The nonwhite/white ratio of the percentage of each group employed in professional and technical occupations rose from .35 in 1958 to .69 in 1973 (U.S. Department of Labor, 1974a: 269). In 1970, non-Southern black families with a male head of household under 35 years of age earned 96% of what comparable white families earned (Scammon and Wattenberg, 1973: 36). But these families accounted for just 6% of all black families. Such "parity" results in part from the higher percentage of young black wives who work year around. And even these gains are being eroded. In 1973 the 96% figure had dropped to 93% (Bryce, 1976: 6). The movement of some racial minorities into the middle class represents a polarization within the nonwhite community rather than progress towards equality with whites. While almost all groups of people earn more money, hold better jobs, are less likely to live in poverty, and in general enjoy a higher standard of living than they did thirty years ago, the economic status of racial minorities as a group has not improved relative to the majority population. Few would argue that formal education, in and of itself, could eliminate racial discrimination, or that absolute economic equality should be a policy objective. But the expansion and equalization of educational attainment should have resulted at least in a reduction of existing inequalities if the techno-democratic model accurately reflected social reality. In conjunction with the previous section, these findings support the class conflict model which contends that inequality is rooted in the class structure inherent in a capitalist mode of production, that educational credentials are used to rank workers and to allocate them to unequal slots within the occupational structure, and that until the class structure is confronted, educational expansion or reform will not substantially alter the distribution of rewards.

WHAT ARE EMPLOYERS LOOKING FOR?

Another way to test the validity of these two models is to ask employers what attributes they seek in their employees and what attributes they associate with educational credentials. According to the techno-democratic model employers should cite specific technical or cognitive abilities. The class conflict model would predict that employers express greater concern for behavioral, noncognitive traits. Schooling does cultivate such non-cognitive charcteristics as discipline, obedience, and acceptance of traditional norms and values in general, while frequently discouraging such traits as creativity, initiative, and unorthodox beliefs (Gintis, 1971; Rist, 1970; Howe and Lauter, 1972; Cottle, 1974). The issue is whether employers value education more for its technical training component or its socialization function.

The Emphasis on Personality

Over the last thirty years many surveys have been conducted to elicit information about what employers want. Invariably such noncognitive traits as personality, motivation, ability to get along and work with others are rated higher than indicators of cognitive ability like previous work experience, knowledge of a specific subject, or grades (Thomas, 1956: 326-

337; Drake, Kaplan, and Stone, 1972; Keyser, 1974; Ma, 1969; Michigan State University Placement Services, 1974: 41-43; Berg, 1971). I asked Frank Endicott, Placement Director at Northwestern University, if his office had conducted any studies to determine whether employers were more concerned with personality and other noncognitive traits or technical abilities and other cognitive abilities. He replied in the winter of 1975:

> It seems to me that we have nailed this one to the wall. PERSONAL QUALITIES are most important in getting a job, in keeping a job, and in succeeding in it over a long period of time, with special reference to college graduates (emphasis in original).

Employers don't mind admitting it is the noncognitive rather than the cognitive traits learned in school which makes college graduates good employees. In a series of twenty-five discussions I had with recruiters at Michigan State University in the spring of 1975, the following were typical of the comments they volunteered:

- college graduates are more productive retail sales representatives not because of the information learned in school but because of the social interaction skills developed in school . . . the content of most courses is irrelevant to the outside world . . . a bachelor's degree is an important indicator of the kind of employee we are seeking because the degree indicates a tendency on the part of an individual to complete a program;
- college graduates are sought [for sales, managerial, and junior executive positions] because a person develops a sense of maturity in college;
- we like our engineers to have a college degree not because of the specific knowledge learned in school, but for the social skills developed in school.

Perhaps the best statement of employers' attitudes toward a college degree is the following line in a Mobil Oil advertisement aimed at future marketing representatives:

> You need a bachelor's degree to apply. We really don't care what it's in. Because the most important requirements are sales ability and motivation. And those are things you can't major in (Michigan State University Placement Services: Fall, 1973: inside front cover).

The Issue of Control

These testimonials raise the question why employers value these noncognitive characteristics. According to the class conflict model these preferences reflect an underlying concern for the maintenance of social control within the firm and throughout the class structure in general.

Evidence for this perspective appears in many sources. In a study of one hundred Lockheed employees in California, recently graduated from a Los Angeles high school, Brenner (1968) found that teachers' ratings of student work habits and cooperation, grade point averages, and school absences were correlated with supervisors' ratings (Brenner, 1968). Analysis showed that when teachers' ratings of student work habits, cooperation, and school absences were controlled, grades had no additional predictive value of job performance. In other words grades predicted job performance only through their noncognitive component (Bowles, Gintis, and Meyer, 1975). Educational requirements for jobs are highest for those positions and within those organizations where employers express the greatest concern for the behavioral characteristics of workers and for social control in general. Concern for job related technical skills or the extent of technological innovation are not as closely related to educational requirements as is the concern for stability and control (Noland and Bakke, 1949: 176-177, 183-185; Collins, 1969: 202-209; Collins, 1974; Edwards, 1975).

Employers are more concerned with the noncognitive, behavioral characteristics of their employees than with the cognitive abilities they possess, and the value of formal education is viewed in terms of the noncognitive traits it imparts. This does not mean that employers are uninterested in the technical capabilities of their workers. But when they choose among several prospective employees using educational credentials in that process, they seek primarily noncognitive attributes of workers. This emphasis reflects employers' underlying concern with the maintenance of social control within the organization.

TECHNOLOGY, IDEOLOGY, AND EDUCATION

This study evaluated two competing perspectives of the relationship between education and the occupational structure, and the dynamics of social stratification in the United States. The evidence presented shows that the expansion of formal education and the upgrading of educational requirements of jobs cannot be explained in terms of the changing technical skill requirements of jobs. And it shows that educational expansion and reform have not reduced economic inequality.

Educational requirements of jobs are frequently raised in response to the increasing supply of better educated workers and educational attainment of workers is used to allocate workers to unequal slots within the occupational structure. One consequence, no doubt, is that individuals have responded by seeking higher levels of educational attainment to improve or maintain their competitive position within the labor force, thus completing the vicious circle of spiralling attainment and requirements. The ranking of employees according to their level of educational attainment has not been a completely arbitrary practice on the part of employers. Better educated workers, particularly college graduates, are valued for the noncognitive attributes imparted by the schooling process because such workers provide employers with a more stable work force. Therefore the class conflict model provides a more adequate explanatory framework.

The basic problem with the techno-democratic model, as well as the functional and human capital theories it rests on, is its focus on the assumed differences among individuals in terms of their cognitive abilities. The structural constraints under which individuals compete are either ignored or treated as unalterable givens. The private ownership of productive resources, the operation of those resources for the personal enrichment of the owners, and the exploitive set of relationships in that system permitting selected individuals to accumulate wealth, are not recognized as central determinants of who gets what and why in American society.

By recognizing that inequality and exploitation are rooted in the class structure of American capitalism rather than in the marginal productivities of individuals who interact within that system, it becomes clear that some ideological mechanism must be created to maintain the system's stability. The inability of technological change to account for the expansion of formal education, the resilience of economic inequality in the face of substantial reduction of educational inequality, and employers' expressed concern for the behavioral characteristics of workers and the socialization function of education make it clear that formal education has long constituted a key element of that ideological mechanism.

Implications for Policy and Research

Educational reform is still viewed by many observers as a key to reducing economic inequality. But to expand or improve educational opportunities, to direct more resources to manpower development or job training, or to implement any other conceivable strategy aimed at altering the characteristics of individuals, are basically marginal approaches to consequences of distributive processes rooted deeply in the institutional framework of society. Attempts to create equal opportunities focusing on characteristics of individuals, the approach of the 1960's which failed to achieve the desired result, are not likely to succeed in the future. If the reduction of economic inequality is a policy objective, it will not be sufficient to equalize opportunities in hope that greater equality automatically follow. The institutional mechanisms generating inequality must be confronted directly.

Future research will be more productive if it focuses on the dynamics of structural or systemic determinants of social phenomena rather than on the characteristics of individuals within that social environment. We should not calculate rates of return to education or correlation coefficients between education and occupational status or socioeconomic status and education, income, or occupation. Rather, we should focus on the historical development of institutions and social relationships, the social as well as the technical forces which dictate change, and the sources of not only consensus but dissent rooted in the structural framework of American society.

REFERENCES

Aronowitz, Stanley
1973   False Promises. New York: McGraw-Hill Book Company.
Becker, Gary
1964   Human Capital: A Theoretical and Empirical Analysis, with Special Reference to Education. New York: Columbia University Press.
Berg, Ivar
1971   Education and Jobs: The Great Training Robbery. Boston: Beacon Press.
Bendix, Reinhard and Seymour Martin Lipset
1959   Social Mobility in Industrial Society. Berkeley: University of California Press.
Bird, Caroline
1975   The Case Against College. New York: David McKay Company.
Blau, Peter M.
1973   The Organization of Academic Work. New York: John Wiley and Sons.
Blau, Peter M. and Otis Dudley Duncan
1967   The American Occupational Structure. New York: John Wiley and Sons.
Bowles, Samuel and Herbert Gintis
1976   Schooling in Capitalist America. New York: Basic Books, Inc.
Bowles, Samuel, Herbert Gintis, and Peter Meyer
1975   "The long shadow of work: education, the family, and the reproduction of the social division of labor." The Insurgent Sociologist, (Summer).
Braverman, Harry
1974   Labor and Monopoly Capital. New York: Monthly Review Press.
Brenner, Marshall H.
1968   "Use of high school data to predict work performance." Journal of Applied Psychology 52 (February): 29-30.
Bright, James R.
1958   Automation and Management. Boston: Harvard Business School.
1966   "The relationship of increasing automation to skill requirements." The Employment Impact of Technological Change. Washington, D.C.: Government Printing Office.
Brookover, Wilbur B. et. al.
1973   Elementary School Social Environments and Achievement. East Lansing, College of Urban Development, Michigan State University.
Bryce, Herrington
1976   "Economics." The Urban League News (January): 5-9.
Business Week
1972a   "The job gap for college graduates." 2247 (September 23): 48-58.
1972b   "Who has the wealth in America." 2240 (August 5): 54-56.
Carnegie Commission on Higher Education
1973   College Graduates and Jobs. New York: McGraw-Hill Book Company.
Coleman, James et. al.
1966   Equality of Educational Opportunity. Washington, D.C.: Government Printing Office.
Collins, Randall
1969   "Education and employment: a study in the dynamics of stratification." Unpublished Ph.D. Dissertation, University of California at Berkeley.
1971   "Functional and conflict theories of educational stratification." American Sociological Review 36(December): 1002-1019.

1974   "Where are educational requirements for employment highest." Sociology of Education 47(Fall): 419-442.

Commager, Henry Steele
1950   The American Mind. New Haven: Yale University Press. Cited in Colin Greer. The Great School Legend [1972]. New York: Basic Books, Inc.

Cottle, Thomas J.
1974   "What tracking did to Ollie Taylor." Social Policy 5(July-August): 21-24.

Cremin, Lawrence
1961   The Transformation of the School. New York: Knopf. Cited in Colin Greer. The Great School Legend. [1972] New York: Basic Books, Inc.

Cubberley, Ellwood P.
1909   Changing Conceptions of Education. Boston: Houghton Mifflin: Cited in Richard C. Edwards, Michael Reich, and Thomas Weisskopf (Eds.) The Capitalist System. [1972] Englewood Cliffs: Prentice Hall.

Diamond, Daniel E. and Hrach Bedrosian
1970   Hiring Standards and Job Performance. Washington, D.C.: Government Printing Office.

Drake, Larry R., H. Roy Kaplan, and Russell A. Stone
1972   "How do employers value the interview." Journal of College Placement 32(February-March): 47-51.

Edwards, Richard C.
1975   "The social relations of production in the firm and labor market structure." Politics and Society 5:83-108.

Fine, Sidney A.
1964   The Nature of Automated Jobs and Their Educational and Training Requirements. McLean: Human Sciences Research, Inc.

Forum on Graduate Student Employment
1974   Michigan State University. (October 24).

Franklin, Raymond S. and Solomon Resnik
1973   The Political Economy of Racism. New York: Holt, Rinehart and Winston, Inc.

Friedenberg, Edgar
1965   Coming of Age in America. New York: Vintage Books.

Gintis, Herbert
1971   "Education, technology, and the characteristics of worker productivity." American Economic Review 61(May): 266-279.

Goodman, Paul
1964   Compulsory Mis-Education. New York: Vintage Books.

Goodman, S. M.
1959   The Assessment of School Quality. Albany: New York State Education Department.

Gordon, Robert A. and James E. Howell
1959   Higher Education for Business. New York: Columbia University Press.

Greer, Colin
1972   The Great School Legend. New York: Basic Books, Inc.

Griliches, Zvi and William M. Mason
1972   "Education, income, and ability." Journal of Political Economy 80(May-June): 74-103.

Harrison, Bennett
1972   "Education and underemployment in the urban ghetto." American Economic Review 62 (December): 796-812.

Hechinger, Fred
1976   "Murder in academe: the demise of education." Saturday Review (March 20).

Horowitz, Morris A. and Irwin L. Herrnstadt
1966   "Changes in the skill requirements of occupations in selected industries." The Employment Impact of Technological Change. Washington, D.C.: Government Printing Office.
1969   The Training of Tool and Die Makers. Boston: Department of Economics. Northeastern University.

Howe, Florence and Paul Lauter
1972   "How the school system is rigged for failure." Richard C. Edwards, Michael Reich, and Thomas E. Weisskopf (Eds.) The Capitalist System. Englewood Cliffs: Prentice-Hall.

Illich, Ivan
1971   Deschooling Society. New York: Harper and Row.

Jaffe, A. J. and Joseph Froomkin
1968   Technology and Jobs. New York: Praeger Publishers.

Jencks, Christopher et. al.
1973   Inequality. New York: Harper and Row.

Johnston, Denis F.
1973   "Education of workers: projections to 1990." Montly Labor Review 96(November): 22-31.

Karier, Clarence J.
1972   "Testing for order and control in the corporate liberal state." Educational Theory 22(Spring): 154-180.
Katz, Michael
1972   Class, Bureaucracy, and Schools. New York: Praeger Publishers.
Kerr, Clark et. al.
1974   "The logic of industrialism." Bertram Silverman and Murray Yanowitch (Eds.) The Worker in "Post-Industrial" Capitalism. New York: The Free Press.
Keyser, Marshall
1974   "How to apply for a job." Journal of College Placement 35(Fall): 63-65.
Killingsworth, Charles C.
1966   "Automation, jobs, and manpower: the case for structural unemployment." The Manpower Revolution. Garden City: Anchor Books.
Lampman, Robert J.
1962   The Share of Top Wealth Holders in National Wealth. Princeton University Press.
Ma, James C.
1969   "Current trends in recruiting practices." Journal of College Placement 29(April-May): 113-114.
Marglin, Stephen A.
1974   "What do bosses do?" The Review of Radical Political Economics 6(Summer): 60-112.
McDill, Edward and Leo Rigsby
1973   The Academic Impact of Educational Climates. Baltimore: John Hopkins University Press.
Michigan State University Placement Services
1973   Placement Manual. Rahway: Placement Publications, Inc. (Fall)
1974   Recruiting Trends Survey. East Lansing: Michigan State University Placement Services.
Miller, Ann
1971   Occupations of the Labor Force According to the Dictionary of Occupational Titles. Washington, D.C.: Office of Management and Budget.
Mollenkopf, W. G. and S. D. Melville
1956   A Study of Secondary School Characteristics as Related to Test Scores. Princeton: Educational Testing Service.
Mueller, Eva
1969   Technological Advance in an Expanding Economy. Ann Arbor: Institute for Social Research.
National Urban League Research Department
1975   Quarterly Economic Report on the Black Worker. Washington, D.C.: National Urban League.
Noland, E. William and E. Wright Bakke
1949   Workers Wanted. New York: Harper and Brothers.
O'Toole, James
1975   "The reserve army of the underemployed." Change Magazine 7(May): 26-33, 63.
Pettigrew, Thomas F.
1974   "The case for racial integration." E. A. Schuler, T. F. Hoult, D. L. Gibson, and W. B. Brookover (Eds.) Readings in Sociology. New York: Thomas Y. Crowell.
Pierson, Frank C.
1959   The Education of American Businessmen. New York: McGraw-Hill Book Company.
President's Commission on Higher Education
1947   Higher Education for American Democracy. Washington, D.C.: Government Printing Office.
Rawlins, V. Lane and Lloyd Ulman
1974   "The utilization of college trained manpower in the United States. Margaret S. Gordon (Ed.) Higher Education and the Labor Market. A Report of the Carnegie Commission on Higher Education. New York: McGraw-Hill Book Company.
Risk, Ray C.
1970   "Student class and teacher expectations: the self-fulfilling prophecy in ghetto education." Harvard Educational Review 40(August): 411-451.
Rosenthal, Neal H.
1973   "The United States economy in 1985: projected changes in occupations." Monthly Labor Review 96(December): 18-26.
Rosenthal, Robert and Lenore Jacobson
1968   Pygmalion in the Classroom. New York: Holt, Rinehart, and Winston.
Scammon, Richard M. and Ben J. Wattenberg
1973   "Black progress and liberal rhetoric." Commentary 55(April): 35-44.
Sewell, W. H. and V. P. Shah
1968   "Social class, parental encouragement, and educational aspirations." American Journal of Sociology 73(March): 559-572.
Shingleton, Jack
1972   "Prognosis of employment for future graduates." Presentation to Administrative Group at Michigan State University (January 4).

Spring, Joel
  1972   Education and the Rise of the Corporate State. Boston: Beacon Press.
Squires, Gregory D.
  1976   "Education, jobs, and the U.S. class structure." Unpublished Ph.D. Dissertation, Michigan
          State University.
Stiglitz, Joseph E.
  1975   "The theory of 'screening,' education, and the distribution of income." American Economic
          Review 65(June): 283-300.
Stone, Katherine
  1974   "The origins of job structures in the steel industry." Review of Radical Political Economics
          6(Summer): 113-173.
Taubman, Paul and Terence Wales
  1974   Higher Education and Earnings. A Report of the Carnegie Commission on Higher Education.
          New York: McGraw-Hill Book Company.
Thomas, Lawrence
  1956   The Occupational Structure and Education. Englewood Cliffs: Prentice-Hall, Inc.
Thurow, Lester C.
  1972   "Education and economic equality." The Public Interest 28(Summer): 66-81.
  1975   Generating Inequality. New York: Basic Books, Inc.
U.S. Bureau of the Census
  1960   Historical Statistics of the United States: Colonial Times to 1957.
  1973a   Statistical Abstract of the United States 1973.
  1973b   Earnings by Occupation and Education: 1970 Census of Population.
  1973c   Age and Earnings by Occupation for the United States: 1970 Census of Population.
  1974a   Statistical Abstract of the United States 1974.
  1974b   The Social and Economic Status of the Black Population in the United States.
  1974c   Current Population Reports. "Money Income and Poverty Status of Families and Persons
          in the United States: 1974."
  1975   Current Population Reports. "Household Money Income in 1974 and Selected Social and
          Economic Characteristics of Households."
U.S. Commission on Civil Rights
  1974   Twenty Years After Brown: The Shadows of the Past.
U.S. Department of Labor
  1957   Estimate of Worker Trait Requirements for 4,000 Jobs as Defined in the 1949 Dictionary
          of Occupational Titles.
  1964   Formal Occupational Training of Adult Workers.
  1965   Selected Characteristics of Occupations, (Physical Demands, Working Conditions, Training
          Time) 1966—A Supplement to the Dictionary of Occupational Titles.
  1969   Employment of High School Graduates and Dropouts, October 1968. Special Labor Force
          Report 108.
  1973   Employment of High School Graduates and Dropouts, October 1972. Special Labor Force
          Report 155.
  1974a   Manpower Report of the President 1974.
  1974b   Employment and Unemployment in 1974. Special Labor Force Report 178.
U.S. National Center for Education Statistics
  1875   Digest of Educational Statistics, 1974.
U.S. Office of Management and Budget.
  1973   Social Indicators 1973.
Weiss, Randall
  1970   "The effects of education on the earnings of blacks and whites." Review of Economics and
          Statistics 52(May): 150-159.
Wool, Harold
  1976   "Future labor supply for lower level occupations." Monthly Labor Review 99(March):
          22-31.

MARGINAL YOUTH AND SOCIAL POLICY

HERMAN SCHWENDINGER and JULIA R. SCHWENDINGER
University of Nevada, Las Vegas

Marginalization of a portion of American youth is described as a result of the structure of the major socialization agencies, the family and the school, in contemporary capitalist society. The family and other agencies mediate the process of marginalization created by economy. To eliminate marginalization, social policies must change the economic structure of society.

THE PROCESSES OF MARGINALIZATION

Whether it includes behavior inside or outside of school, the most sustained official reactions to delinquency usually involve a marginal population of youth, that has existed since the early centuries of capitalism. In those early centuries, however, many marginal youth were integrated within a larger population, composed of unemployed or subemployed laborers and debt-ridden artisans and farmers (Schwendinger and Schwendinger, 1976). Prior to the 19th century, marginals were originally produced and then "chastized for their enforced transformation into vagabonds and paupers," before manufacturing establishments could absorb their labor power (Marx, 1959:731-734). The process of marginalization subsequently annihilated urban artisanry and filled the debtors prisons with artisans bankrupted by the rise of pre-industrial manufactories and the domestic cottage industries. Afterward, the expansion of industrialism marginalized the toilers who had worked within the cottage industries. Simultaneously, this expansion absorbed millions of other marginals while it was producing a relative surplus population. With the rise of monopoly-capitalism, this population was generally restricted to the secondary labor market.

Long-term trends toward stagnation, also a characteristic of modern capitalist societies, inevitably occur and have only been overcome periodically. In colonial and semi-colonial capitalist societies, the effects of these trends on marginalization are particularly evident. Marginals in Venezuela, for instance, constitute almost one third of the population. The agrarian marginals live on subsistence payments or work without explicit wages. On the edges of the cities, rural migrants and urban marginals, who are underemployed, intermittently employed, and just plain unemployed, live in rat-infested slums. Some of these persons are employed in part-time or otherwise unproductive jobs, largely concentrated in the inflated tertiary sector (Hein and Stenzal, 1973). These persons are the menial "service workers" or the "penny capitalists," who desperately shift for themselves by scavenging, huckstering, working at odd jobs, and performing a variety of personal services for minimal payments.

The United States is also beset by long-term trends toward stagnation. The American economy no longer expands sufficiently to absorb most of its technologically displaced labor force—much less the new generations of workers. The rate of absorption has only surged for short periods during wartime or during a post-war boom. Generally the younger, the older, and the most oppressed workers have been excluded from the labor market. Millions have become marginal. From an economic standpoint, these persons at any given time are either absolutely or relatively superfluous.

Advanced capitalism prolongs the dependent status of youth. This prolongation elevates the theoretical importance of certain factors in the socialization agencies, which include the family, yet center on the modern school. These factors, as we shall see, uniquely recreate the process of marginalization *within* the socialization agencies themselves.

Analysis of the family and the school indicates that significant economic functions, which undoubtedly effect delinquent relations, are performed by these agencies. Most socialization agencies concentrate on youth who will generally become proletarians and who, therefore, require certain types of services for the production of their labor power. These services are largely provided by parents and by teachers, whose efforts are exerted in the family and the school. With regard to the reproduction of their labor power both socialization agencies seem to operate separately while, in fact, they are quite interdependent.

Various kinds of interdependent relations characterize these agencies: obviously, a child's success in school is dependent upon other family relations. Empirical studies also indicate that the family is a stronger determinant of the child's eventual "success" as a labor force participant. But *determination* of individual success cannot be equated with *domination* of the general standards which regulate successful striving. The family is forced to regulate its own productive relations according to the meritocratic and technical standards exerted by the school. For the long-term reproduction of labor power, therefore, the school is the dominating agency.

The reproductive relations in the school are in turn largely dominated by industrial relations. Social scientists have clearly demonstrated that educational standards "correspond" to the hierarchical and segmented organization of the labor force (Bowles and Gintis, 1973). The standards used to reward and punish a student's behavior within the school, therefore, are synchronized with the standards that are used by managers to control workers.

The reproductive relations within the family are also dominated by industry, but this form of domination is partly mediated by the school. As indicated, the school, in spite of appearances, essentially organizes its production relations around industrially related standards. By dominating production relations within the family, the school as well as industry imposes these standards upon parents and children.

At least two general consequences flow from these serial relations of domination. First, the reproductive relations within socialization agencies are synchronized with the alienated social relations that generally characterize commodity production. These synchronized relations are not confined to the youngsters who are in the process of acquiring the power to labor. They include both the parents and the teachers, who are involved in the long-term production of this commodity.

Second, these dominating relations are expressed in the same general laws of investment and profit maximization which culminate in the uneven development of various groups and nations (Bluestone, 1972). This means investments in the development of the labor force are allocated unevenly. Such investments concentrate on those groups of persons considered to have a greater potentiality for meeting the meritocratic criteria prevailing in educational institutions. Conversely, unless political struggles broaden educational policies, the investments of private or public resources—calculable in terms of money, equipment, facilities, faculties, and even in the teacher's time, attention, and expectations—will be minimal for the development of those groups of persons who do not appear to meet these criteria.

Consequently, the allocation of educational resources favors the youth who have already been the recipients of superior resources. They are recipients because of the advantages that are passed on to the members of certain ethnic, racial, or occupational strata, or because of the compensatory time and energy expended on them by self-sacrificing parents. During the elementary school period, a mutually reinforcing relationship is established between the activities of youth who show the productive signs of superior familial investments, and the patterns for selectively allocating resources within educational institutions. Throughout the child's formative period, educational capital continuously builds on the most favored students.

Simultaneously, the competitive position of the least favored students deteriorates and a process, analogous to marginalization within the economy, occurs in the context of the school and the family. This inherently contradictory trend results in anarchic behavior patterns, created by students who are not strongly motivated to achieve, and who do not make any disciplined effort to achieve. These are also the students who actually do not achieve the cognitive and non-cognitive traits that generally favor sustained labor force participation in the future. Although their chances for future employment are somewhat independent of their status in socialization agencies, these children manifest early in life the adaptive characteristics that evolve in capitalism among numerous owners of the least valuable forms of labor power.

Thus, the relations that favor the uneven development of labor power early in life generate a youthful population of *prototypic* marginals, whose status is not actually determined directly by economic institutions. The members of this population are not usually counted among "the employed" or "the unemployed." Instead, they are usually regarded as students and, during most of their adolescent years, workaday life is very far from their minds.

Within communities across the United States, adolescents speak about these prototypic marginals. Such names as Greaser, Vato, Dude, Honcho, Hodad, and Hood appear whenever they are mentioned in conversations. These metaphors refer to individual marginals and, among other social regularities in their personal behavior, to their conduct, carriage, attitudes, gestures, grooming, argot, clothing, and delinquent acts.

The marginalization process under discussion is not directly determined by labor market relations. Here the term "marginal" simply refers to the "prototypic" rather than labor force marginal. The effects of this process will therefore be reflected in family and school relationships, but they are not classified by any official economic category.

It is taken for granted that certain types of family conflicts or "breakdowns" will definitely enhance the possibilities of marginalization. But these possibilities are also mediated by parental resources. Wealthy families can employ such "absorption mechanisms" as psychiatric counseling, boarding school, and the tutorial trip abroad to cushion the effects of family disturbance on the child. If these mechanisms are unsuccessful, then their wealth further provides children who are becoming marginalized with a second chance later in life. Some of these children, in fact, never have to concern themselves with labor market activity: they can be sustained by inherited property.

By contrast, working class families are exposed to greater hardships and difficulties. Absorption mechanisms are relatively unavailable and family problems directly influence the parents' and child's active contribution to the production of the child's labor power. They interact with the already disadvantaged competitive relations engendered by the school.

Consequently, traditional socio-economic attributes, such as the parents' income, education, and property, which represent the most widespread family characteristics, directly effect the likelihood of marginalization. Because of the long-term effects of the uneven development of capital, a greater proportion of marginal youth can be expected among lower status families. Alternatively, marginalization can certainly be expected among *higher* status families (or among "middle class" families), but to a lesser degree. This observation is important, because the literature on "middle class" delinquency has glossed over the differences between marginal "middle class" delinquents and *other* types of delinquents.

Let us now consider youth who, from the standpoint of the school, represent the most highly developed forms of labor power. As high academic achievers, they strikingly epitomize the division of labor among mental and manual workers in capitalist societies. They are usually very articulate, and some have broad interests in politics, culture, and science. Others, noted for their narrow academic and technical interests, symbolize how much young personalities have been influenced by the extreme labor force segmentation among mental workers. Their personal interests are "overspecialized," and they are organized largely by experiences based on the appropriation and dispensation of technical knowledge.

In this work, the term "prototypic intellectuals" will be used to characterize the youth mentioned above. The word "intellectual" classifies those persons who devote their occupational activities to the formulation of ideas, to the creation of artistic representations of ideas, or to the application of ideas, such as the application of scientific-technical knowledge to human affairs. The development of modern intellectuals can be traced back to the early capitalist period. But this development has been accelerated enormously by expansion of monopoly capitalism and the modern state (Schwendingers, 1974:143-158, 360-361). Today the category of intellectuals includes writers, artists, librarians, social workers, city planners, teachers, and scientists.

The prototypic intellectual, on the other hand, refers to youth showing the personal interests and characteristics generated among adults by the developments mentioned above. Historically, educational institutions have played a very important role in regulating the formation of this particular population. Certain families, however, have contributed candidates disproportionately. Bourgeois families, including the small farmers as well as independent professions, have supplied the greatest proportions. In recent years, the established families of such "mental workers" as teachers, technicians, and scientists, also contribute relatively higher numbers of prototypic intellectuals.

On the other hand, because of bourgeois educational policies and the intergenerational effects of uneven investment, young women, youth of both sexes who belong to racially oppressed groups, and children of unskilled workers become candidates to a less degree. It has been chiefly the white families of higher socio-economic status that have established a mutually dependent relation with the school. The children cf families that *have* more *get* more, because the public educational system converts human beings into potential commodities and builds upon *that* human material which already has considerable investment.

In communities across the United States, one finds that metaphors for this latter youth also appear in peer conversations. Included among these names are Intellectual, Brain, Pencil-Neck, Egg Head, Book Worm, and Walking Encyclopedia (See Schwendingers, forthcoming). For now, it should be noted that by contrast with many marginals, these youth are paragons of virtue. In fact, they are foremost members of the least delinquent population in a local society of youth.

SOCIAL POLICY

What social policies are required for the elimination of marginalization, uneven development and delinquency? Unfortunately, a theory of fundamental causes cannot provide either quick or direct answers to this question. Social policy formulation requires more than a causal theory. The level of the productive forces and hence the actual resources available in a given society must be considered. Conflicts over resources are also important. In fact, among the general determinants of social policies, class forces and political conflicts over control of these resources are most important.

In our opinion, an examination of both fundamental causes and social policy determinants lead to but one conclusion. The best possibilities for eliminating marginalization, uneven development, and delinquency exist in socialist societies. This conclusion, however, cannot be applied universally because socialist nations diverge in the course of their development, and the divergences have retrogressive as well as progressive consequences. Furthermore, some socialist nations, such as Yugoslavia, still retain anarchic market systems, which produce marginalization. Nevertheless, genuine socialist developments are numerous and they counter marginalization, uneven development, and delinquency.

As socialist societies overcome the anarchy of the market through economic planning, then marginalization and delinquency are curtailed sharply. The virtual elimination of unemployment and subemployment enormously decreases the numbers of adolescent marginals, and the size and stability of their delinquent group formations. (In capitalist societies, these groups are concentrated in slums and ghettos.) Walter O'Connor (1972:93), a liberal scholar, reports,

> Soviet delinquents tend to commit their offenses in groups . . . these groups, however, are generally rather small in number and fluid in composition, bearing little resemblance to the organized fighting gangs of large American cities in the 1950's. On the whole, it seems doubtful that we can speak of 'gangs' at all in the Soviet case. The instances of Soviet delinquents acting in concert frequently seem to reflect a spontaneous and temporary coming together for the purpose of some relatively specific act.

China provides additional illustrations of the decrease in marginalization and delinquency. American journalists have been struck by the relative absence of crime in the People's Republic of China today. This absence cannot be due to cultural differences between the Eastern and the Western hemispheres, because the differences between "liberated China" and "nationalist China" were discerned long ago by American observors. William Hinton (1970:19), for instance, worked during the post war years in China as a representative of the United Nations Relief and Rehabilitation Administration. He observed that in 1947,

> The most striking thing about the [communist] towns was the absence of beggars . . . It was unbelievable but true. The same went for prostitutes: there did not seem to be any. I was never opportuned even though I wandered day and night in the main streets and back alleys of the biggest towns in the area. In Nationalist-held Peking, on the other hand, clerks and roomboys in the main hotels doubled as pimps, while little children touted for their sisters on the sidewalks.

Futher illustrations can be obtained from Cuba and the German Democratic Republic. In the pre-revolutionary period, Havana was the center of organized crime in the Carribean. In addition, Cuba, like other Latin American countries, had an enormous population of marginals. Today, marginalization and organized crime, and their effects on children and adolescents, have disappeared from Cuba. Additional comparisons referring to unemployment that favor socialism can be made between the German Democratic Republic and the Federal Republic of Germany. With regard to crime, there has been a long-term decreasing trend in ordinary crime within the German Democratic Republic, but no comparable decline in West Germany. Again, since similar national groups are involved, such differences are due to their social orders.

The complete elimination of marginalization and delinquency depends upon advanced socialist changes. Socialism does not emerge full grown from the womb of class societies; it bears the imprint of thousands of years of class developments. Under socialism, school and family relations continue to reproduce the labor force, and some of these reproductive relations are not changed radically because certain bourgeois rights are maintained in industry. Such rights include equal pay for equal units of work; hence, they also include differentials in pay resulting from variations in individual skills, talents, and physical abilities. Consequently, since the products of labor are distributed during this transitional period "from each according to his or her ability; to each according to work performance," certain pre-existing socialization functions, social distinctions, and competitive relations are sustained. They are gradually eliminated, however, as their material basis is transformed, and the prevailing distributive principle becomes " . . . to each according to need." Consequently, as the state becomes a genuine expression of workers' power, and as the economy becomes regulated by "a settled plan," and as the creative powers of labor are devoted to social needs, then the social inequalities between town and country, between intellectual and manual workers, and between sexes, races, and nationalities will be eliminated. Marginalization, uneven development and delinquency will finally disappear.

Obviously, the formation of social policy planning in the United States is generally organized around different possibilities. The United States remains a capitalist society and, consequently, policy makers underwrite capital accumulation. They defend multinational interests through C.I.A. activity in Latin American countries and they enrich commercial interests through urban renewal programs in North American cities. By developing educational-industrial, police-industrial, and other social-industrial complexes, they exploit domestic problems to maintain profits (O'Connor, 1974; McLaughan, 1975). Such developments undermine attempts to prevent marginalization, uneven development and delinquency.

Because of the domination by capital, social policy planning usually avoids conflict with essential structural relations, but this accomodation is self-defeating. Since they are subordinated to the very forces that cause these problems, social policy planners cannot deal with the problems successfully. Instead, they attack the problems piece-meal without regard to long-term strategies for structural changes. Although direct intervention into the immediate causes of marginalization, uneven development and delinquency is required even for the *amelioration* of these problems, such intervention is rarely attempted.

Take the numerous manpower training programs, which have concentrated on black marginals. The programs have failed to make any improvement in black communities, because they do not lower unemployment directly. Surveys report, therefore, that

> without a direct transformation and augmentation of the demand for their labor, significant improvement in the economic situation of ghetto dwellers is unlikely. Attempts to change the worker himself—whether to remedy his personal 'defects' or to move him to a 'better' environment—have not worked up until now, and the [several sources of data reported] in this study provide little if any evidence to support the belief that such attempts will be sufficient in the future (Harrison, 1975:159-160).

Thus, without significant attempts to expand and stabilize the labor market directly through public works, the socialization of industries, and economic planning, the social investment in reducing marginalization through manpower training is irrational.

As indicated, such manpower programs are not integrated with policies that change structural relations in the economy; hence, their effects on marginalization are negligible. Similar relations apply to the school. Since compensatory education policies are also restricted by capital, they are not related to strategies that change structural relations in either the school or economy. Hence their effects on the equalization of school achievement are very limited.

While compensatory education has some positive effects on racial, ethnic, or economic groups that have higher proportions of prototypic marginal youth, the relative magnitude of these effects is questionable. Martin Carnoy's (1975:233-242) survey of studies about teacher performance indicates that compensatory programs have strikingly similar results.

> They generally show a positive relationship between so-called higher 'quality' characteristics of teachers and exam score. They also show significantly different teacher input-school output relationships for different ethnic groups and, in Puerto Rico, for different class groups. Finally, they show that even if increasing teacher quality results in higher achievement, average achievement scores will at best bring them only part of the way toward equality with presently high scoring groups . . . even if substantially higher-quality teaching is made available to the low-scoring than to the high-scoring students, the change would result in only a partial reduction of exam-score difference between the two. In the case of ethnic and racial minorities in the United States, the reduction may well be negligible.

Such findings are not surprising. Social investments do effect student development, but the combined effects of intergenerational and governmental investments, generally favoring groups with higher statuses, far outweigh social investments into compensatory education. Consequently, the effects of that education are, of necessity, limited, and they cannot neutralize the tendencies toward uneven development. Furthermore, certain other limitations of compensatory education policies are not revealed by studies of isolated programs. The most severe test of these policies would be made if they were instituted everywhere. Under such conditions, various mechanisms (e.g., grading by the "thirds," or by other standardized scores) would maintain the same competitive and hierarchical school relationships, despite the fluctuations in average levels of individual productivity. Hence, marginal youth would still be produced, but with a higher achievement score than before.

With regard to the labor market, value-determining and price-making mechanisms accomplish similar ends. The distribution of educational investments has improved considerably over the last three decades. But, Carnoy (1975:369-370) points out,

> the payoff to schooling changes in a way that makes lower levels of schooling worth less over time relative to higher levels. Thus, the number of people who receive secondary schooling has increased markedly in the United States between 1939 and 1959, but the payoff to that level actually fell. So just as the poor begin to get higher levels of schooling, the relative value to the labor market of those levels falls. Even when a society invests more in schooling for the poor, therefore, the labor market values that schooling less than before the poor were getting it.

The same dismal pattern characterizes delinquency policies. Numerous studies indicate that piece-meal and accommodative social policies have insignificant effects on delinquency. The failure of these policies, which involve counseling, job training, or diversion programs, simply reinforces the necessity for socialist strategies for change. To be successful, short-term programmatic solutions must be part of long-term strategies which support working-class movements that are primary agents of fundamental structural change. The linkage between short-term programs and these long-term strategies represents the central challenge to social policy analysts. There will be no magical solutions by professionals working to eliminate marginalization, uneven development, and delinquency, as long as structural relations in our society are disregarded.

REFERENCES

Bluestone, Barry
1972 "Capitalism and poverty in America: A discussion." Monthly Review 2:64-71.
Bowles, Samuel and Herbert Gintis
1973 "I.Q. in the U.S. class structure." Social Policy 3:65-96.
Bremner, Robert H.
1970 Children and Youth in America, A Documentary History, I. Cambridge, Massachusetts: Harvard University Press.
Carnoy, Martin
1975 Schooling in a Corporate Society, the Political Economy of Education in America. Second Edition. New York: David McKay Company, Inc.
Carson, Robert B.
1972 "Youthful labor surplus in disaccumulationist capitalism." Socialist Revolution 2:15-44.
The Editors
1975 "Capitalism and unemployment." Monthly Review 27:1-13.
Harrison, Bennett
1975 "Education and underemployment in the urban ghetto." Pp. 133-60 in Martin Carnoy (ed.), Schooling in a Corporate Society. New York: David McKay Company, Inc.
Hein, Wolfgang and Konrad Stenzal
1973 "The capitalist state and underdevelopment in Latin America—the case of Venezuela." Kapitalistate 2:31-48.

Hinton, William
    1970 Iron Oxen. New York: Monthly Review Press.
Marx, Karl
    1959 Capital, I. Moscow: Foreign Languages Publishing House.
McLaughlan, Gregory
    1975 "LEAA: A case study in the development of the social industrial complex." Crime and Social
        Justice 4:15-23.
O'Connor, James
    1973 The Fiscal Crisis of the State. New York: St. Martin's Press.
O'Connor, Walter D.
    1972 Deviance in Soviet Society, Crime, Delinquency, and Alcoholism. New York: Columbia Univer-
        sity Press.
Reich, Michael, David M. Gordon and Richard C. Edwards
    1973 "A theory of labor market segmentation," American Economic Review 63:359-365.
Schwendinger, Herman and Julia R. Schwendinger
    1974 The Sociologists of the Chair, A Radical Analysis of the Formative Years of North American
        Sociology (1883-1922). New York: Basic Books.
    1976 "The collective varieties of youth." Crime and Social Justice 5:7-25.
        Forthcoming The Collective Varieties of Youth Book.

CLIENT CONTROL AND ORGANIZATIONAL DOMINANCE:
THE SCHOOL, ITS STUDENTS, AND THEIR PARENTS*

MONIKA WITTIG
Pädagogische Hochschule Westfalen Lippe, Abteilung Münster
West Germany

This paper examines client control as an important aspect of the organizational dynamics in a large educational institution. School personnel attempt to control students *and* their parents (duality of clientele) to fulfill their two main responsibilities: serving their clientele and functioning effectively and efficiently as members of an organization. Two dominant strategies for action in these processes are: attempts to secure parent cooperation through persuasion or coercion and attempts to evade or actively hinder parent interference with the school. The selection of strategies is based upon labeling and especially co-labeling activities which are identified as organizational imperatives resulting from the service institution's need to fulfill its two main responsibilities.

The Problem

Service institutions—and schools belong to this category (cf., for example, Becker, 1953, and Bidwell, 1965)—are charged with the dual responsibilities of serving their direct clients (students) and indirect clients (parents) (Bidwell, 1965:978) while functioning effectively and efficiently as organizations. These dual responsibilities produce tension. An important part of the school personnel's daily work is to ease this tension. School personnel experience conflict especially when managing students considered troublemakers. Such internally defined deviants undermine the effective and efficient functioning of the school organization by disrupting the normal school work routine.

Such trouble potentially threatens the organization's relationship with its clientele. Students, and especially their parents, are likely to demand services from the institution it cannot and will not provide because they endanger organizational effectiveness and efficiency. To retain effectiveness, school personnel want to maintain sufficient latitude for their professional judgments (and implicitly for their own and the organization's autonomy) in choosing the services to be provided. Efforts to secure this autonomy involve efforts *to control* clientele. The process of client control requires activities and strategies to obtain client cooperation. If such cooperation cannot be obtained, different strategies emerge: attempts to evade or eliminate what is now seen as interferences with the organization.

The following report will illuminate elements of client control processes as they become manifest in the activities of specialized personnel in a large, organizationally complex high school. At the same time the data analysis makes visible labeling and co-labeling (Suchar, 1972) among school personnel who are expected "to do something" about troublemakers. In contrast to other recent work on deviant labeling in educational settings (Fisher, 1972; and Foster et al., 1972) this report focuses on definitional processes (Kitsuse and Spector, 1973) and especially the contextual framework in which such processes occur.

---

*Some of the material presented was drawn from the author's unpublished Ph.D. dissertation: *Identification and Processing of Troublemakers in School*. Northwestern University, 1973. Data collection for the dissertation and the present work was financially supported by a Spencer Foundation Research Grant, a Northwestern University Dissertation Year Fellowship and a Research Grant from the Ohio State University, College of Education Research Committee. I am especially indebted to Howard S. Becker, John I. Kitsuse, Barbara Rosenblum, and Charles Suchar who commented critically on earlier drafts and helped with invaluable suggestions and encouragement.

The Research Setting

The school, Midwestern High, is a large comprehensive four-year high school near a large midwestern city offering its students a wide variety of programs. Midwestern High has approximately 2,400 students. The 1970 US Census indicates that the community is middle class, with a median annual income of $16,423 and a mean annual income of $19,108. Of the population twenty-five years and over almost seventy-six percent have a high school diploma, and 12.8 is the median years of school completed. More than ninety-seven percent of the children between the ages of fourteen and seventeen are in school.

Study Design

Four sets of data were collected: (1) fourteen months of field notes on informal conversations, general occurences in the school, weekly meetings of specialized school personnel who discuss problem students, and classroom observations; (2) in-depth open-ended interviews with student services personnel and teachers; (3) transcripts of administrative meetings relevant to the research concerns; and (4) excerpts from students' cumulative records.

Elements of Problem-Management

The school has an efficient referral system to manage problem students. Two deans are responsible for the disciplinary actions deemed necessary for educational or organizational reasons. Teachers, sometimes supervisory personnel or administrators, write disciplinary referrals to the student's dean. The dean calls the student to the office, discusses the referral and imposes sanctions spelled out in the student handbook.

The referral system, however, is more elaborate. Any faculty member may seek out the student's counselor for advice and/or suggest a referral to the Committee, a weekly meeting of student services personnel who discuss problem students and make recommendations for action. Faculty may also refer to the Committee directly. All these referrals are sent first to a secretary who solicits information on a special form, the Teachers' Report, from each of the student's teachers. She sends this information to the assistant principal for student services, the Committee chairman. During the meeting, the counselor usually presents the "case" and requests suggestions for actions.

Before the student is discussed in the Committee, the "problem" has gone through a double transformation. First, when teachers fill out the Teachers' Report, behavior, attitude, and personality problems in the classroom are transformed into problems located in the student's character. So classroom problems become descriptions of the student's actual social identity (Goffman, 1963:2-3). Second, on the referral sheets to the Committee, such character problems are interpreted as psychological or pathological difficulties.

More specifically, teachers see two broad categories of trouble in their classrooms: (1) Student behavior, which is observable and interferes with teacher expectations; and (2) student personality, independent of observable conduct.

Teachers are expected to establish a classroom atmosphere conducive to learning: without noise, boisterous students, movement about the room, inattention, obstinate and discourteous behavior, tardiness, or other activities detracting from learning. Students who interfere in these ways are problems. Others are classified as problems because they exhibit certain idiosyncratic characteristics incompatible with the teacher's positive self-evaluation. These are students who do not suppress personality conflicts with the teacher. Students who are seen as holding different values, being immature, considering school irrelevant, lacking sincerity, not achieving, displaying negativism, and as truant are also considered problems. Teachers are especially concerned with truancy—in addition to more obvious educational concerns—because their superiors and they themselves interpret high truancy rates as indicators of poor teaching. Since teachers have to report frequent truancy to the deans' office, it can become a means by which their administrative abilities are evaluated. Students who threaten the teacher's position of authority—especially publicly—are considered problems. Refusing to take correction or to follow instructions, talking back to the teacher, or disobeying orders are examples of such threats (for more detail, see Wittig, 1973:91-99).

The teacher has various options in managing such problems. She will first try to solve the problems in the classroom. If this attempt fails, the most common approach is referral to the deans. The teacher, however, will refer the student to the student service personnel if she perceives the causes as other than disciplinary.

Managing problem students is a feature of the ordinary work of school personnel. This creates observable events to illuminate important features of the school's social organization and its management of routine work. In the course of such management, school personnel must select and transform classroom problems so that their descriptions become meaningful to the next level in the school's hierarchy (cf., Cicourel, 1968:16 and passim). The first transformation occurs in the Teachers Reports, a confidential form requesting information on a student's "academic, behavioral, and social progress including attendance, health factors, and present status in class." The completed forms become part of the student's record. In addition to the information directly requested, teachers frequently add their assessment of the student's motivation toward school and his/her ability to do the work required for class. Most important, teachers comment on the student's character, providing the reader with a perception of the student's actual social identity. Such character assessments are positive or negative, some students are defended as essentially good, friendly, and positive human beings. Others are characterized as bad, unworthy, and pitiful. Such assessments are presented without behavioral evidence. If the student's actions are described at all, they serve only as illustrations of imputed core characters.

Two categories unsolicited by the Teacher's Report deal with the common-sense causation of problems: "emotional problems" and "home problems." References to emotional problems tend to be vague; but some are very explicit. Perceived faults in the student's characters are treated as implicit or explicit symptoms of emotional problems. A student who seems "strange" to the teacher, "lies, is deceitful, immature and insecure," who "lacks motivation," or "does not have clearly expressed goals in life yet" is described as "sick" or as "having emotional problems." Although teachers seem reluctant to make written statements about a student's family, the information they record links the problems to those seen in the family. This Teacher's Reports contain assessments of the parents' ability as parents and of their emotional as well as marital stability. In writing these records, teachers actively manage their environment. Their judgmental, perceptual, and typifying work makes sense of their world and prepares the scene for further inference and action (Cicourel, 1968: 111).

Teachers are able to accomplish such management of their environment because they have frequent contact with student services personnel—especially with the Committee members and can thus anticipate the kind of information expected by the Committee. This information together with the Committee members' knowledge of the students and their cumulative records form the basis for the second transformation.

When asked to identify the most problematic case they had worked with during the past year, all but one Committee member mentioned students they saw as having emotional problems. While the emotional problems are vaguely described and the indicators are not clearly relevant, the classification is understood by most faculty members.

The indicators fall into three categories: infraction of school rules, attitudinal indicators, and school performance. Certain infractions of school rules trigger the imputation of a sick label: use of drugs, truancy, destruction of school property, fighting, acting out, instigation of a disturbance (such as setting off a smoke bomb), disobedience, defiance of authority, and use of obscenities or swear words. Attitudes identified with a "sick" identity are: being withdrawn, hostile, or belligerent. "Lack of motivation, disinterest in school, flight from reality (manifested in the refusal to accept the allegation of having problems and to accept help), and a resemblance of a depression" are further indicators. "Low self-image, immaturity, tics, and running away" result in an imputation of "sickness" as do "too frequent visits to the nurses' office" or "having an affair with an older man." School performance serves as another important signal for expected problems. Low ability and overachieving as well as high ability and underachieving are symptoms that "something is wrong." The low ability student—inferred from test results—with high aspirations is seen as unable to accept reality. A student with high tested intelligence who doesn't achieve is seen as having emotional problems preventing better performance.

When student services personnel consider a "case" serious enough to be discussed at a Committee meeting, they state the reason for referral on a "Referral Sheet." These forms confirm the predominant interest in the emotional dimension of trouble. Truancy, the most frequent reason, is interpreted as a symptom of emotional instability, as are "home problems" and "behavior problems." A "recommendation for one of the special programs" is also interpreted within the framework of emotional problems. The written reasons for referral confirm the second transformation: the tendency to interpret problems in psychological terms. The actual classroom problems, then, are transformed into concerns over the emotional health of the student through the necessary and successful preparation of the scene for the Committee meetings. During these meetings personnel discuss courses of action and accomplish the work of client control.

Dynamics of the Management of Client Control

The Committee's work is marked by a tension between an internal concern: the smooth and efficient functioning of the school as an institution concerned with client control; and an external concern: the preservation of the image of an innovative, effective educational institution. In the Committee meetings, this pressure is translated into attempts to secure the essential cooperation of parents and the necessity to prevent parents (and the community) from interfering with the Committee work.

During the Committee meetings, the referee, usually the counselor, sometimes the dean or the social worker, presents the "case" by summarizing the problem. This includes details of the student's previous performance, problems, and complaints from other school segments, information on the student's background, discussions of earlier parent contact and general information on the student's family. Such information is extracted from the student's file and from first-hand experience with students and parents. Anecdotal material, including hearsay about an impending separation of a student's parents, and material collected unsystematically by elementary and junior high school officials who formerly knew the student are included. All Committee members are encouraged to offer their assessment of the student's character, personality, ability, attitudes, potentials as well as home and parents. If available, the psychologist will interpret test results. Teacher's Reports are only read if they contain new information. Next "ways to help the student" are discussed, i.e. means available within the school as well as help from outside sources. After reaching agreement on a course of action, a member is advised to contact the student and initiate the neccessary steps. A special Committee meeting is scheduled four times a year where all members responsible for such action report on the results.

The Committee's activities show an essential feature of its work: the need for parent cooperation. The following account will highlight the Committee's efforts to gain parental permission to administer placement tests for special programs, to gain parental participation in treatment efforts, and to convince parents of the school's leadership as a progressive educational institution, thereby avoiding potential parental action considered harmful to this image. Such efforts are the positive elements of client control.

The Committee deals with two categories of problem students: those of "normal character" and those of "disturbed character" (Emerson, 1969). While problem students of normal character take little of the Committee's time, those with disturbed character are the focus of most deliberations. In these discussions, the Committee tries to analyze the student's problem, considers treatment possibilities and inquires into the student's home to learn more about the parents. Questions about home life focus on parental competence and previous accomodations to the school's suggestions and actions. General information on the family is also collected: on marital status of the parents, possible marriage problems, pending separation or divorce, the financial situation, parentage of the child, parents' history of physical or mental illness, problems with siblings, and the parents' educational and occupational attainment. For example, a referral sheet contained the following information on a boy:

> obnoxious behavior in class; mother has been to the superintendent, the boy has seen a superintendent, the boy has seen a psychiatrist, will not see the social worker. . . . Lives with guardians now, parents live in M., Indiana; he is a ward of the state.

The Committee discussions provide more information:

> His guardians don't want to realize that the kid has some problems. When they were approached, they didn't even come to school, they immediately contacted the superintendent. They were working at a halfway house before and are likely to project other problems than the ones we are confronted with. . . . They are the kind of people who want to make good what the boy's harsh fate messed up.

While the counselor's comments hint at child abuse by the parents, he describes the guardians' attitude toward school and its efforts "to help," and their unwillingness to accept the Committee's recomendations. Such information is shared in order to prepare the Committee for potential difficulties with these guardians. The inferences made cast doubt on the guardians' capabilities as guardians, their willingness to work with the school, and their particular philosophy in interpreting the boy's difficulties. At a later discussion, the social worker adds:

> There seems to be some kind of jealousy in the foster father. He complained that D. still respects his real parents; they always told the boy that he was a real failure. . . . The foster father feels that the boy is fulfilling his parents' prophesy in all he does. . . .

The guardians are described as unable to "cope" with the boy's lasting attachment to his parents; and once identified as having "problems" themselves, they are co-labeled (Suchar, 1972, passim).

After exchanging such information, the Committee discusses possible "ways to help." From the Committee's point of view, helping consists of finding means in or outside school to help the student adjust to the normal routine of the school day. Student adaptation is an important aspect of the personnel's work since they are responsible for the uninterrupted flow of school activities. The "helping stance" requires an examination of the school's resources to see if any of them can provide help the student seems to need. It also requires an investigation into obstacles which might occur in the process of providing help. Here information on the student's parents is vital to the Committee's work since parental cooperation is required but cannot be assumed:

> One mother refused to give permission to have her son tested. The test was a state require-

ment for placement in special school programs financially supported by the state. The special education teacher related: the boy 'was all for it [to enter the program], wanted to take the tests. . . . But the mother came up with this refusal. . . . '

Information on the parents is necessary to head off any potential refusal to cooperate since it limits the effectiveness of the Committee's recommendations. Information on parents provides the basis for dealing strategically with difficult parents. Such strategies range from persuasion to coercion. In connection with the permission for testing, the special education teacher reports on such persuasion efforts:

I wrote a letter and got no response. . . . I wrote about a month later. I called . . . and said 'let me explain even further what it is.' She [mother] was obviously threatened by the term psychological testing. I explained and she said 'oh, that's all it is?' You know, I told her what it is used for, for placement purposes. . . . I have to admit I snowed her a little bit, embellished it a little bit to make it sound as pleasant as possible. . . . She agreed to sign the permission slip but never did. The persuasion failed. (Since the boy improved, no further parent cooperation was needed.)

In another case, indirect coercive measures were suggested:

The psychologist reported: 'There is a long history of problems. His parents never cooperated. . . . We have to get them to cooperate. . . . They don't see that there is a problem and that he needs help. . . . We have to get him, *do* something so that we have a lever for getting him psychiatric help. The parents have to be told that he cannot be in school with that kind of behavior.' The social worker related an incident which occurred outside of school: 'A. was picked up by the police . . . because he was found pointing a knife at another kid in a fight. Maybe we can use this to get the parents to cooperate with the school.' And later: 'We can use the knife-incident as a lever to force them' to get psychiatric help for the boy.

The Committee tries to force parent cooperation in cases they consider "dangerous" and where physical harm to other students may be involved. Such cases are considered serious enough to warrant forms of coercion to achieve parental cooperation. This coercive approach carries an implicit judgment about the parents. They are seen as unwilling or unable to accept the school's assessment of the student's problem. "Lacking insight" is interpreted as a sign of the parents' lack of realism, flight from reality, or obstinacy. All these signs are considered indicators of emotional problems in students. Similar inferences are made about uncooperative parents. In a later conversation, the boy's counselor made these inferences explicit:

See, the parents have always denied that there is something wrong with him. . . . How can someone in his right mind deny that the kid is sick, seriously sick? This is one of the problems we face, we not only have sick kids but also sick parents. Many parents in this community are emotionally unstable, there are lots of problems in the homes!

Parental cooperation is essential for treatment inside the institution. The efforts of teachers in special education programs are particularly vulnerable to counteractive measures of the parents. Therefore, special education teachers frequently try to involve parents in what they call "treatment" and ask them to participate in various activities designed to "help the kid." Such participation was designed for a student considered immature, disinterested in school, a low achiever but clever manipulator of people:

Well, we had an excellent thing worked out with the kid about his class attendance in relation to the use of the family car on weekends. The mother said it was a great idea. . . . Three days later he is driving the car to school every day. . . . When I called her she said she didn't understand the agreement. . . . There was no cooperation. She was buffaloed [by her son]. She made all these promises and never carried them out!

The evaluation of the mother is negative. She is seen as unable to control her son. Such frequent inferences regarding the parents' abilities are mitigated, however, by their willingness to cooperate.

> (In another case) There was an effort made, [the parents] are fairly realistic. They got in touch with a psychiatrist and the treatment was done. . . . They have become more realistic in what has to be done and are taking people's advice.

The way cooperation can lessen negative inferences points to the organizational function of the co-labeling process. Negative inferences—documented in the student's record—diminish the parents' credibility and make them less successful should the parents try to intervene in school measures. Parents "in need of help" can be approached from two vantage points: cooperation with school will not only help their children but also themselves.

The Committee discussions suggest another element of school personnel's work. As "helping agents" they stress as their work's main rationale "helping the student adapt to the normal routine of the school day." This helping aspect has to be understood dialectically. Help is often extended to students who were identified as problematic by other school segments. The Committee, therefore, is called upon to eliminate the problems for them; i.e., to work for the smooth functioning of the school. The Committee has to be seen also as a group of specialized professionals charged with client control:

> (One counselor elaborated) You teach a kid to survive and to adjust to the situation. . . . I think too often we find it easier and more expedient to change the kid's environment instead of saying 'look, you find yourself in this world, you are the one who is going to learn . . . how you've got to respond.'

The social workers who define their role as more student oriented and are organizationally expected to do so, are also concerned with student control, though less obviously:

> See, some people are overly concerned with a student not achieving. . . . But they don't realize that this may be one way for the student to 'get even with his father.' If we take this outlet away from the kid he may cause much more trouble, he may act out in a much more serious manner.

Acting out with the potential for dangerous consequences clearly means a more serious threat to the school's smooth functioning than low achievement. The social worker's plea for the school not to impose its standards upon the student has to be seen as a measure of client control rather than as an attempt to defend the student's interest. The Committee often objects to what it interprets as the faculty's unjustified expectations of "instant results," an indication that the Committee is generally expected to fulfill control functions.

Parent cooperation as a measure of client control has to be considered from yet another aspect: parents who are unwilling to cooperate challenge the professionalism of personnel and so trigger reactions to protect it:

> You know, we . . . are professionals and know what we are speaking about. . . . We cannot work when parents give us a hard time.

School personnel see their professionalism challenged especially when parents "go over a Committee member's head" to supervisors or to the superintendent. This tendency to ignore or to countermand school personnel's advice results in fear that their decisions might be overturned by higher echelons of the administration. Such reversal is seen as an implicit negative evaluation and as a loss in the credibility of professional judgment. This fear is intensified through sterotypic views about the parents. They are perceived as unusually active and aggressive in pursuing their rights regarding the school and the education their children receive there. They are seen as extremely education-oriented but often unqualified to make proper educational decisions. To persuade or coerce parents into cooperating with the school, then, helps control a potential challenge to professionalism and so preserves the Committee members' self-image and self-worth.

Parent cooperation with the school is also important to the school's image. The faculty is very conscious of working in a school nationally known for quality education and for taking an innovative and progressive approach. This image can be perpetuated only if the parents and the community cooperate to incorporate new programs and educational philosophies into the school. Lack of parental cooperation endangers organizational effectiveness and so threatens the school's image and is, therefore, avoided.

When all school attempts to secure parental cooperation nevertheless fail or are expected to do so, then the school refuses to cooperate with parents and actively exludes them from "interfering with school affairs." Such exclusion occurs with both, "problem" and "normal" students.

> A mother known as 'weird and unrealistic' was concerned over her daughter's political orientation and contacted the dean who reported: 'B.'s mother is concerned over the leftist tendencies her daughter is displaying. . . . She requests help . . . from school.' The girl's counselor remarked: 'Well, her grades show no signs of concern. . . . When the mother called *me* I told her that the school could do nothing about the political orientations of its students. . . . ' The dean added: 'We also must point out that she should not take up our time with *that* kind of a problem!'

The student is no problem, while the mother is known as difficult, so the mother's desire to initiate school action is rejected and her request is considered an interference.

Cases in which parents try to interfere directly with school personnel's assessment of a problem are considered as serious. Parents are, again, seen as very education oriented and as likely to voice their demands toward school. The Committee feels that such demands are often unreasonable and unrealistic. The parents' insistence upon such demands becomes an open threat to personnel, especially to counselors who have to advise students and their parents.

Another facet of the prevailing stereotype is regarded as even more threatening. Parents are seen as overprotective and as siding with their children in cases of dispute with school personnel.

> The principal mentioned: ' . . . when you are disciplining a student, or correcting a student, or when you point out weaknesses of a student, I could think of some communities where—if the school said it was the case—it would be supported by the parents. Here it's not the case. It is more likely to be questioned by the parents. . . . They are more willing to take the student's point of view. . . . '

Committee discussions frequently contain statements about an "overprotective home, an overprotective mother." Such inferences lead to specific actions:

> A student known for constantly requesting a change of courses was discussed: 'There is another problem, Momma! Momma just picks up the phone and expects us to change her daughter's program. She gives that rap about how sensitive her daughter is. . . . The girl is always very pleasant but you never get really through to her; and Momma is straightening it out for her daughter. It is very difficult to work with such an overprotective parent.' It is decided that a final change will be made. Two weeks later the counselor reports on the case: 'I told [the mother] clearly that we will make this last one change. I stressed that . . . with her protective attitude the girl will never learn to handle her own affairs. . . . Apart from Momma, I have the feeling the girl started to respond; I think we'ge got a larger problem with Momma than we have with the girl.'

The emphasis shifts from the student's "problem" to that of the mother. The school responds by eliminating the parental interference through setting conditions and trying to educate the parent about the educational mistakes she makes. In addition, the counselor uses another strategy to reduce parental interference. She takes the girl's request to the forum of the Committee. She solicits and receives support for the planned action and presents it to the mother as a group decision. Since the Committee involves a group of professionals who all agreed on the suggested action, it becomes very difficult for the parent to challenge. Parents are also, to some extent, feared for their specific plans and concepts in educational matters, and so the avoidance strategies described above are developed. At the same time, a contrary set of inferences exists. Parents are seen as permissive, unrealistic, and as having problems themselves. These inferences, combined with a lack of cooperation, trigger more potent efforts to exclude parents from effectively interfering with planned school actions. The following "case" will illustrate coercive measures first and then show attempts to undermine the basis for effective challenge to school actions.

In "serious cases" school personnel use coercive measures: threats of expulsion and conditional readmission after an expulsion.

> A student had been a problem for over a year. His mother was described as emotionally unstable, his father had a stroke a few years ago and was seen as 'unwilling to serve any kind of disciplinary role . . . ' The boy was 'constantly searching for structure,' and that 'had to manifest itself in school.' He set fires in waste baskets, cut classes, smoked on school grounds and did other things to ' . . . indicate that he needed help. We all began to work to get his family into . . . family counseling which they were unwilling to do . . . although at the time of the suspension for lighting fire he and his family were coerced by the pressure of the school to go to a family counseling service. . . . After he got back into school they dropped off.'

Later the boy set off a home-made smoke bomb which caused no injuries or physical damage. When questioned, he defied school officials by being abusive and obscene.

> And because of this we were forced to take him to the school board for expulsion. . . . [It] was not necessarily meant to be punitive to the child . . . it was to enable us to get some lever on the kid to be able to get him some help. . . . For him to get back into school this is what they had to do: we forced him and his parents into a therapy situation with a psychiatrist . . .

Frequently, parents will successfully thwart all such school approaches. This attitude becomes a clear indication for school personnel that there "is something wrong with the parents," that they need help, too. Parents are no longer "next of relation" who aid personnel, but become "co-patients" (Suchar, 1972). Parents who are known to be uncooperative are seen as "sick," as having problems themselves:

> We have to know what kinds of parents we are dealing with (sic). When they have problems themselves, how can we deal with them to help the kid?

As co-patients, parents become potential subjects for "treatment." In this case, they are not accepted as competent in educational decisions. At the same time, their position as adversaries of the school is weakened:

> The Committee discussed a girl: 'We should recommend outside help again; the parents are overprotective, and maybe we are overprotective, too. The parents can't be reached, they don't cooperate. The father hits easily, so we cannot send all the information on the girl's problems to the home.' The dean then reported progress in her behavior. The following decision was made: Her 'apparent success should be used to get the family into family counseling so that more progress can be made.'

The parents are included in the school's efforts to adapt the student to the normal school routine. By labeling them "sick" and maintaining case histories on parents and students, the school justifies its actions and eliminates effective parental resistance to the school's objectives. To preserve organizational control and autonomy, the parents are rendered incompetent in their parental tasks and are not provided with all information. So they become less effective whether they take their "case" to higher echelons of the school administration or to court. In extreme situations, such as attempted expulsion from school, the parent's legal position is weakened because school records contain information on efforts to "help parents and child" which were refused. Such record content disqualifies the parents and strengthens the school's position:

> The expulsion '(was for us to get a lever on the kid [the boy who set fire in waste baskets], to be able to get him some help. The parents had never before taken our suggestions. . . . We suggested that he and his family get . . . psychiatric help. The parents had rejected this idea entirely. . . . ' The boy was expelled and later readmitted under the condition that he and his parents submit to psychiatric treatment. All involved signed a contract documenting these conditions.

Further resistance by the parents to school recommendations is unlikely—and if it occurred would probably be ineffective against such counter strategies.

Committee discussions show concern over "correct procedures" in school contacts with parents. Due process[1] is stressed in contacts with parents who are critical of the school and, therefore, expected to litigate against it. Situations which touch upon legal issues such as expulsion, extreme truancy or endangered graduation due to truancy and related loss of credits, are vulnerable to breaches of due process.

> In a truancy matter, a mother complained about unfair treatment of her daugher. During Committee discussions, the chairman stated: 'All I want to make sure is that the parents were fairly warned of the consequences [of the truancy]. I'm merely concerned with . . . due process. If due process was honored, then there is no basis for a revision in the appeals procedure.'

Due process is a potent weapon to prevent parents from successfully attempting to interfere with school decisions. Committee activities are visibly influenced by the perceived need "to cover our own grounds," a concern which reflects school personnel perceptions of the community. It is assessed as highly education oriented and the parents are seen as using all means at their disposal to reach their educational goals for their children. Perceived "exaggerated educational ambitions" for their children, especially in problem cases, is interpreted as a sign of parents' pathology. Frequently told anecdotes about such exaggerated ambitions to attain educational prominence for their children describe the parents as unrealistic and prone to use or condone devious means in educational competition.

> A student was caught cheating in a college record exam: 'The boy's parents came in . . . threatening to sue the school to make sure that [the cheating] didn't go on his records.'

Such aggressiveness coupled with a proclivity for devious means to achieve educational aims and with achievement pressures on the students leads school personnel to assess such parents as unrealistic, "driven," or "sick" and results in the above strategies of excluding parents from potential interference with school activities.

---

[1] Here elements of due process are notice of charges, right to counsel (especially in expulsion cases), right to confrontation, privilege against self-incrimination, right to transcript of the hearing, and right to appeal. With regard to the Committee work, right of appeal and notice of charges are relevant elements of due process.

Conclusion

The descriptive account of the process of dealing with organizationally defined deviants reveals features of the school personnel's daily work and of the organizational structure. Both influence the processes of defining and dealing with internal deviance. Through the bureaucratic channels for problem solving a double transformation in the definition of what constitutes a problem student occurs: first, from behavior, attitude, and personality problems to problems in the student's character; and second, from character problems to psychological difficulties. These transformations are the preparations for a team approach to solving such problems. This team of specialized professionals first attempts to secure needed parental cooperation. When such attempts fail, the team members make efforts to prevent parents from what is now interpreted as interference with the school's work. Both parental cooperation and attempts to avoid parental interference are measures of client control—an important element of the service institution's organizational imperative: to account to higher echelons of the school administration and the community that the school is doing successful and efficient work.

The analysis directs attention to the processes of co-labeling. The results indicate that co-labeling takes place under the assumption that the deviants' familial or associational network functions to maintain the individual in the deviant role. More important, however, the analysis identifies labeling and co-labeling as organizational imperatives which result from the service institution's need to control clientele. In organizations with minors as direct clientele (e.g., children's hospitals, day-care centers, or schools) the control of the direct clientele alone does not guarantee the realization of organizational goals. The parents of the children have a keen interest in the outcome of organizational efforts and can directly influence the organization's operations. Such potential is either coopted by enlisting parental cooperation for organizationally defined ends or rendered ineffective through excluding parents from affecting organizational activities. Co-labeling and actions resulting from it provide potent means of controlling indirect clientele in addition to internal means to control direct clientele.

REFERENCES

Becker, Howard S.
  1953   "The teacher in the authority system of the public school." Journal of Educational Sociology 27:128-141.
  1963   Outsiders. New York: The Free Press.
Bidwell, Charles E.
  1965   "The school as a formal organization." in J. G. March (ed.), Handbook of Organizations. Chicago: Rand McNally.
Boocock, Sarane S.
  1972   An Introduction to the Sociology of Learning. Boston: Houghton Mifflin.
Cicourel, Aaron V.
  1968   The Social Organization of Juvenile Justice. New York: Wiley.
Douglas, Jack D.
  1970   Deviance and Respectability. Princeton: Princeton University Press.
Emerson, Robert M.
  1969   Judging Delinquents. Chicago: Aldine.
Fisher, S.
  1972   "Stigma and deviant careers in school." Social Problems 20:78-83.
Foster, J. et al.
  1972   "Perceptions of stigma following public intervention for delinquent behavior." Social Problems 20:202-209.
Garfinkel, Harold
  1967   Studies in Ethnomethodology. Englewood Cliffs, N. J.: Prentice Hall.
Goffman, Erving
  1963 . Stigma. Englewood Cliffs, N. J.: Prentice Hall.

Kitsuse, John I.
    1964   "Societal reaction to deviant behavior: Problems of theory and method." in H. S. Becker (ed.). The Other Side. New York: The Free Press.
    1975   "The 'New conception of deviance' and its critics." in W. R. Gove (ed.). The Labelling of Deviance. New York: Sage Publication, Inc.
Kitsuse, John I. and Malcolm Spector
    1973   "Toward a sociology of social problems: Social conditions, value-judgments, and social problems." Social Problems 20:407-419.
Kitsuse, John I. and Malcolm Spector
    1975   "Social problems and deviance: Some parallel issues." Social Problems 22:584-594.
Lauderdale, Pat
    1976   "Deviance and moral boundaries." American Sociological Review 41:660-676.
Lemert, Edwin M.
    1951   Social Pathology. New York: McGraw-Hill.
    1967   Human Deviance, Social Problems, and Social Control. Englewood Cliffs, N. J.: Prentice Hall.
Lofland, John
    1971   Analyzing Social Settings. Belmont: Wadsworth.
Marshall, H. and R. Purdy
    1972   "Hidden deviance and the labeling approach: The case for drinking and driving." Social Problems 19:541-553.
McHugh, Peter
    1970   "A common sense perception of deviance." in J. D. Douglas (ed.). Deviance and Respectability. New York: Basic Books.
Scheff, Thomas
    1974   "The labelling theory of mental illness." American Sociological Review 39:444-452.
Schutz, Alfred
    1970a   On Phenomenology and Social Relations. Chicago: University of Chicago Press.
    1970b   Reflections on the Problem of Relevance. New Haven: Yale University Press.
    1971   Collected Papers, Vol I. The Hague: Martinus Nijhoff.
Suchar, Charles S.
    1972   The Social Organization of Child Therapy. unpublished Ph.D. Dissertation: Northwestern University.
Wittig, Monika
    1973   Identification and Processing of Troublemakers in School. Unpublished Ph.D. Dissertation: Northwesteern University.

SCHOOLING AND WORK:
SOCIAL CONSTRAINTS ON EQUAL EDUCATIONAL OPPORTUNITY

KATHLEEN WILCOX
PIA MORIARTY
Research Associates, Center for Economic Studies

In order effectively to socialize children to competence in the adult roles available to them, schools must produce a highly differentiated pool of graduates to fill the requirements of hierarchically stratified work roles in the United States. In this paper we compare how two public elementary schools in an upper-middle class and a lower-middle class neighborhood socialize children along the dimensions of cognitive competence, self-image, and relationship to authority. Our findings suggest that schools differentially socialize children to respond to authority so as to be competent in adult work roles similar to those currently held by their parents.

Americans believe in equal educational opportunity, and they have been willing to spend their tax dollars on public schools in the attempt to make it a reality. During the 1960's, the public became increasingly aware that certain groups of people—the poor, minorities, and women—were not enjoying the full benefits of the educational system, and special programs were instituted to supplement the educational resources offered these groups. However, a combination of factors including the questionable effectiveness of these programs, the current recession, and the sudden popularity of the political theme that "government can't do everything," indicate an apparent shift in attitudes away from public and governmental support for educational spending.

Although we share a concern about the future direction of education in the United States, we feel that the current predicament of the school system reflects a number of serious misconceptions on the part of educators and others about the role of schools in society. Cultural and social scientific beliefs in the importance of equal educational opportunity and the possibility of upward mobility through individual achievement have led to the prevalent assumption that schools are able to develop and sort out individual differences in an equable and neutral fashion (See: Harvard Educational Review, 1968, Special Issue on Equal Educational Opportunity, and McMurrin, 1971). What has not been recognized, however, is that this individualistic approach to the function of schools fails to address fundamental issues of schooling as a social institution and the importance of schooling in socializing children for available adult roles.

Like other industrial societies, the United States has financed schools to socialize its children to competence as adults. Society pays for schools; schools, in turn, attempt effectively to deliver children prepared to function in the full range of adult social roles. As social institutions, schools are not isolated and autonomous constructs, but integral parts of a social whole where institutions interact with and affect one another. In particular, schools must attend realistically to the demands of the workplace where most of their children will move as adults.

In this paper, we examine the nature of that workplace, arguing that its differentiation and hierarchical stratification require a similar range in the levels of preparation students are given in schools. We argue that schools must produce a highly differentiated pool of graduates to match the reality of the world of work. To support this view, we present an anthropological investigation of the functioning of two public schools in an upper-middle class and a lower-middle class neighborhood, relating the experiences of children in those schools to the experience of their parents in another major social institution, work.

The idea that schools have institutional obligations selectively to allocate students to future adult roles is not a new one, although, as indicated, earlier studies have seen that function as based on differing individual achievements (Parsons, 1959). More recently, a number of studies have examined the role of schools in socializing groups of students who differed from some comparison population (Leacock 1969, Herriott, 1966). Social class has been treated as an additional phenomenon in these studies (e.g., upper-class white schools compared with lower-class black schools), but has been less often examined as a phenomenon in itself, particularly among white students. In this study, we have attempted to look specifically at the influence of social class by comparing two primarily white schools.

Children move from schools into the world of work, widely recognized in the United States today as consisting of a finely differentiated hierarchy of occupational roles. *Work in America*, the report of a special task force to the Secretary of Health, Education, and Welfare, describes the conditions of work the 1970 Census indicates for over two-thirds of the employed population:

> . . . the trend is toward large corporations and bureaucracies which typically organize work in such a way as to minimize the independence of the workers and maximize control and predictability for the organization (HEW, 1973: 21).

As a human activity, work is inescapably both a technical and a social process. In our investigation of the functioning of schools to prepare children for future work roles, we have included both these dimensions by focusing on three aspects of work roles: cognitive and technical skills; differential relationships to authority; and psychological attributes such as self-image, aspirations, and self-presentation.

First, we examine cognitive and technical skills, because work roles are often assumed to be distinguished solely according to that dimension. The most well-established and widely-known example of this perspective is the human capital model (Becker, 1967):

> Nearly all economists who use human capital models believe either explicitly or implicitly that the major components of productivity under modern technological conditions are cognitive abilities and technical skills. Schooling imparts cognitive skills, increases "capacity to learn," and teaches some technical skills . . . . Differences between individuals in personality traits, values, modes of self-presentation, etc., are assumed to be completely secondary components of productivity and hence are seldom discussed and never systematically incorporated in human capital models (Levin, et al., forthcoming).

Bowles and Gintis present extensive evidence to suggest that the cognitive aspect of job performance has been greatly overemphasized. They point out that the dollar payoff of education in the work world is related to IQ only tenuously, if at all (Bowles and Gintis, 1976: 9). They document the importance of personality traits and personal attributes to job performance. Nonetheless, cognitive and technical skills are inevitably an aspect of competence at work, and therefore we have included this area in our study.

Next, we look at the personal attribute that corresponds most directly to the hierarchical nature of the workplace, one's relationship to authority. A number of researchers have explored this aspect of work (Kohn 1969, Gintis 1971, Edwards 1976, Levin forthcoming, Carter and Carnoy 1974). Kohn's (1969) impressive statistical study establishes a dichotomy between jobs where those at lower levels must submit to *external* authority, while those at higher levels rely on an *internalized* motivation for direction. Kohn contrasts jobs along this internal/external dimension, implying that jobs with high levels of (internal) occupational self-direction offer the opportunity for autzomonous, truly self-actualizing modes of conduct.

Bowles and Gintis' review of the literature on work roles leads to a modified view of the occupational structure, where professionals and managers are not autonomous, but must necessarily rely heavily on internalized norms and standards of practice in order to plan and carry out responsibilities in the best interests of the firm without direct supervision. At the same time, those workers who execute the managers' plans and directives must do so reliably in order for the enterprise to function smoothly. They must respond positively to the external procedures and rules that are defined for them, rather than spontaneously revise their work assignments. In the workplace, an orientation in terms of an internal control scheme is a fundamental executive attribute, just as an orientation toward following rules and external controls is essential to performance in compartmentalized, lower-level jobs (Bowles and Gintis, 1976: 53-148).

Third, we explore some of the psychological attributes identified with work roles and reinforced in the schools—self-image, aspirations, and self-presentation—because we recognize that social influences motivate people towards particular roles. Meyer emphasizes this view in his summary of the literature on anticipatory socialization, discussing the tendency for people to take on those qualities related to widely-legitimated definitions of themselves and of their futures. He points out that the more it is clearly defined and socially agreed that an individual will acquire a certain position, the more likely s/he is to take on the attributes of that position (Meyer, 1970). In another vein, Goffman's work (1959) illustrates the centrality of self-presentation to all aspects of human social behavior, including behavior at work; Bowles and Gintis underline its relevance to differential work roles (Bowles and Gintis, 1976: 141). Sennett and Cobb's (1972) interviews with American workers reflect the consequences of school experience for future self-image on the job.

In order to function effectively to prepare children for existing adult roles, schools must socialize their pupils with skills and attributes consonant with those required by the structure of the economy, including those just indicated. To match a highly differentiated and stratified collection of work roles, schools must produce an equally differentiated pool of graduates. They must produce drop-outs for the drop-out level jobs just as they produce Ph.D.'s for the Ph.D. level jobs. The process of socialization is not an open-ended one.

In a society with a work hierarchy such as ours, schools act as gatekeepers to the world of work. Meyer (1976) speaks of schools as each having a charter, an institutionalized social definition of what it is expected to produce. Students from some schools (or particular tracks within a school) are institutionally identified as potentially valuable commodities in a way recognizable to other institutions which guard the gates to influential levels of the social hierarchy, such as universities and major employers. Different schools are recognized for producing different kinds of products. Brookover and Erickson (1975:383-4) comment on the process producing these different products:

> . . . . society defines the level of ability and learning which will be achieved. Almost all children can and will learn whatever is defined as appropriate and required in the culture, and will fail to learn those types of behavior that society defines as inappropriate, improper, or not expected of them. . . . . Almost 100% of Americans learn to drive on the right-hand side of the road and almost all Britishers learn to drive on the left-hand side of the road. At a more abstract and verbal level, we recognize that almost 100% of the children in every society in the world learn to speak and communicate in an abstract, complex set of verbal symbols which we call language. . . . (Yet) Unlike our demand that all children learn to speak the langjage, our educational system demands that some children not learn algebra or physics and a wide range of other behavior. The result of . . . . the(se) educational practices . . . . is a school system that produces widely varied types of achievement in student groups classified and labelled as different in ability, interests, and needs.

From this perspective, the skills a child learns in school depend more on the social expectations for that child than on something inherent in that child. There is considerable evidence that the social expectations leading to the classification and labelling process Brookover and Erickson discuss are directly related to the identification by the society of different groups of people with different work roles. We are referring to groups such as class, sex, and ethnicity—all linked to recurring patterns of occupational roles. Indeed, in terms of sex and ethnicity, it has become almost trite to note how most company presidents are white males, while most people in jobs at the lowest level—domestic servants, cannery workers, farm laborers—are women and minorities. And, in terms of social class, although there is some individual mobility in the society, the majority remain in a class position similar to that of their parents (Stanley et. al., 1956: 219). Occupational role has been statistically demonstrated to define social class status better than any other variable (Kahl and Davis, 1955).

A developing body of material analyzes how groups of people are allocated to positions in the labor market. This theory of labor market segmentation sees role allocation not as a result of differing amounts of "human capital" possessed by groups, but rather as the result of a multitude of structural and historical characteristics fundamental to the economy. Space prevents a detailed description of this theory here; the interested reader is referred to other sources (Carter and Carnoy, 1974; Levin et. al., forthcoming).

We have chosen to explore one group allocation mechanism, that of social class, in terms of its effect on classroom socialization for future work roles, according to the three dimensions previously outlined.

INVESTIGATING THE FUNCTION OF SCHOOLS:
SAMPLE AND GENERAL METHODOLOGY

The literature suggests that these characteristics—cognitive and technical complexity, differential relationship to authority and personal attributes like self-image—delineate important differences between upper-middle and lower-middle class jobs. However, they can only be accurately observed in the context of subtle interaction patterns that lend themselves neither to statistical survey techniques nor short-term intensive studies. In order to observe these particular phenomena, it was necessary to adopt a long-term, in-depth methodology. Consequently, we narrowed our sample to two classrooms in the hopes that this more focused comparison would yield a richness of data that could not be obtained by other methods.

We sought two public elementary schools that fit the research design in terms of three criteria: socioeconomic status in mainstream upper-middle and lower-middle class neighborhoods (especially by income and occupation), representativeness of the two teachers (respected, experienced, and well integrated into their respective districts), and permission to observe intensively and to collect additional information from parents essential to an in-depth study. After an exhaustive screening of 31 classrooms in 10 different schools, we selected Collis P. Huntington Elementary School and Joe Smith Elementary School, focusing on one first grade classroom in each school. We chose first grade rather than a later year to observe the initial socialization impact of schooling. The principals directed us to the particular classroom we observed at each school. The teachers they chose were a comfortable part of their respective worlds; both were highly regarded by colleagues, and both had taught for over 10 years. Initial observations satisified us that both classrooms met our criteria for selection.

Collis P. Huntington School serves an upper-middle class neighborhood where many residents (50% of the fathers of children we observed) are self-employed, and most work as professionals, managers, and administrators. The 1970 Census reports their median annual income at $14,535 and median educational level at 15.4 years. With inflation, salaries have clearly risen since 1970; we have no accurate measure of this rise, although we do know that current housing values in the area start around $90,000. The Huntington neighborhood is virtually all-white.

The neighborhood around Joe Smith School is a good example of a lower-middle class community—certainly not a slum, but a rather rundown suburb where most parents are employed in skilled blue collar jobs and routinized, low-pay work. This trend is reflected in the 1970 Census estimation of their median annual income at $9,826, and in the corresponding current valuation (under $40,000) of their tract homes. Median education is 12.2 years, or slightly more than high school graduation. But in its socioeconomic background and in its ethnic composition (mostly white, with a representative sprinkling of families from various minority groups), the Smith neighborhood comes close to being an all-American average place to live.

In addition to socioeconomic characteristics that made these two neighborhoods a desirable choice in terms of our research design, patterns of school performance on state-mandated achievement tests also reflected the dynamic we wished to observe. Smith scores fell close to the state median, and Huntington scores were well above it. While children at Smith scored in the 67th and 69th percentiles on Grade 2 and 3 reading tests in 1974-75, by the 6th grade they had dropped to the 55th percentiles. At Huntington, on the other hand, 2nd and 3rd graders started at the 99th percentile, and maintained their reading scores at the 96th percentile level in 6th grade.

Although we had begun with some definite ideas about the nature of work roles, our purpose was to record actual classroom behavior, rather than to observe in terms of predetermined categories. Following an anthropological methodology, we spent several days making generalized observations in the two first grades in order to extract a sense of the *emic* (Goodenough, 1970), or the people's own way of categorizing meaningful objects and activities in their own setting—the classroom. After this initial groundwork, we developed simplified observation instruments. They focused on three areas of classroom behavior that corresponded to our analysis of significant differences between upper-middle and lower-middle class work:

- discipline and values taught (including internal/external control schemes),
- role of the student in the classroom (structured self-presentation and child participation), and
- presentation of cognitive materials.

We spent a minimum of 12 in-class hours recording all interactions in the single area of observation agreed upon for a given time period. Fieldwork in the classroom extended over three months, for a total of almost 60 in-class hours at Huntington and 106 hours at Smith going into the preparation of statistical summaries alone. Many more hours were spent observing in other classrooms, talking with teachers, counselors, and administrators, and interviewing most of the parents of children in both rooms in order to reassure ourselves that the teachers we had chosen were not atypical of their schools as a whole. Having only one continuous observer in each school made it impossible to control completely for observer bias, but we met regularly, sometimes daily, to coordinate perceptions and systematic recording techniques.

We are prevented by space limitations from painting a complete picture of the systematic techniques we developed to record the subtle yet pervasive characteristics that link schooling and work. Instead, we offer an example of our treatment of the special methodological problems posed by only one area of classroom behavior, that of discipline and the transmission of values. Research findings in other areas developed through the same, or similarly detailed and specialized, methodologies.

DISCIPLINE AND THE TRANSMISSION OF VALUES: METHODOLOGY

Like other aspects of the socialization process, the teaching of discipline and values has both present and future implications. It communicates principles of conduct for the child to use in making and acting on decisions. At the grade school level, values define both present priorities and future aspirations. Since work is an integral part of the futures of most children, it is important to look at the kinds of discipline and values they are taught, and how these things prepare them for future roles in the world of work.

In order to define the value structure in both classrooms, we devised a means of systematizing the teachers' discipline or control schemes using teacher/child interactions (verbal exchanges) as the unit of observation. We noted both the form and approach (strategy) the teacher used, and the value content (message) of each interaction, and developed these observations into an elaborate classification system of 53 strategies and 30 messages, all reflecting the teachers' own (emic) categories. This provided a very rich data base, accurate though unwieldy in its details. Consequently, after a careful analysis of patterns revealed by this emic system, we re-classified our observations into an *etic*, or analytical, system of eight variables relevant to our inquiry and reasonably representing the more detailed information we had gathered. Our re-classification was based on four contrasting pairs of variables:

- internal/external source of responsibility,
- present/future orientation,
- positive/negative affect, and
- cognitive/behavioral application

Although the distinctions between these contrasting variables blur occasionally in practice, we found them a useful construct for conceptualizing and recording patterns in the behavior we observed.

To identify significant differences between the teachers' control schemes, we computed school scores for each of these eight variables based on the mean number of interactions/child (n = 45; 20 children at Huntington and 25 at Smith). These scores reflected the percentage of total observations in each classroom (571 interactions at Huntington and 509 at Smith) that contained at least one occurrence of a given variable. An arc-sine transformation normalized the distribution of these scores (Eisenhart, 1947) so that t-tests and an analysis of variance could be performed to test the relative effects of four independent variables: school, sex, high/low ability group and white/non-white ethnicity.

Although this analysis of variance showed that some patterns of effects could be explained by various combinations of sex, ability group, and ethnicity, the vast majority of significant differences were best explained by school identity, while controlling for the other three variables. Again, space limitations prevent us from presenting the full array of research findings confirmed by this statistical technique. Instead, we summarize our results for only one pair of contrasting variables, that of internal vs. external source of responsibility. To our knowledge, these two variables have not been systematically observed in schools before. Their inclusion in this study represents a conceptual innovation that helped us look more closely at class differences between schools because of its close correspondence with hierarchical authority structures in the world of work.

INTERNAL/EXTERNAL DISCIPLINES: RESEARCH FINDINGS

As already noted, internal/external control schemes reflect stratification in the workplace, where higher level workers who function without immediate supervision must be able to make decisions based on internalized standards, and lower level workers must be depended to follow directions reliably. Blue collar jobs require an ability to respond positively to procedures and rules defined by an external authority source. Professional and managerial jobs require an ability to function independently. This view does not imply independence from all norms and standards of practice; rather, it necessitates particularly reliable adherence to them:

> That is, the vast majority of workers in higher levels of the hierarchy of production are by no means autonomous, self-actualizing and creatively self-directed. Rather, they are probably supersocialized so as to internalize authority and act without direct and continuous supervision to implement goals and objectives relatively alienated from their own personal needs (Bowles and Gintis, 1976: 145).

This understanding of the nature of higher levels of work led us to expect an emphasis on internalized values and standards of achievement at Huntington. Conversely, we expected that the socialization of Smith children would emphasize the same reliance on external rules and directives suggested as essential to performance in the blue collar jobs held by their parents.

In schools, the internal/external distinction is reflected in both teacher expectations and the nature of responsibilities given to the children. We classified as *internal* those interactions where the teacher treated the child as a self-directed person capable of managing a process in an independent way and choosing the consequences of his/her activity. In an internal interaction, the teacher throws the responsibility back to the child to think and shape activity in a manner that promotes or relies upon internalized values, self-images, standards or goals. The following examples from the Huntington classroom illustrate internal interactions:

> Tommy, talk to yourself quietly and tell yourself where you are and what's expected of you.

> You really goofed off. Why do you do this to yourself?

> Now you boys don't use good judgment when you come to the circle. Your legs are touching his, so pretty soon you're going to be kicking each other. See, the way you sit can help you study.

> Our fifteen minutes are up. Have you used them wisely?

At Smith, many of the teacher's internal-based control statements had applications in the affective domain, rather than in the area of academic skills. She was consistent in her refusal to mediate disagreements among the children, forcing them to take the initiative to resolve their own difficulties:

> (to two children who came asking her judgment as to which could use a particular game)

> I don't know what happened. You two will have to decide that yourselves.

These are all internal means of control, because the teacher is asking the children to think for themselves; she expects them to further their own best interests without her direct supervision.

By contrast, in an *external* interaction, the teacher is the one who does the thinking. She treats the child as a person who is expected to follow certain standard rules, procedures or directions laid down by herself and made salient by her authority and direct power. The following examples from the Smith classroom illustrates external interactions:

> You have a responsibility to get that paper done and I want it done now.

You have an assignment. Sit down and get busy.

You guys have to take the responsibility of learning. Come on, you should be with the program. Eyes should be up here, pencils down.

Two ways of establishing order within the classroom that were common at Smith—commands resting on the authority of the teacher or some other adult, and rule repetition—are external means of control, because they reinforce a pattern where the impetus for behavior does not come from the children themselves, but from some external rule or authority figure who issues rules and directives.

As expected, Huntington showed a consistently higher proportion of internal-based interaction than did Smith, and the difference between the two schools was very significant ($p = .001$), especially for interactions involving academic skills ($p = .001$). However, both schools showed high levels of external *behavioral* controls.

These results indicate that children at both schools were socialized to respond to external behavioral standards, but only the Huntington children were taught that they were personally responsible for maintaining the quality of their academic work. The Huntington teacher took time to establish internalized standards of achievement that would motivate them to perform well without her constant supervision. The internalized sense of responsibility she emphasized parallels the internal controls demanded of their professional parents on the job.

At Smith, this internal component was largely missing. Smith children were taught to rely heavily on external controls provided by the teacher, particularly in the area of academic tasks. By default, they had little exposure to the process of internalizing standards of achievement, although they were taught internalized norms for settling disputes among themselves. When the dominant Smith control scheme based on external restrictions is applied to future work situations, it seems a good preparation for lower-level jobs where reliable rule-following is an essential component.

CONCLUSION

Patterns of internal/external relationship to authority stressed at Huntington and Smith correspond closely to the relative positions of those children's parents in upper-middle and lower-middle class jobs. What can we conclude from this information?

From an anthropological perspective, the principal function of schooling is to socialize children so they will be capable of assuming the adult social roles available to them (Gearing, 1973). Informed by an examination of the differentiated nature of those adult roles in the world of work, we have systematically observed the functioning of two public elementary schools to socialize children along three dimensions, presenting our results only in the area of relationship to authority. These research findings are only part of a larger comparative ethnography to document significant differences between the schools in the areas of cognitive skills and self-image as well. Our results suggest that schools are differentially socializing their students to fill adult work roles similar to those currently held by their parents (Wilcox and Moriarty, 1976).

Children in the upper-middle class school are not taught in the same way, nor are they receiving the same content as those in the lower-middle class school. The dominant bias in American culture points to an individualistic interpretation of these results—that the differences we have documented are simply a reflection of the personal idiosyncracies of the two teachers involved. We would argue that retraining these teachers or even replacing them with new ones would not significantly change the patterns observed. Children are treated differently at Smith and Huntington not because the teachers are different or because the teachers are not both committed to the ideal of equal educational opportunity, but because the social context is different. Interviews with other teachers and observations in other classrooms at both schools, together with a fuller ethnographic comparison of both neighborhoods, confirm and define those differences along the lines of social class. The two teachers reflect the larger social dynamic where family background is perceived as an index of inevitable adult roles. At Smith, teachers saw that background as "culture of poverty," and made a number of disparaging remarks about the neighborhood, while those at Huntington were very aware of the wealth and status of the parents there (Wilcox and Moriarty, 1976). Children in both schools were unconsciously yet consistently socialized in particular ways congruent with their parents' level of participation in the world of work. Social class background was obvious to both teachers and children at the two schools, and it structured in the same imbalance in social relationships at the schools as might be found in any bureaucratic organization. Until inequalities in the structure of work are changed, it is unrealistic to expect any teacher, however trained, to be free of the pervasive stereotyping fostered by everyday social experience that constantly recognizes and draws conclusions from social class status.

Our research findings imply that without significant changes in social stratification by class background and its basis in the hierarchical structure of work, it is not likely that similarly structured patterns will be eliminated from schools, no matter how much money is spent toward equalizing educational opportunity. Schools must prepare children for roles in a real, not an idealized world. Equality and full human development can only be fostered by the schools when the adult social roles the children take are changed to support and rely upon these qualities as well.

We would suggest that much of the energy used in school reform should be redirected into democratizing our economic institutions. We believe this is the most direct path to those familiar goals of equality and justice, and choosing a path through the schools will be longer and much more tortuous, if not an outright failure.

We are not saying that schools are not important. We disagree strongly with Jencks' conclusion that variations in what children learn in school depend largely on variations in what they bring to school, rather than on variations in what schools offer them (Jencks, 1972:53). This study has outlined the substantial effect that schools have in recreating the social distinctions that the society needs in order to have adult citizens functioning in all the necessary roles in its economy. Contrary to popular beliefs, schools relate effectively to the real, stratified world of work in this society. Because of this effectiveness, only a fundamental restructuring of the economy can affect basic changes in the way schools socialize children.

BIBLIOGRAPHY

Becker, Gary
 1967 Human Capital and the Personal Distribution of Income. Ann Arbor, Michigan: The University of Michigan Press.
Brookover, Wilbur B. and Edsel L. Erickson
 1975 Sociology of Education. Homewood, Illinois: The Dorsey Press.
Bowles, Samuel and Herbert Gintis
 1976 Schooling in Capitalist America. New York: Basic Books.
Carter, Michael A. and Martin Carnoy
 1974 "Theories of labor markets and worker productivity." Discussion paper, Palo Alto, California: Center for Economic Studies.
Edwards, Richard C.
 1976 "Individual traits and organizational incentives: What makes a 'good worker?" Journal of Human Resources (in press).
Eisenhart, Churchill
 1947 "Inverse sine transformation of proportions." in Eisenhart et al. eds., Techniques of Statistical Analysis. New York: McGraw-Hill.

Gearing, Frederich O.
1973 "Where we are and where we might go: Steps toward a general theory of cultural transmission." CAE Newsletter 4: 1-10.

Gintis, Herbert
1971 "Education, technology, and the characteristics of worker productivity." American Economic Review, 61 (May).

Goffman, Erving
1959 The Presentation of Self in Everyday Life. Garden City, New York: Doubleday.

Goodenough, Ward
1970 Description and Comparison in Cultural Anthropology. Chicago: Aldine.

Harvard Educational Review
1968 Special Issue on Equal Educational Opportunity. 38, No. 1 (Winter).

Herriott, Robert E. and Nancy St. John
1966 Social Class and the Urban School: The Impact of Pupil Background on Teachers and Principals. New York: Wiley and Sons.

Jencks, Christopher, et al.
1972 Inequality: A Reassessment of the Effect of Family and Schooling in America. New York: Harper and Row.

Kahl, Joseph A. and James A. Davis
1955 "A comparison of indexes of socio-economic status." American Sociological Review 20 (June): 317-25.

Kohn, Melvin
1967 Class and Conformity: A Study in Values. Homewood, Illinois: The Dorsey Press.

Leacock, Eleanor
1969 Teaching and Learning in City Schools. New York: Basic Books.

Levin, Henry M., et al.
Education and Work: The Development of a Radical Hypothesis. Palo Alto, California: Center for Economic Studies (forthcoming).

McMurrin, Sterling M.
1971 The Conditions for Educational Equality. New York: Committee for Economic Development.

Meyer, John W.
1970 "The charter: Conditions of diffuse socialization in schools" in W. R. Scott. Social Processes and Social Structures. New York: Holt, Rinehart & Winston.

Parsons, Talcott.
1959 "The school class as a social system." Harvard Educational Review, 29, No. 4 (Fall).

Rosenfeld, Gerry
1971 "Shut Those Thick Lips!": A Study of Slum School Failure. New York: Holt Rinehart & Winston.

Sennett, Richard and Jonathan Cobb
1972 The Hidden Injuries of Class: Knopf.

Stanley, William O., et al.
1956 Social Foundations of Education. New York: Dryden Press, Inc.

Wilcox, Kathleen and Pia Moriarty
1976 "Schooling and differential socialization to competence." Discussion paper, Palo Alto, California: Center for Economic Studies (forthcoming).

WHAT FREE SCHOOLS TEACH*

ANN SWIDLER
Harvard University

Alternative schools are no more, and often less effective in teaching academic skills than are traditional schools. Alternative schools do, however, teach a "hidden curriculum," a set of norms nearly the inverse of those traditional schools teach. Using the work of Dreeben, *On What Is Learned in School* (1968), and contrasting his findings with those from a two-year study of two alternative high schools, it is argued that in place of the values of individualism and achievement, alternative schools teach group skills. Students do not learn to cope with the stress of evaluation and the risk of failure; instead they are encouraged to develop autonomy, self-direction, and emotional openness. In contrast to the universalistic, specific norms of traditional schooling, free schools stress diffuse, particularistic, intimate relations between teachers and students and within the student peer group. The paper concludes with an analysis of the social class implications of the norms which free schools teach.

Alternative schools, like traditional schools, teach norms of conduct and patterns of social organization as well as skills. This paper, based on two years of field research at two contrasting alternative high schools in Berkeley, California, examines the "hidden curriculum" of free schools—what they teach implicitly through their organization, their methods of social control, and their impact on the student peer group.

The two alternative high schools studied (here called Group High and Ethnic High) were not quite typical of other free schools. First, they were larger. Group High had about 230 students, and Ethnic High about 95. Second, the two schools were part of a public school system, established as independent sub-schools within a conventional, though liberal, high school. In racial and class composition they were perhaps representative of the two major strands of the free school movement. Group High was predominantly white, middle and upper-middle class, with a strong counter-cultural ideology. Though Ethnic High had elements of a free-school ideology, its approach was primarily political and "multi-cultural," emphasizing ethnic identity, basic skills, and mutual respect among ethnic groups. Its students, approximately a third blacks, a third whites and a third Chicanos, were largely from working-class families, and many had histories of school failure.

Despite differences in student bodies and philosophy, both alternatives were "free schools" in that they rejected hierarchical authority. Both schools shared decision-making power with students and encouraged them to choose their own educational directions. Students and teachers acted like equals, and students were freed from traditional patterns of deference, formality and discipline.

NORMS AND VALUES
Dreeben (1968:44) argues that schools, through the structural arrangements they make for handling children, teach pupils to "accept principles of conduct, or social norms, and to act according to them." Students in school learn to act in a public arena, according to rules

*Revised version of a paper presented at the Annual Meeting of the American Sociological Association, August 30-September 3, 1976, New York City. The full study upon which this paper is based can be found in Swidler (1975). To preserve confidentiality, pseudonyms have been given to the two schools studied, and citations to studies which contain specific reference to the schools have been omitted. I would like to thank Carole E. Joffe and Claude S. Fischer for helpful comments on an earlier draft of this paper.

resembling those in the market-place and the world of work, rather than those organizing the intimate life of the family. In this sense, as Eisenstadt (1956) suggested some time ago, the school provides a bridge between the values of intimacy, acceptance and authority pervading the family (what Parsonians would identify as ascription, particularism, affectivity and diffuseness), and the more demanding, impersonal rules of the larger society. Dreeben (1968:65) argues that

> pupils, by coping with the sequence of classroom tasks and situations, are more likely to learn the principles (i.e., social norms) of *independence, achievement, universalism* and *specificity* than if they remained full-time members of the household (emphasis added).

The structure of life in free schools, although it also provides children with experience in a public realm outside the family, teaches a set of norms contradictory at many points to those implicit in the traditional school setting. An exploration of these contrasts will begin to provide an answer to the question of what free schools teach.

ACADEMIC SKILLS

Before examining the norms and values free schools teach, we must first look briefly at their success in teaching conventional academic skills. Despite the arguments of the early free-school proponents such as Neill, Dennison, Kohl, and Holt that children learn quickly and easily if only they are freed from humiliation, constraint, and anxiety, there is no evidence to date, in either my own work or in published studies, that free schools do a better job of teaching academic skills than do traditional schools. Indeed, there is considerable evidence that students actually learn less in alternative schools (Minuchin, *et al.,* 1969; Bane, 1972b; Bennett, 1976; Stallings, 1976).

An evaluation of Group High after its first and second years compared Group High's students to controls who had applied for admission and had been excluded by lottery. During the first year the Group High students seemed to make slightly greater gains in verbal and mathematical skills than the controls, but during the second year these gains disappeared, and the Group High students also showed no superiority on tests of cognitive functioning or ego maturity. Although no reliable evaluation of Ethnic High was ever conducted, tests administered throughout the school district showed no overall differences in achievement for students in alternative schools (there were, in all, more than 20 alternative schools in the district) as compared to students in regular classrooms. These results are particularly disappointing since the students who choose to attend alternative schools tended to be slightly more white and more middle-class than students in the regular schools, and since the alternative schools had very small student-teacher ratios and substantial supplemental funding.

Other studies confirm these findings. Mary Jo Bane (1972b: 274n), in a review of research on pre-school programs, concluded that:

> more structured programs . . . are more effective in raising the cognitive scores of disadvantaged children than unstructured programs like those of traditional nursery schools.

In her own study of two contrasting first-grade classrooms Bane (1972a) found no significant differences in reading achievement between students assigned to an open vs. a traditional classroom. Similarly a national study by the Stanford Research Institute (Stallings, 1976) concluded that for economically deprived children "highly controlled" classrooms were much more effective in improving reading and math scores, though children in less traditional classrooms showed superior gains on non-verbal tests, were absent from school less often, and were more willing to work independently. The findings are consistent: although students seem to learn no more, and sometimes less, in free schools, they like them better, identify more with the school, and like their teachers more (Minuchin, *et al.*, 1969: 179), than do students in traditional schools.

If free schools do not, as some have hoped, make children blossom intellectually, the question of what they do teach becomes all the more pressing. In my research at Group High I was struck with this question very directly. Here were the bright, lively children of educated upper-middle class families, sitting through long, boring meetings, spending hours in classes largely involving desultory personal discussion, and feeling satisfied, even exhilirated, by the process. Group High was so popular with students that it was oversubscribed from the beginning, and parents seeking admission for their children badgered school administrators. In response to these demands, the school board established another alternative high school the year after Group High opened. In a survey of Group High students most of the students reported that they liked the school, and in contrast to 41% in a sample from traditional schools, 72% said that Group High "was doing a good job of preparing them for the future." In addition, the parents of Group High students (surveyed during the Group High evaluation) were more satisified with the school, evaluated their sons' and daughters' school experience as better, and thought their children were learning more than did parents of the controls. What, then, made these students want an alternative school experience? We can begin to answer this question by examining what free schools—in contrast to traditional schools—teach through their informal structure.

INDEPENDENCE AND ACHIEVEMENT

Take first the traditional-school norm which Dreeben (1968:66) calls "independence:"

> Pupils learn to acknowledge that there are tasks they must do alone, and to do them that way. Along with this self-imposed obligation goes the idea that others have a legitimate right to expect such independent behavior under certain circumstances.

The focal point for learning the norm of independence, Dreeben argues, is in formal testing situations where students are judged on their performance as individuals. The value schools place on independence is expressed by the prohibition against "cheating"—one of the primary breaches of school morality.

Students must also become accustomed to being judged. Learning "achievement" values means learning to be evaluated, to cope with both success and failure.

> Classrooms are organized around a set of core activities in which a teacher assigns tasks to pupils and evaluates and compares the quality of their work. In the course of time, pupils differentiate themselves according to how well they perform a variety of tasks, most of which require the use of symbolic skills.

> These activities force pupils to cope with various degrees of success and failure, both of which can be psychologically problematic (Dreeben, 1968: 71).

Both my own research and other studies of alternative schools (Minuchin *et al.* 1969; Bane, 1972a) indicate that they differ from traditional schools precisely in that they do not teach the norms Dreeben calls independence and achievement. Free schools subordinate individual achievement to the development of group life.

Bane's (1972a) study of first graders in two contrasting classrooms gives some hint of the link between learning group skills and the failure to learn norms of individualism and achievement. Bane systematically recorded the way twelve lower-ability children in two contrasting first grade classrooms actually spent their time. Children in the open, unstructured classroom engaged in more varied activities, moved around more, and made more choices about what activities to pursue than did children in the traditional classroom. These differences did not, however, lead children in the unstructured classroom to concentrate for longer periods of time on the activities they had chosen. Although children in the unstructured classroom spent significantly less time in activities coded "solidary non-productive"—that is sitting at their desks doing nothing—and were less often overtly bored, they also spent less time in learning activities. Instead, children in the open classroom spent their time in social interaction with teachers and peers.[1]

> [T]here is more social activity of all types in the unstructured room than in the struc-tured. There are more conversations and there are also more competitive and aggressive interchanges. Because both types of interactions, positive and negative, exist together, it can be suggested that open classrooms provide opportunities for a wider range of personal relationships than structured classrooms do (Bane, 1972a: 99).

Minuchin and her colleagues (1969) conducted one of the most persuasive studies of the effects of classroom structure. The Minuchin group studied fourth-grade children in four contrasting schools, ranging from a very conservative parochial school to a progressive private school emphasizing freedom, expressiveness, and independent exploration. Despite the advantages of smaller classes and more positive student attitudes toward school, the pro-gressive-school children scored substantially lower than others from more traditional schools on several measures of intelligence and achievement: the Stanford Achievement Test, the Kuhlman-Anderson Intelligence Test, and the Wechsler Intelligence Scale for Children. These differences were not accounted for by family background (Minuchin, et al., 1969: 185). There were no significant group differences on tests of imaginativeness (215-220) or self-confidence and satisfaction (290).

When we explore the causes of the poor performance of the progressive-school students in the Minuchin study, we find failure to learn achievement norms, inexperience with being evaluated, and anxiety over the stresses of coping with success and failure. The progressive-school children were unfamiliar with the psychological and practical demands of the testing situation itself. First, they had not learned to put forth that burst of concentrated effort that allows good test-takers to work at top speed and peak effort. Hence, they attempted fewer items on each test, even though, of the items they attempted, they got about the same proportion right as children from the traditional schools. The progressive-school children also had particular difficulty with tests requiring use of words out of context simply to prove that one understood them. They performed poorly on subtests that

> required the child to search short lists of nouns and identify those which he was told were related in some specific way: pairs which constituted opposites, single words which were not members of the general class to which the others belonged (Minuchin, et al., 1969: 186-7).

In addition, the progressive school children had not learned to cope with the anxiety of evaluation in a testing situation. During the Stanford Achievement Test,

> The stress created by this more difficult test battery became so great that a contagious banter and protest gradually developed during two of the subtests to the point where the test administration had to be curtailed just short of the allotted time period (Minuchin, et al., 1969: 188).

---

[1] Other studies (Bennett, 1976: 141-148; Evans, 1975; Brandt, 1975) seem to confirm Bane's findings. Bennett found that students in informal classrooms worked less and spent more time in interaction with other pupils than did students in traditional classrooms. Evans (1975) found that there was a great deal more reading activity in U. S. traditional classrooms than in either U.S. or British open classrooms, though open and traditional classrooms were similar in the frequency of math and science activities. Brandt (1975: 118) reports that there was almost twice as much peer interaction in two British open classrooms he studied as in comparable observations of children in American children, though he was also struck by the degree of task involvement in the British open classroom.

But it was not simply that the progressive-school children had failed to learn test-taking and individual performance skills; in their place, they had learned extensive group skills their peers in traditional schools had failed to learn. The Minuchin team gave children in all four schools a modified version of the Russell Sage Social Relations Test. The test involved asking the children as a group to build a bridge out of large blocks to match a demonstration model. On this test children from the progressive school were strikingly superior. Students from the most traditional schools showed the most tension and competition, the greatest rigidity of group structure, and the highest percentage of non-participants. Only the progressive-school students were able to finish the task in the allotted time. Furthermore,

[t]he performance of the [progressive-school] children had the qualities of an effective group effort, carried through with considerable *esprit de corps*. Planning was vigorous and relevant; building was self-propelled, effective, and technically accurate (204).

The progressive-school group was more cooperative and included all the children in the task.

The spontaneous activitiy which followed completion of the second construction bears mention. The children re-formed the test blocks to fashion the figure of a man, likened it to George Washington, and finished by adding a "wig" which they shaped out of cotton lying on a nearby shelf. The activity was characterized, as was most of the session, by a sense of productive autonomy, a flow of ideas that built on each other, harmonious relations among the children, and general pleasure in what they were doing (205).

The progressive-school children had not only learned group skills; they had also learned a set of norms emphasizing peer ties rather than relations with authority. In attitudes toward authority they, unlike the children from more traditional schools, had passed the "conforming stage" and showed a "rational, objective" attitude toward authority (Minuchin, *et al.*, 1969: 266). In tests of moral development, they were more peer-loyal, saying, for example, that they "would refuse to reveal the guilty child to the teacher" (279).

They were most concerned about direct or indirect violations—through deceit or manipulation—of what they regarded as the code of fair play in the life that children lead with each other. The emerging principles seemed to be expressive of a child society in active formation (279-280).

GROUP SKILLS

If anything describes what, in my research, free schools teach, it is group skills. At Group High students spent endless hours in meetings—all-school meetings, Tribal[2] meetings, counseling group meetings—meetings which spilled over past the hour, after school, to the next day. Every discussion turned into a discussion of basic principles, and debates over ultimate goals took priority over efficient decision-making. An outside research team at Group High reported that:

At frequent intervals during the first two years, the total school would meet for as long as necessary (half days to two days) for self-evaluation sessions. Discussion called for expressions of opinions about how things had been going (what was good, what was bad, analysis of the strategies, tactics, values) and then drawing up, on the basis of the evaluation, plans for change. There was always controversy as to how [Group High] should meet as a whole school for these discussions (as a whole? in small groups?) because of the continuing concern about large-scale participation and involvement. . . . [P]eople were shocked that [Group High] changed the school so drastically from semester to semester.

---

[2] The school was divided into four sub-units called "Tribes" which served as foci for group solidarity.

The importance of this group spirit for students' experience at Group High was nicely illustrated in a note one student passed to another during a particularly long, heated school meeting: "Let's not go to college next year. This is where life is really happening."

Both students and staff judged the school by the success of its group life, not by its effectiveness in traditional sorts of teaching. When students were asked whether they liked school, they answered in terms of the ability of their Tribe, or of the school as a whole, to "get it together." A successful group project—a picnic, communal breakfast, or retreat, or a meeting which produced honest discussion—could create temporary euphoria. Students also reacted with great distress to crises such as one Tribe's failure to agree on decorating its Tribal room or another Tribe's apathetic response to the suggestion of a picnic. The ups and downs of school life for both students and teachers depended on the success or failure of group life, not on the success or failure of individuals. Another symptom of this emphasis on group life was that the kind of disruptive, distancing behavior that often marks stressful situations occurred in group meetings where something had gone wrong—not, as in traditional schools, in confrontations over teacher authority or demands for individual performance.

Although Ethnic High was less concerned with the ideology of community, it also substituted an emphasis on group life for attention to individual achievement. The school year was held together by a string of social events—parties, picnics, weekly lunches, and a weekend retreat—rather than by a formal structure of classes. Many students, while skipping their own classes, stayed at school all day, talking to their friends and teachers. The importance students attributed to group activities was nicely exemplified during an early Ethnic High meeting where a retreat was being planned. The Director, teasing the students, asked why they were already talking about a retreat when they hadn't buckled down to work yet. A student replied, "You go away, get to know everybody, and then you can work." When, at a meeting called to discuss school problems, a few students complained about classes, the Co-Director asked, "Classes? Is that the major thing you do at [Ethnic High], go to classes?" The student mentioned education beyond the classroom, but the Co-Director probed again: "What about personal relationships? Do you think you get to know people the same way at [Ethnic High] that you do in other schools?" When students began to praise the school's virtues, the Co-Director insisted that there were "real problems" in the school—problems of insufficient group commitment.

Ethnic High gave little attention to formal classes, often only disorganized, watered-down versions of conventional classroom instruction. Both students and teachers let whole days slip by without attending to academic matters. Only group events really aroused the school, symbolizing success or failure. Ethnic High organized a large fair to which students from the regular high school were invited. The fair was to include dancing exhibitions, an art show, a band, and as a climax, a school play. However, the teacher who was directing the play came late, failed to organize the students, and finally came out on the stage to announce that the play would not be shown. The school was humiliated by this failure and afterwards there were recriminations, apologies, and a lingering sense of shame.

Another highly charged group challenge was the retreat. Early in the year students began suggesting a retreat to increase school solidarity. The teachers agreed, but left the planning to a student committee which, after several weeks, had not solved the problem of fundraising. At a large school meeting students again pressed the question of a retreat, and a teacher said, quite sarcastically, "You aren't going to have a retreat, because you are never going to do anything about it." This challenge galvanized the students who set to work with great energy and organized a successful fund-raising scheme. Finally, a semester late, the retreat was held. But the essential issue is that the school saw students' willingness to work for and participate in group events as much more important than individual performance in the traditional classroom setting.

FREEDOM FROM FAILURE

Free schools also make an explicit effort to avoid teaching students the aspects of "achievement" norms involving learning to cope with success and failure. Kohl, Dennison, Holt and other free-school spokespersons argue that it is precisely the experience of being evaluated, and the consequent fear of failure, which prevent students from learning. Dennison (1969: 79) says of his favorite problem student, José:

> [H] is failure to read should not be described as a problem at all, but a symptom. We need only to look at José to see what his problems are: shame, fear, resentment, rejection of others and of himself, anxiety, self-contempt, loneliness.

José's failure to read was "school-induced behavior" in response to the brutalizing process of evaluation he had endured in school. The first job of the free school is therefore to teach children self-confidence and self-respect. These then provide the only sound basis for learning.

Group High and Ethnic High avoided teaching students about achievement, about success and failure. They concentrated instead on teaching students self-confidence and self-respect. The first element in increasing students' self-confidence was reducing the inequality in status between teachers and students. Casual, friendly relations between teachers and students lessened students' fear, and made the teachers seem approachable, non-intimidating friends. Students felt important precisely because, as one student put it, "The teachers were really friends with the students." Second, the schools reversed the whole structure of values that normally define students as inferiors. At Ethnic High the major source of status was ethnic pride and ethnic identity. This the students, largely Third-World, possessed to a much greater extent than their teachers. Indeed, precisely by becoming teachers, even teachers from minority backgrounds had shown themselves somewhat "inauthentic." The teachers not only respected, but were actually a little in awe of students' street wisdom, their toughness, and their difficult life experiences. Rather than defining academic skills as the core goal of the school, the school builit an inverted status system where the students were superior.

A second way to avoid evaluating students, and to build student self-confidence, is to construct assignments with few possibilities for failure. At Ethnic High, for example, writing free verse became a very popular activity. Students could be encouraged to express themselves, without fear of failing at some academic task. Other open-ended assignments serve the same function. They allow the teacher to approve whatever effort the student makes and students can afford to try, since whatever they do will be acceptable. Often, for example, Ethnic High class assignments were to make collages from magazine pictures expressing one's feelings, or to write poems or stories about one's own experiences, or to discuss issues in one's own life.

Most of the students at Group High did not start out with histories of school failure. Yet Group High also avoided judging students' work—not to overcome blocks to learning, but to encourage autonomy and individual growth. The ethic was that anything anyone did was good if it "expressed their true feelings" or "made a contribution to the group." Students were praised and rewarded for "sharing their ideas with the group," not for having the right answers. Indeed, right or wrong answers, correct or incorrect facts and ideas, were subordinated to psychological and socio-emotional considerations. Students were not judged; they were encouraged to develop their individual potential.

Most classes at Group High were organized as group discussions, combined with individual presentations by students. This structure avoided putting the teacher at the center of the classroom situation, and maximized the value of individual autonomy and of community—both precious to students. Students made presentations of work they had done on their own outside of class. But these assignments, which might have created pressure for performance and subjected students to the risk of evaluation and possible failure, in fact served the opposite function. Students "presented" whatever they liked—a novel read recently, a movie, or a friend of the family whom one student brought to class. The ethic of individuality meant that whatever a student was involved in—from reading *The Sensuous Woman* to bike riding—was good because it grew out of that student's own unique interests.

The emphasis on sharing and community further contributed to an environment of appreciation rather than criticism. Students listened to each other with great respect and consideration, because they believed in participation and sharing. A tedious report on English kings received the same careful attention as any other project a student wanted to present. Students quite frequently said to each other, "I appreciate having you in this class. I've learned a great deal from you," and solemn thanks often followed a student's particularly honest expression of a personal problem or an unpopular opinion. In this atmosphere of self-conscious mutual appreciation, it was difficult for questions of success or failure to arise.

Even regularly assigned work in classes tended to be open-ended, demanding personal involvement but precluding evaluation or judgment of the contribution of individual students. Courses required students to keep journals of their dreams, to draw pictures representing their feelings, or to discuss aspects of their personal lives. But such assignments made evaluation in the usual sense irrelevant. The pressures on students were for participation, honesty, self-expression, and sharing—not for achievement. The lessons learned at Group High were that one should pursue one's own needs, and not look to others for direction and evaluation, yet that group cooperation is more important than individual achievement.

UNIVERSALISM AND SPECIFICITY

The last two norms Dreeben discusses are universalism and specificity. While in the family children are treated as unique individuals, loved on the basis of intimate, particularistic attachments, in schools children learn to accept treatment as members of a general category. They learn they will be held accountable for distinct tasks (such as obedience to rules or performance on specific assignments) rather than evaluated as whole people. Students, Dreeben says (1969: 79), learn to accept the norm of "fairness," so that they themselves come to demand treatment on the basis of general, objective criteria rather than personal liking or attachment.

> When children compare their lot—their gains and losses, rewards and punishments, privileges and responsibilities—with that of others and express dissatisfaction about their own, they have begun thinking in terms of equity.

At both Ethnic High and Group High, education was designed to involve the whole person. Teachers and students were friends involved in diffuse, personal relationships. Students were taught to express themselves and to search for personal growth within the school setting. They were not taught to expect treatment as part of a generalized category. Indeed, the norm for both teachers and students was that one must always deal with the other person as a whole person. Both students and teachers found their non-academic attributes an important part of their status in the school, and demands on students often bypassed the academic altogether, concentrating on personality, character and self.

Group High required personal involvement and participation; demands for a more functionally specific definition of the school's claims were openly rejected. When one young woman in a class said she wanted to audit the class, but that she did not want to have to do a project, the other students turned on her. One said, "I don't like what you said. That's [Traditional] High talk." They agreed that if she wanted to be in the group, she would have to participate fully. Another student concluded, "I don't care whether you actually do a project. I just want you to care enought to say you'll do one." In the same spirit, Group High's evaluations were long written descriptions of how each student had grown and changed during the semester. Some teachers explicitly told students that they wanted to evaluate how the student had grown as a person during the whole semester rather than evaluating participation or performance in the specific course where the evaluation was written.

At Ethnic High the curriculum was somewhat more traditional, and yet relations were, if anything, more diffuse and particularistic than at Group High. As I noted earlier, students were encouraged to develop their own unique qualities. In addition, teachers and students were involved in a complex web of particularistic relationships. Teachers and students shared details of their love lives, went to parties together, visited each other at home, and knew each others' families. When a student was in trouble with the police the teachers helped. When another student had trouble caring for her sick child, the teachers were happy to suspend all assigned work. When a student was in conflict with his parents, helping him resolve that conflict was considered much more important than getting him to class or teaching him vocabulary words. Indeed, a "therapeutic" approach to education, seeking first to cure students of the psychological barriers to learning caused by family or society, necessarily implies an individualized, personal approach to students, rather than an insistence on universalistic, specialized relationships.

One of the most striking characteristics of teacher-student relations at Group High was that fairness was not an issue. Teachers, while they pressured students in subtle ways, did not often assign tasks or evaluate them, so Group High lacked that continuing debate over the fairness of assignments, tests, and grades—the major language of conflict in traditional schools. What replaced this authority-oriented language (language about the rights and obligations of superiors and subordinates) was an intense attention to individuals that made general comparisons inappropriate. If students were told that they were not open enough with their feelings, did not listen to other people, or did not believe in themselves enough, they might object, but they could not cry "unfair, you didn't tell us we were going to be tested on that." More typically, if a student, asked to share a fantasy with the group, felt insecure, inadequate, or indifferent, the issue of fairness did not arise.

Grading and evaluation mattered more at Ethnic High, but the issue was primarily how much the teachers would let the students take advantage of them, or how much they could demand of students, rather than the fairness of one student's grades compared to another's. Indeed, most of the arguments by students were on purely particularistic grounds—a teacher should let a student by with a B because they were friends, or because the student had had a bad semester, or because the student needed the grade to help him qualify for cheaper car insurance. The mesh of personal ties between students and teachers was so thick that grades were almost always determined by a process of personal negotiation, with students bringing to bear all their anger, charm, or persuasiveness to improve their grades, while teachers tried to use their grading powers to extract a little more work. There was never a pretense that students with the same grade had worked equally hard. If a student who never came to class and rejected any form of testing showed good faith by trying to write a story for one class, that student might well be rewarded with the same B as a more diligent student who did regular assignments.

At both Ethnic High and Group High what replaced traditional norms of fairness were concerns about participation: commitment versus withdrawal, giving versus taking, community versus individualism. Although there were dramatic contrasts between the two schools, Group High and Ethnic High were both concerned with questions of who would contribute to the group and who would "rip-off" the school. At Ethnic High these concerns were expressed in discussions about who would contribute money for food for a school lunch, or who had taken money from the school treasury, while at Group High people were more likely to discuss abstract issues of sharing, commitment and participation. But at both schools group issues were the dominant focus. The schools were much less concerned with the norm of fairness governing authority relationships—problems of obedience versus defiance and equity versus injustice—than with norms relevant to community. The norm was not fairness, but mutuality.

CONCLUSION

Dreeben argues that the norms taught by schools—independence, achievement, universalism, and specificity—are the norms governing formal institutions, such as work, secondary associations, and the political order, in contrast to the norms operating in the intimate, personalized world of the family. Schools intervene on behalf of public life, teaching the child to adapt to the world outside the family.

When we try to analyze the social-structural role of alternative schooling, what are we to make of the diffuse, particularistic, collectivist, supportive qualities of the free school experience? Do alternative schools represent an attempt to run a large, secondary organization on the same principles as a family? To a certain extent we may say that organizations attempting to operate collectively often fall back on family life for ideology, norms, and patterns of psychic functioning. We need only note the prevalence of the terms "brother" and "sister" in many social movements or communal groups and the explicit desire of many contemporary collectives to be "families." When teachers use bonds of affection to replace authority, when the school insists on treating students as whole people rather than producing discrete skills, when students insist on sharing rather than achievement, free schools are certainly closer to family life than are most formal organizations in our society. And yet there are some important differences.

First, free schools are much more egalitarian than families. They are more like a large group of siblings—a purely peer-oriented society without parents or children. The teachers are "really friends with the students," and statuses are equalized to counterbalance the traditional advantages from the age, experience, and structural position of teachers. Love is adopted as a norm from the family, and guilt also, but not the combination of love and domination so characteristic of family life in our society.

Second, free schools are diffuse and particularistic in one sense, but extremely universalistic in another. Group High rejected universalistic achievement standards and tried to deal with students as unique individuals; yet in other respects the universalistic ethos at Group High was much stronger than in any traditional school. Universalism was so strong that teachers could not discriminate among students *even* on the basis of achievement. The standard of achievement was redefined so that it referred to each student's obligation to inner growth, but offered no external criteria for judging students either against teacher demands or in comparison with each other. the school's emphasis on group cohesion also made friendship a universalistically distributed commodity. The mode of friendship itself was socialized. Students and teachers apportioned warmth, attention and support with amazing impartiality. Teachers did not pick, on particularistic grounds, students they liked or disliked, allowing their personal preferences to govern their behavior. As members of the community, everyone in the school had claims on the others. Even students were supposed to, and did to a considerable extent, suppress personal preferences, and offer all their fellow students warmth and appreciation. Within the school context, students were to extend to their fellows the kind of consideration, affection, and concern they might, outside of school, reserve for their own intimates.

Kanter (1972) and Zablocki (1971) both talk about similar, but more extensive socialization of affection in intentional communities. Personal intimacy is encouraged, but it cannot be exclusive.

> Bruderhof love . . . is not *eros* but *agape*. That is, it is love based not on attraction to personal attributes of another person, but on a shared feeling of partaking in God's all encompassing love. "Likes and dislikes of people are no part of this life. They can be no part of it," said the wife of the Servant of the Word at Woodcrest (Zablocki, 1971: 169).

Kanter (1972: 87) similarly points out that successful utopian communities, in order to increase group cohesion, set limits on exclusive emotional attachments by prohibiting exclusive two-person sexual bonds.

While restrictions on personal intimacy were not as severe in Group High as those in successful intentional communities, they followed the same logic. The rejection of specific, universalistic achievement values in favor of ascription and particularism was thus not quite what it seemed. The demand was really that every person be treated in a special way—not liked or disliked according to his or her individual characteristics, but listened to, encouraged, included, because he or she was part of the school.

Rejection of the norms of independence and achievement in Group High and Ethnic High was also an ambiguous phenomenon. While students learned to subordinate individual achievement to collective goals, they also were encouraged to develop individuality and autonomy. Independence was defined not as learning to work alone and to be evaluated on that work, but as learning personal autonomy, self-confidence and the pleasure of self-expression. One of the fascinating questions about free schools—and other alternative organizations spawned by the counter-culture—is, of course, how they handle the tension in their own ideologies between the values of individualism and community. That question is too complex for this discussion. Suffice it to say that the kind of individualism traditional schools teach is discouraged in alternative schools, while other sorts of individuality are encouraged.

Alternative schools do not then represent a regression from the universalistic, achievement-oriented, specific, independent norms of modern public life to the diffuse, particularistic, ascriptive, dependent norms of the family. Group High taught norms appropriate to public life, to creating and sustaining cooperative group life. But the norms governing the group-oriented organizational life of Group High were different in many respects from those found either in families or traditional schools. These norms subordinated achievement to the ideals of personal growth and community, while within an equalitarian ethos they encouraged individual uniqueness.

What does this "hidden curriculum" of alternative schools imply for their relationship to social class and social change in contemporary America? It has been clear throughout this analysis that the free-school ideology was acted out more fully at Group High than at Ethnic High. Students at Ethnic High, while they valued the freedom and autonomy an alternative school provided, still wanted to learn basic academic skills. At times they seemed confused or resentful when teachers did not assert authority and insist on academic performance. This paradox, I think, has been typical of the free school movement. While alternative teaching techniques have been proposed as a remedy for the failure of traditional schooling to reach the educationally disadvantaged, such schools have had their greatest success and their greatest popularity with the educated upper-middle class. In Berkeley, the alternative schools with predominantly minority students and staff began to insist on increasingly structured education, while they retained an emphasis on ethnic history and culture. Katz (1971: 136) and Joffe (1977) have also pointed to the tension between the goals of educational reformers and the demands of many parents who want a traditional but more effective education for their children.

What is striking about the values free schools teach is that, at a number of points, they seem to be so compatible with the needs of an educated upper-middle class. Students practising autonomy and self-direction, doing independent projects without waiting for assignments from teachers, sound a little like young graduate students in the making. While we would, of course, argue that an educated person requires discipline and rationality as well as autonomy and self-direction, it may be part of the goal of alternative schools to set right what they see as an imbalance in traditional education—to free students from an excessive reliance on authority and external direction.

Learning group skills seems a useless accomplishment in a competitive capitalist society, but even here I am impressed by how team-work and the management of human relations have become important to the corporate world. The search for community in the counterculture has often been interpreted as rebellion against the impersonal competitiveness of modern life (Roszak, 1969; Slater, 1970). Yet it is possible to argue that, for a specialized segment of the upper-middle class, education encouraging flexibility, autonomy, and group skills is good preparation for professional roles in the most innovative sectors of the public and private economy. Whatever the final verdict on the "success" of free schools, it has become increasingly clear that alternative education does not appeal equally to all groups in contemporary society. If we wish to understand why it appeals so strongly to some, we do well to look at the ways alternative schools teach an implicit curriculum of norms and values, rather than at the ways they teach traditional academic skills.

From our analysis of Group High and Ethnic High, we may justifiably conclude (as have others, both friends and foes of free schools, [Graubard, 1972; Friedman, n.d.,; Bowles and Gintis, 1975]) that free schools are not likely to reduce economic or educational inequality. Free schools may be more humane than traditional schools, but on the whole they reflect rather than challenge the class structure. Yet this is not quite the whole story. While the hidden curriculum of free schools is primarily designed to benefit the children of the educated upper-middle class, it has some advantages for less privileged students.

Ethnic High offered its students certain concrete benefits. It was a liberal dispenser of educational credentials, so that students who might otherwise have dropped out of school were able to earn high school diplomas. If educational credentials are more important for occupational success than the skills schools teach (Jencks, *et al.,* 1972; Collins, 1971) then Ethnic High served its students well.

But there were also advantages to Ethnic High's hidden curriculum. While Ethnic High's students ignored or resisted many aspects of the free school ethos, they learned two sorts of skills which are of great value. First, Ethnic High taught students to manipulate bureaucratic machinery. The ability to get around high school requirements, fight one's way into special programs, or persuade administrators to bend rules came naturally to Group High's students. Students at Ethnic High, encouraged by their teachers, came to expect, and to be willing to fight for, similar special treatment. Second, Ethnic High's students developed increased self-confidence. Being treated as important, valuable members of the community gave students a sense of entitlement, even if it did not give them academic skills. If this sounds like a dubious virtue, we must remember how much the success of middle-class people is based on having learned to demand things—whether or not they deserve them—from presuming that they are among the deserving. For some of Ethnic High's students, like the young man who decided that no one would stop him from going to law school (and who then entered the University of California on a special admissions program), this was a valuable lesson.

REFERENCES

Bane, Mary Jo
    1972a   "The effects of structure: a study of first grade children in open and traditional classrooms." Unpublished Ed.D. dissertation, Graduate School of Education, Harvard University.
    1972b   "Open education." Harvard Educational Review 42:273-281.
Bennett, Neville
    1976   Teaching Styles and Pupil Progress. London: Open Books.
Bowles, Samuel and Herbert Gintis
    1975   Schooling in Capitalist America: Educational Reform and the Contradictions of Economic Life. New York: Basic Books.
Brandt, Richard M.
    1975   "An observational portrait of a British infant school." Pp. 101-125 in Bernard Spodek and Herbert J. Walberg (eds.), Studies in Open Education. New York: Agathon Press.
Collins, Randall
    1971   "Functional and conflict theories of educational stratification." American Sociological Review 36:1002-1019.
Dennison, George
    1969   The Lives of Children. New York: Random House.
Dreeben, Robert
    1968   On What Is Learned in School. Reading, Ma.: Addison-Wesley.
Eisenstadt, S.N.
    1956   From Generation to Generation: Age Groups and Social Structure. New York: Free Press.
Evans, Judith T.
    1975   "An activity analysis of U.S. traditional, U.S. open, and British open classrooms." Pp. 155-168 in Bernard Spodek and Herbert J. Walberg (eds.), Studies in Open Education. New York: Agathon Press.
Friedman, Neil
    n.d.   "Inequality, social control and the history of educational reform." Unpublished paper, School of Social Welfare, State University of New York at Stony Brook.
Graubard, Allen
    1972   Free the Children: Radical Reform and the Free School Movement. New York: Random House.
Jencks, Christopher, Marshall Smith, Henry Ackland, Mary Jo Bane, David Cohen, Herbert Gintis, Barbara Heyns, and Stephen Michelson
    1972   Inequality: A Reassessment of the Effect of Family and Schooling in America. New York: Basic Books.
Joffe, Carole E.
    1977   Friendly Intruders: Childcare Professionals and Family Life. Berkeley: University of California Press. In Press.
Kanter, Rosabeth Moss
    1972   Commitment and Community: Communes and Utopias in Sociological Perspective. Cambridge, Ma.: Harvard University Press.
Katz, Michael B.
    1971   Class, Bureaucracy, and Schools. New York: Praeger.
Minuchin, Patricia, Barbara Biber, Edna Shapiro, and Herbert Zimiles
    1969   The Psychological Impact of School Experience: A Comparative Study of Nine-Year-Old Children in Contrasting Schools. New York: Basic Books.
Roszak, Theodore
    1969   The Making of a Counter Culture: Reflections on the Technocratic Society and Its Youthful Opposition. Garden City, N.Y.: Doubleday.
Stallings, Jane A.
    1976   "How instructional processes relate to child outcomes in a national Study of Follow Through." Menlo Park, Ca.: Stanford Research Institute.
Slater, Philip E.
    1970   The Pursuit of Loneliness: American Culture at the Breaking Point. Boston: Beacon Press.
Swidler, Ann
    1975   "Organization without authority: A study of two alternative schools." Unpublished Ph.D. dissertation. University of California at Berkeley.

Zablocki, Benjamin
    1971   The Joyful Community. Baltimore: Penguin.

TRYING TIMES: HAITIAN YOUTH IN AN INNER CITY HIGH SCHOOL

PAULE VERDET
Boston University

Volunteer-teaching of English and Mathematics to Haitians at an inner city high school in New England offers special, if painful, opportunities for participant observation to a sociologist. Some of the unique problems of figuring in a foreign tongue are considered—as are the successes and failures at communication by teachers and students.

(A test is given in this Algebra II class. I observe Matthew, age 18)
He starts working in his slow, cautious way. He finds the right answers to problems which involve recognizing and combining like terms ($3x + 6y + 2y + 8x =$). Then he figures $10 - 3 - 2 - 4 = +7$. But as he copies his answers on the test sheet, he hesitates for several minutes. He can't decide that $+7$ is right, but apparently he can't decide what is wrong about it either. I see him try to rearrange the terms of the expression, taking them two at a time. Finally he gets the right answer. What is going on in this mind? what blockages? Is it his very slowness that makes it impossible for decision and assent to take shape in him?
. . . At the end I speak to the teacher, underlining how hard Matthew tries, and that he goes slowly not for lack of attention but the very opposite. He says that in a little while he will send Matthew to the program for problem students. I push on, telling him my concern for all these students so handicapped by their language that they never finish the tests and thus get poor grades even if all their answers were right. Well, what can he do about that? They still might get through with a C⁻ (i.e. pass). This is not what I had in mind. I say that perhaps a few words of appreciation or encouragement might compensate for the grades. As I leave, I have some hope that he will do something about it (Excerpt from field notes, 10/10/75).

How have I, as a sociologist, access to what goes on inside a high school classroom? I am a volunteer. When desegregation through busing was ordered in my city, in the Fall of 1974, the public schools held three days of open house for students, parents and members of the community. I went to several of them. At Inner City High I found a bilingual program in great need of extra help. The native French speakers were students from Haiti. They did not have special classes in Math and Sciences. I volunteered to help with Math, reasoning that a minimum investment in a subject where words are of secondary importance should pay off handsomely. I decided to spend one day there each week. I have continued to go for two years under the joint sponsorship of the head of the bilingual program and of the chairman of the Math Department. I have been welcomed in all classes where I could find a Haitian in trouble, by teachers and students alike. How slow my progress has been, and still is, in discovering the dimensions of the problem, has perplexed me. I have also had to resolve the conflicting demands of the two roles of volunteer and researcher.

Who are these Haitian students? Having befriended them in classroom and cafeteria, I was invited by some to Haitian events: a feast in honor of their Independence Day, several masses, their Mothers' Day celebration, youth group meetings, graduation party. There is an ever-swelling influx of their families to our North Eastern city. Not only teen-agers and fathers come, but grandmothers and young children. Many families are divided, however: some members here, supporting those who stayed on the island.

Haiti, a French colony, gained its independence in the wake of the French Revolution. Haitians are proud of the fact; rather proud also of their French cultural heritage. Their school system, in particular, closely parallels that of France. But they come to America because Haiti cannot feed its people. Typical concerns of the students reflect this situation:

- for the present, they seek- and find- part-time (menial jobs;
- for the immediate future, they seek a college education leading to a professional or semi-professional career;
- for the long range future, they dream of returning home to save their country from poverty and oppression.

They love their island. There is little travel back and forth because of the cost, and the illegal status of many. But the ties are real: money and packages are sent regularly; even an infant would be sent by her parents to spend the winter with relatives. And when Mothers' day is celebrated here—not in mid-May but in late May as in Haiti, and in France—there are expressions of feeling that the little American colony and the island are as one. And the American exiles keep dreaming of their island where the weather is mild, the vegetation beautiful, the fruit ripe, the pace unhurried.

Not all Haitian teen-agers attend Inner City High. At social events I have noticed a good many youth (among them some light skinned) whom I never saw before. They attend a parochial school, without a bilingual program but also without Inner City High's bad reputation among Haitian parents as a tough, even dangerous place. Actually Inner City High is neither. It is not much of a school, though. Of its 242 graduates of the 1975 class, 13% have continued to a four-year college, 7% to a junior college, 43% to work, with an ominous 37% listed as "other."[1] Recent newspaper accounts place the total attendance at 1580—which I think an inflated figure; and the racial distribution at 30% white, 67% black and 3% other. It is unclear how the Haitians are classified. There are more than 100 of them at Inner City High. It is possible that only those among them who need placement in the bilingual program are counted among "others." Those who know English may be counted as black—a convenient administrative fiction. For, regardless of their proficiency in English, all Haitians stay among themselves, and almost exclusively speak creole, the lively unwritten patois of their island.

On the basis of my observations so far I should say that these coal black people are not Blacks. They are different. They are not struggling for their freedom, they have *had* their freedom for a long time. Their *de facto* oppressors have not been whites, but men of their own race, not only Papa Duvalier but those before and after him. I don't think that they comprehend the race problem in America. Last year, when interracial violence erupted in various spots of the city, two of our Haitian students were beaten up by a band of white youth upon leaving the trolley: "Why???" they asked the head of the bilingual program the next day, "we hadn't stolen anthing!!" Theirs is not a "minority" mentality. They have no cause for militancy or argumentation.[2]

There is a large contingent of Haitians at Inner City High, anyway. Twenty-four graduated in 1975, more than fifty in 1976. The bilingual staff consists now of two people. A young woman heads it: a fair skinned Haitian, with degrees in law and education from both Haiti and the U.S., she is a first-rate teacher of English as a second language. Her speech to the 1975 graduates, at the lively and well-attended party she gave them, was vibrant with the pride of an older sister, the love of-a parent, the wisdom of an established immigrant. She

---

[1] In comparison, the high school nearest the domicile of the judge who ordered enforced busing had 225 graduates in 1975: of these 75% went to a four year college, 12% to a junior college, 6% to work, with 7% left in the "other" category. In sum: 20% continue to college from Inner City High vs. 87% from Outer Suburb High.

[2] I am speaking of high school students here. Haitians in college may become involved in various movements, where they join forces with blacks, or illegal immigrants, or political radicals.

started the program with just a few of them. How long will she be able to maintain this style in the face of their ever increasing numbers? In the Fall of 1974 a man, also a Haitian, with a law degree, was hired as her assistant. She did not have a say in this choice and they do not work closely together. As a teacher of French and Haitian literature, and of American and Haitian history (taught in French), he seems to do a creditable job. These last courses are not required of the Haitians. Only about half of them take one or the other, whether by choice or because of the vagaries of the registration procedure, I don't know. I use the word "vagaries" advisedly, having seen students whose English was practically non-existant placed in a Geometry class when a slow moving Algebra class would have been far more appropriate. On the other hand a bright college-bound 12th grader, without a language problem, was placed in Algebra I instead of Algebra II.

But my prime acquaintance is with the trying times of students taught Math in a tongue they do not quite understand. One would think that Math, Algebra in particular, relies so much on sheer logic, simple rules, and memorized formulae, that the language for teaching it would be almost irrelevant. Besides, aren't French and English at their most identical when it comes to speaking of "additions," "fractions," "resolving" an "equation?" Yes—and No. Take the rule for the addition of two integers: If they have the same sign, add the values and keep the sign; if the signs are different, take the sign of the larger, and substract the value of the smaller from that of the larger. "Integer" in French is "nombre entier;" "smaller" is "plus petit." The rest is close enough. But mathematical understanding demands complete clarity. Shadows produce uncertainty, slowing one down and, worse, keeping one from developing greater and greater agility and self-confidence in the manipulation of symbols. Other instances of disturbing differences include: different use of concepts such as "to reduce" and "to simplify;" different ways of managing long division; different systems of measures (I discovered one day, much to my dismay, that one of my charges did not know what an "inch" was); different ways of saying the same thing (In French, to solve the simplest of equations, $x + a = b$, you substract from both sides; in English, at Inner City High, you *add* the opposite of a). I could lengthen the list further: when you write a number in French, the point and the comma have the exactly reverse function of what they have in English; in geometry, English distinguishes clearly between "straight angle" ($180°$) and "right angle" ($90°$), but both words translate as "droit," reserved in French for the $90°$ angle.

Thus the simplest, most straightforward demonstration by the teacher at the blackboard is likely to acquire complex twists in the mind of the French speaking student, and to lose its economy, its consistency. Students have to approach that strange stuff with great caution. They may discover its meaning, by themselves or with help, only to be faced, over and over, with new mysteries.

Still, sheer repetition of the same formula, problem after problem written on the blackboard, manages to register in the student's mind. Especially so since the teacher, at the blackboard, usually enunciates clearly when explaining something. When turning to ordinary matters, however, such as, "Open your books on p. 52 and do problems 12 to 18," the teacher tends to speak very fast, even to mumble. He is resting from the effort at the blackboard, throwing the ball to the students now: it's their turn to apply themselves, right away. But the student who is not a native English speaker is going to miss that ball. The instruction conveys nothing to him or her. He or she has to watch what others are doing and then, maybe, catch up. I have observed Haitians told, for instance, to "start with the right hand column" of a full page of problems. They did not understand, and the teacher did not realize, until I pointed it out to him, that they *could not* have understood it. Or this: as the bell rings at the end of a period, the teacher writes on the board: "H W p. 251 #5-17." What's that? I wonder. And as I suddenly understand the short-hand I quickly ask two or three of the

Haitians, who are starting to leave, "Do you know that Mr. X assigned some home work for tonight?" "No!" they all answer, much surprised. I tell him. He is astonished.

The teacher does not understand why his messages are not received. He sees that students don't do what they are asked to do, or do it late. To him, they look slow, inattentive, un-interested and/or incapable. A parallel misinterpretation occurs when students fail to understand what they are asked to do on a test: e.g. "simplify . . ." a whole list of algebraic expressions. What does "simplify" mean here? When they ask me, I must admit that I answer on the basis of my knowledge of Algebra as a whole—obviously something they cannot be expected to have. Several times I have been told by a teacher: "I am giving a test today," as if to say that I was not needed. Again, the teacher does not realize where he fails to communicate.

What he realizes only too well is the remedy the students have found to the situation. They consult among themselves. The one who can understand best, or least badly, cues in the others. They are quick to follow his/her lead. But of course this principle of When In Doubt Consult, gets easily extended to asking for the answer to a tough problem. Thus, in some home rooms or even at the beginning of a class, one can observe some students copying a whole list of answers from the best Haitian student in the class. No wonder that the teacher is annoyed when he realizes that a small Haitian mafia confronts him every day. Their use of creole as they talk to each other must accentuate his feeling of helplessness. No wonder that he should become punitive when he gives a test in class. No wonder that he should feel inclined to grade them strictly on their own merit, that is, not taking into account their slower pace, their need for explanations. The teacher reasons: if you don't understand something, just ask *me*, don't copy from your neighbor! *But* all teachers should know that it is often harder to formulate a good question than to understand the explanation in the first place—especially if your difficulty lies with language . . .

Besides, it is not part of the Haitian student role to ask questions publicly from the teacher. Even the good student who knows English well does not. In this regard there is a striking difference, at Inner City High, between black, white and Haitian students. The good, or only interested, black student bombards the teacher with questions: "Why do you find $12x^2$ here?" "Do you want our answer, or how we get it?" He or she (often she) bombards the teacher with complaints: "Why do you give us something so difficult? (Or so easy?) (Or with so little time?)" The tone is aggressive but the intention is clearly to communicate, and to make sense together.[3] The good, or interested, white student never demands anything. He or she is prompt, attentive, docile. The Haitians would be all that if they understood the language; as soon as they do, they fall into that same pattern.

Or do they? In two years I have encountered case after case of Haitian students whose English was quite passable, yet whose mathematical performance was deplorable. At first I warned the teachers: his/her problem is not with English but with Math. Then I found a student, here in the U.S. for three years, who did not remember that 1 meter equals 100 centimeters. Strange, I felt, I would have thought the metric system would be engraved in a mind forever. I was also shocked by the frequent ignorance of their multiplication tables displayed by average students. And yet, in one of the classes that I now hold for those who are learning English as a second language, I found my students enthusiastically reconstructing the complex procedure for extracting the square root of a number! Only recently have all those disparate observations come to fall into something of a pattern. I happened to be observing a youngster in the process of answering, or rather failing to answer, a test in basic

---

[3] Parenthetically the most tangible accomplishment of integration in my eyes so far is the great good humor of white teachers answering those black demands.

arithmetic skills (He was mistakenly assigned to the 9th grade instead of the 7th or 8th; he has been in the U.S. for three years and speaks good English). He did not know how to divide, how to factor, nor even how to do a long multiplication. Upon further inquiry I discovered that he did not know his multiplication tables at all. He performed the necessary additions instead. I took him aside to make him understand that he should learn his tables seriously and to start him on the process. But at that point I had to ask myself: in which language shall we do it: English, or French? I opted for English, since he knew it well enough. Was I right? *I* do all my figuring in French, my native tongue, because only in French do I get that almost imperceptible mental signal that tells me when I am making a mistake. If *they*, my Haitians, are made to figure in English, will they have to abandon that internal compass, and never truly replace it? This possibility would help explain their slow pace, their hesitations, their perplexity, and at times the randomness, the mindlessness of their answers. Could it be that one of the underlying problems of the whole bilingual enterprise is that basic arithmetic is treated as just another part of civilized discourse, when it might rather be a pathway, once traced, not to be disturbed but carefully tended and maintained? Shouldn't the students be taught *Math* in French rather than U.S. and Haitian History, at least until they have mastered all its basic skills once and for all?

Trying times indeed. They want to learn, they never go to sleep in class the way the other students do. Toward the end of the school year they are the only students on whose daily presence the teachers can count. Still, save for shining exceptions, they are treated as if they were stupid, because they are slow. They can't show what they know because they don't quite understand what is asked of them. As they learn English, they forget basic arithmetic. They can't win. Neither can their teachers. This powerlessness of the teacher is as hard on the students as it is on the teacher himself. A teacher is supposed to explain, to *teach*. And those Haitians, who are admirable with their teacher of English as a second language, get unruly if they become the majority in an ordinary class. This obstreperousness relieves their frustration, but increases that of the teacher to the point of desperation. When they are a minority, on the contrary, they suffer in silence, and one worries at the harm done their self-image by the grades and rebuffs received.

In this research note I have tried to communicate the things I discovered through continuous observation of the small world of the classroom. My main conclusion so far is methodological. I am studying a problem I thought held few secrets for me. I was a student (a graduate) in this country at a time when my knowledge of English was scanty. I thought I had been through it all. I had not. When I entered Inner City High, I had planned to observe, from my role as a volunteer, the inter-racial tensions expected to surface. None did. Only little by little did I realize that there was more to the students' predicament than I had thought at first. I am astonished, even now, at how long it took me to discover some now obvious dimensions of the situation—more than a year, for instance, to notice the difference in the teachers' pattern of speech when at the blackboard and when giving practical commands or asking personal questions. Were I working along lines established ahead of time, as one does under a grant, I would run a great risk of continuing to ignore what I am now slowly discovering. Had I been in a hurry to publish, again I believe that I would have missed much. I am curious to discover how long I can successfully mine that field of information.

For there is no question but that I will be at Inner City High a long time yet. Not primarily for the sake of this research but for the sake of these kids. It is the first time that I have had to reconcile the demands of the double role. Volunteering is an all-absorbing task. In the classroom my focus of attention is not on the whole situation but on such items as: how much does Rene follow of what Mrs. O. is saying right now? how could these two girls be persuaded to do their exercises without copying from each other? how can I best convey to

Palmyra that a number divided by itself does not equal zero? Accordingly, I have to push myself to take notes about what is going on, at the blackboard and in the classroom. And if by chance I get so absorbed in that task that I forget to help one of my charges at the right time, I feel as if I had deserted my post. On the other hand, I have repeatedly abandoned a first-rate observation post to respond to the needs of this or that student.

Still, going systematically in the direction where the students' needs take me has emerged as a good exploratory technique. For instance, I was moved, in the Fall of 1975, to volunteer in two periods of their class in English as a second language once a week to tutor arithmetic and elementary Algebra. At first, I would utter twice each of my statements: once in French, once in English. Little by little, however, I moved towards teaching exclusively in French. I *did* it *before* I developed consciously the insight I have presented above about the importance of reinforcing their early training in arithmetic. Another positive result of my choice of priorities has been the friendship developed between the students and myself. I would think that, were I ever to do a study in depth of the Haitian community, I would have more than enough willing respondents—not only "my" kids, but their parents, their relatives, their friends, their priest. Likewise, at Inner City High, I have become a familiar presence, welcome to look at any record, to discuss pedagogy with many teachers—and this in spite of the fact that I reiterate, from time to time, that I am a sociologist.

Some day, then, the researcher may fully benefit from the work of the volunteer. But when? My priorities are not likely to change. There is a joy associated with an active involvement with people, in response to their pressing need, not easily matched by the fulfillment of long range professional goals.

THE SOCIAL CONSEQUENCES OF CHICANO HOME/SCHOOL BILINGUALISM*

DAVID E. LÓPEZ

Department of Sociology
University of California, Los Angeles

A review of the literature on the scholastic consequences of being bilingual suggests that the negative effects of Chicano home/school bilingualism stem from extrinsic factors, particularly the reactions of others to ethnic stigma, rather than from anything intrinsic to bilingualism, and that the effects vary by class and social context. Four models relating home/school bilingualism to subsequent attainments are presented and, contrary to expectations, a model of balanced effects, in which negative effects on educational attainment are cancelled out by the subsequent positive sociometric advantage of knowing Spanish, is best supported by recent data from Los Angeles. However, in middle-class Chicano homes the pattern of effects is reversed.

The consequences of bilingualism have been the subject of considerable research and controversy. Most research has focused on home/school (H/S) bilingualism—reared in one language, usually of a low status ethic group, and schooled in another, usually the socially dominant language—and until recently the predominant view has been that bilingualism is more bad than good (some major reviews of this literature are found in: Arsenian, 1937; Darcy, 1953; Haugen, 1956; Arizona State University, 1960; Peal and Lambert, 1962; MacNamara, 1966). But several studies have also shown that bilingualism does not necessarily retard learning, and may even stimulate intellectual development (Arsenian, 1937; Peal and Lambert, 1962; Balkan, 1970; Mackey, 1972; Lambert and Tucker, 1972). The sociological implication is that the apparent negative effects of bilingualism spring more from variable extrinsic social forces, such as how others react to and discriminate against bilinguals, than from psycholinguistic factors intrinsic to bilingualism.

Substandard verbal test performance by H/S bilingual children is widely if not universally documented (Darcy, 1946; 1953; Anastasi and Cordova, 1953; Jones, 1959). But there have been virtually no studies of subsequent effects. The considerably disadvantaged status of Chicanos and other groups with high degrees of bilingualism has commonly led to the presumption that these groups suffer from a lasting language handicap (e.g. U.S. Department of Health, Education and Welfare, 1974). But this view has never been substantiated for Chicanos or other bilinguals. The belief is bolstered by misleading impressionistic evidence (poor, and frequently immigrant, Chicanos speak Spanish, Q.E.D.) and by published reports showing negative associations between social status and some measure of connection with the Spanish language (U.S. Department of Health, Education and Welfare, 1974: 61; Grebler et al, 1970: 424-426; U.S. Bureau of the Census, 1971: 10-12; 1973a: 20-27). But these reports include large proportions of Mexican immigrants who rank low on indicators of social status and, since they were raised in Mexico, were hardly subject to home/school bilingualism. Moreover, the reports usually relate status to current language. Given the possibility that upward mobility is accompanied by language apostasy (Barker, 1947; Penalosa and McDonagh, 1966), this

---

*This paper is based on data from a survey supported by the United States Public Health Service, National Institute of Child Health and Human Development Contract RD-12215 MOD.5, George Sabagh, Principal Investigator. Analysis was facilitated by a grant from the Chicano Studies Center and Institute of American Cultures, UCLA. The assistance of Maria Iosue and Pat Roos is gratefully acknowledged, as are the comments of Donald Treiman on an earlier version of this paper.

relation further serves to make Spanish look bad.[1] This paper briefly reassesses previous research on the effects of bilingualism and introduces new data to test whether or not child-hood bilingualism has any lasting consequences on the educational, occupational and income attainments of Chicanos. The paper also assesses the relative importance of extrinsic as opposed to intrinsic causation in these effects to understand whether or not language factors are involved, as disabilities or through discrimination, in the considerable socioeconomic gap between Chicanos and Anglos (Duncan and Duncan, 1968; Grebler et al., 1970: 143-149, 181-194; Poston and Alvirez, 1973; Garcia, 1975).

To sociologists the long-run effects of H/S bilingualism are more important and more interesting than school test performance. One need not be an educational psychologist— and indeed it may help not to be—to know that children who do not speak much English will not do so well on tests in English. Moreover, relationships on this level imply little about future lives. Two decades ago a major linguistic student of bilingualism suggested that the great concern for relations between bilingualism and cognitive ability was socially beside the point because, since the latter had so little to do with ultimate social position, any slight reduction in bilingualism would be immaterial in the long run (Haugen, 1956:83). Subse-quent research has confirmed that test scores are poor independent predictors of socioeco-nomic status (Jencks, 1972:220-221; 350). Yet bilingualism is socially relevant. A corollary of the hypothesis of extrinsic causation is that bilingualism may be detrimental even in situations where intellectual function is unimportant.

DATA AND METHODS

Data for this paper come from a 1973 survey of 1129 Chicano households in the Los Angles area (weighted to give a representative sample). Los Angeles is by far the largest Chicano metropolis. It offers a more congenial socioeconomic environment than most of the Southwest, and for this reason is extremely diverse in the social origins of its Chicano popu-lation. Only U.S. *raised* men 25-44 are included in this analysis. When possible results are reported separately for ten-year cohorts. But even in the twenty year band, age is unrelated to occupational status and income, and only mildly associated with Spanish upbringing ($r = .20$) and schooling ($r = .-19$) . . . not enough materially to confound the analysis. For regression analysis, language of upbringing is dichotomized 1/0, Spanish (or H/S bilingualism) and English, respectively.[2] Education, occupation and income are measured in ordinary ways: years, Duncan scores and dollars. Results are presented in a simplified Blau and Duncan (1967) path model, with language added in. Correlational results are supported by the analysis of sub-group means, but space limitations required that most of this be omitted.

The logic of this study is internal analysis. Chicano is compared to Chicano, rather than Chicano to Anglo, thus avoiding a host of complicating differences that can only imperfectly

---

[1] "Chicano" includes all U.S. residents of Mexican or Southwest Hispanic descent or origin. The subject of this paper dictated that only those raised in the United States be considered. About three-quarters of all adult Chicanos raised in the United States were brought up primarily in Spanish (U.S. Bureau of the Census, 1971). But few speak only Spanish—more native Chicanos are monolingual in English than in Spanish—simply because in school and various other social settings they have been obliged to perform in English. Spanish has been maintained in second and third generation homes, and by middle and working-class Chicanos as well as among the very poor. These Chicano subgroups also have considerable proportions of English monolingual homes, providing natural control groups, though previous researchers were not always aware of them.

[2] It may seen odd that those raised in bilingual homes are excluded from an analysis of bilingualism. The survey question on language of upbringing did include a "both equally" category, but it was indicated for only 9% of the men, compared to 64% mostly Spanish and 27% mostly English. These bilingual homes tended to be higher status, and there were too few low status bilingual homes in the sample for analysis in the scheme adopted in this paper.

be "controlled" experimentally or statistically. At the same time the principal research question is how far H/S bilingualism explains Anglo-Chicano inequalities. If no effects of H/S bilingualism appear, then it is fair to conclude that language handicaps (intrinsic or extrinsic) play no part in the social lives of Chicanos raised in the United States. Causal complexes cannot simply be broken down into discrete additive factors. But the attempt made in this paper to understand and directly assess one factor in the Anglo-Chicano disparity is preferable to arbitrarily labeling residual differences left after the most obvious controls as "discrimination" or "cultural differences," depending on one's point of view.

THE BILINGUAL STIGMA

A review of the sociolinguistics and educational psychology of bilingualism (necessarily excluded here . . . see Lopez, 1975) indicates that the only necessary difference between monolinguals and bilinguals is that the latter speak a second language. In addition sociolinguists have shown that the home/school bilingual's sound and syntax in either language is affected by the other. This phenomenon, unfortunately labeled by Uriel Weinreich (1953) as "interference," does not necessarily impair expression but it does make the bilingual a language non-conformist and allows others to identify him or her with a particular ethnic group (Bossard, 1945; Haugen, 1956). When that ethnic identification is prestigious the accent can be an advantage. When it is with a despised lower-class ethnic group it elicits conscious and unconscious prejudice, discrimination and hostility. Like color and other aspects of personal appearance and style, it is a sign of ethnicity. Not bilingualism in itself, but the identity it conveys produces the social consequences of being bilingual.

The voluminous psychological literature on bilingualism contributes little to the understanding of its social consequences. Some of the earliest work showed that bilingualism sometimes depressed IQ scores and other times did not (e.g. Saer, 1923). But rather than investigating the factors that made for this circumstantial variation and whether or not low-scoring bilinguals were handicapped for life, psychologists have instead sought to isolate "pure" bilingualism among young children. What this has really amounted to is surrounding bilinguals with *favorable* circumstances and it is hardly surprising that in such experiments bilingual children do as well as monolinguals, though never really better (Arsenian, 1937; Levinson, 1959; Peal and Lambert, 1962; Mackey, 1972; Lambert and Tucker, 1972). These favorable circumstances include good schools, no ethnic stigma and middle-class or above status . . . usually all three. The problem is that Chicanos and other large home/school bilingual populations are stigmatized, lower-class and attend poor schools. Bilingual instruction in an upper-class Swiss or German school is not bilingualism in the *barrio*.

Arsenian's (1937) data on Italian and Jewish children in New York provides evidence of the stigma effect in schools. Among the Jewish children, where Jewish teachers predominate (according to informal sources,) bilingualism had no effect on IQ tests scores or teacher evaluations. Among the Italian children, who had few if any Italian teachers, bilinguals did moderately worse on the tests and, significantly, were far behind in the evaluations of their teachers. The social status and scholastic difficulties of Italians earlier in this century were not unlike those of Chicanos today. Then, as now, even well-meaning and sympathetic teachers with a patronizing missionary zeal felt they should suppress the native language for the children's own good. But outsiders tend to see low-status ethnic groups as homogeneous, so that while they may have thought they were punishing Italianisms among linguistically homogeneous children, in fact they were really punishing those from Italian-speaking homes, and rewarding those from ethnically Italian but English-speaking homes. The greater effect on teacher evaluations than on outsider-administered tests strongly supports an extrinsic explanation of the scholastic effects of bilingualism.

Published reminiscences (Bossard, 1945; Haugen, 1972: 308-319) and casual interviews indicate that middle-class bilingual children indentified with a stigmatized group have resources to overcome initial learning handicaps and discrimination and sometimes even turn bilingualism to advantage. Their resources include the usual class advantages. But the maintenance of a literate ethnic tradition at home (usually requiring language maintenance as well) may provide a further advantage. Perhaps this complementary literate tradition rather than any difference in "values" explains the high educational attainments of middle-class (at least in culture), second-generation Americans.

The hypothesis of extrinsic causation and ethnic stigma explains the varying findings of educational psychologists better than any intrinsic psychological theory of bilingualism. It also leads to explicit predictions about the social consequences of H/S bilingualism. Lower-class minority children should suffer most in schools, with their emphasis on language conformity, middle-class comportment and de-ethnicization. But later, when lower-class bilinguals confront the blue-collar job market to which their poor schooling channels them they may not be particularly discriminated against for language non-conformity and the ethnicity it symbolizes. On the other hand, middle-class children may have the resources to overcome initial handicaps and stigma and do at least average in school. But if they maintain language non-conformity (and according to linguists they do to at least some degree) they may later suffer from direct discrimination in the white-collar job market where language conformity is highly valued and lower-class stigmatized ethnicity is out of place.

ALTERNATIVE MODELS OF BILINGUALISM AND STATUS ATTAINMENT

The lack of previous findings makes it prudent to consider the various way home/school bilingualism might affect social attainments. These can be summarized by four alternative models, each implying a particular set of relations and non-relations testable against social life cycle data.

I. The Class Correlate Model

If H/S bilingualism appears to have negative effects only because Spanish-speaking homes tend also to be low status ones then one can conclude that H/S bilingualism plays no independent part in Chicano status attainment. For this to be true the association between Spanish and low status homes has to be strong enough that controlling for the latter reduces all partial effects of the former to zero.

II. The Cumulative Effects Model

Various studies have shown that Chicanos, like blacks, suffer in comparison to Anglos at each point in the attainment chain. If the intrinsic and extrinsic effects of home/school bilingualism continue to handicap, then among Chicanos those raised in Spanish should attain lower levels of education, occupational status and income, and the attainment differentials should not be "explained" by previous factors along the line—producing the following set of relations: negative associations of Spanish upbringing with educational, occupational and income attainments; with occupation when education is controlled; and with income even when both education and occupation are controlled. In a path model relating these variables there would be direct effects of language on each succeeding attainment, as well as indirect effects from language all the way to income. In this model and those that follow, language effects must of course remain when parental status is considered.

III. The Mediating Factor Model

While Chicano attainment patterns roughly follow the model for blacks, in the sense that background and mediating factors do not fully explain their lower occupational and income attainments, education is usually a more powerful explanatory factor for Chicanos than for blacks. If education is the crucial mediating variable between home/school bilingualism and income, then the subsequent effects of language would disappear when education controls are introduced. In a path model there would be no direct effect from language to income, but rather all the former's effect on the latter would be indirect through education. There are two variants within this general model, according to where occupation fits in. A direct relation between language and occupation means that language discrimination also takes place in the job market but that, for occupations of equal status, language of upbringing has no further effect. The absence of such a direct relation supports the great emphasis on education and schooling. Either mediating factor model requires that there be zero-order correlations of upbringing language with education, occupation and income, and that these associations not disappear when parental status is controlled.

IV. The Balanced Effects Model

Any explanation of a negative relation between H/S bilingualism and income should conform to one of the models above. Logically there are other possibilities, for example no path through education and occupation but rather only a direct relation with income. But the limited amount known about the effects of home/school bilingualism strongly suggests that its relation to education is the one most likely to appear. However, there is a fourth interesting possibility. Home/school bilingualism may depress educational attainment but have no long-run negative correlation with or effects on ultimate attainments. But there then emerges a curious implication: since education is associated positively with subsequent attainments, the direct effects between Spanish upbringing and these attainments must be positive. The quantitative logic, which path analysis graphically portrays, is inexorable: a negative path between uncorrelated variables must be balanced by a positive path. In other words, the negative effects on education of rearing in Spanish may be counterbalanced by other positive effects.

Of the four alternatives the mediating factor model emphasizing education is best supported by what is known about Chicano status attainment and also by the theory of extrinsic causation. Cumulative effects are also possible. But the evidence of, in comparison to blacks, less direct discrimination against Chicanos (Pinkney, 1963), and the greater salience of education (Grebler et al., 1970: 194; Poston and Alvirez, 1973; Williams et al., 1973; Garcia, 1975), combined with the fact that most Chicanos are in the manual work force, and so less subject to language discrimination, all suggest that the mediating factor model is the more likely. None of the other alternatives is supported by previous findings. One monograph on bilingual Chicano children asserts that bilingualism's apparent effects are really class effects, but provides no substantiating evidence (Arizona State University, 1960).

CLASS VARIATION

If middle-class Chicano children can overcome whatever debilitating effects rearing in Spanish has among the poor then their educational attainments would be no different from English-speaking middle-class Chicanos. On the other hand, if they maintain the language style that continues to identify them as "Mexican" and if, as the extrinsic theory predicts, this stigma is a greater hindrance in the white-collar job market, then their bilingual origins should have negative direct effects on their ultimate occupational and income levels. The clearest way to assess class variation is to replicate the language-attainment model for groups divided according to class origins. A distinct pattern of relations among those raised middle class will not greatly affect the overall results because the vast majority of the sample was not raised (and has not attained) middle-class status.

TABLE 1

*Intercorrelations, Means and Standard Deviations of Home/School Bilingualism
and Status Variables, by Age Groups, for U.S. -Raised Chicano Men in Los Angeles*

25–44	1	2	3	4	5	mean	s.d.
1		−.02	−.24	−.08	−0−	.70	.46
2			.16	.38	.15	22.6	19.1
3				.41	.34	11.3	2.5
4	N = 238				.44	32.3	20.3
5						10144	4723

25–34	1	2	3	4	5	mean	s.d.
1		−.05	−.32	−.22	−.01	.60	.49
2			.06	.23	.05	21.5	17.8
3				.34	.23	11.7	2.2
4	N = 138				.51	32.0	19.5
5						10160	4973

35–44	1	2	3	4	5	mean	s.d.
1		−.01	−.08	.07	.02	.80	.40
2			.28	.54	.26	23.9	20.3
3				.48	.47	10.9	2.7
4	N = 100				.37	32.5	21.2
5						10127	4447

1. home/school bilingualism (Spanish at home)
2. father's occupational status
3. education
4. occupational status
5. income

RESULTS

In contrast to the standard status attainment model (Blau and Duncan, 1967: 169-170), education has an independent effect on occupational attainment no greater than that of father's status and the effect of father's status is mostly direct, not indirect through schooling. An indication that home/school bilingualism is of fundamental importance for understanding these differences comes from viewing English and Spanish-raised Chicanos separately. For the latter the standardized regression coefficient from education to occupation (with father's occupation also in the equation) is only .29. But among English-raised Chicanos it is .65, comparable to the national average.

Despite the distinctive pattern and the apparent importance of language, the first conclusion from our Los Angeles data is that home/school bilingualism has no massive lasting net effects. Educational attainment is clearly affected, and there are interesting interactions and patterns that allow one to choose from among the alternative models. But if enduring effects on occupational and income status are the criteria, then H/S bilingualism ranks well down the list of important factors in Chicano status attainment. On the other hand, if its effects are not spectacular neither are they just artifacts of social class.[3] In fact H/S bilingualism and father's occupational status are essentially uncorrelated in the wide or narrow age bands.

[3] The language effects are not explained away by either generational or rural/urban upbringing variation. The pattern of balanced effects is actually *stronger* among third and subsequent generations. English upbringing and urbanness are strongly related but only about half of those raised lower class and in Spanish were also rural. When rural-urban upbringing is included in the basic path model it has the expected effect on education (beta = −.10) but no other significant effects, and the effect of H/S bilingualism on years of schooling is reduced only slightly, from .23 to .20.

FIGURE 1

Home/School Bilingualism in the Context of Status Attainment.
Los Angeles Chicano Men, 25-44. 1973.

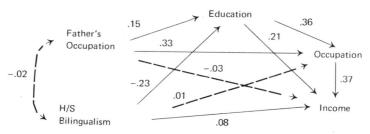

Note: Solid lines indicate effects based on regression coefficients greater than twice the standard error.

Education, Occupation and Income Separately

Table I provides the intercorrelations, means and standard deviations for the entire sample and also the ten-year cohorts. Since home/school bilingualism and father's status are unrelated the zero-order correlations between these independent variables and the three attainment measures indicate the total effects of the former on the latter. Home/school bilingualism has its clearest effect exactly where one might expect, on educational attainment. In every case H/S bilingualism has a negative effect on schooling. The considerably greater effect among younger men may be due to a variety of factors such as more accurate reporting for them, declining discrimination against English-speaking Chicanos, and the greater language heterogeneity among younger men. These and other complications cannot be easily differentiated so the relation of language and occupation in both cohorts combined is probably the best estimate of the true effect. There is also a considerable negative relation with occupational level among younger men. But in the older cohort, which may well better represent ultimate occupational attainment, the relation is actually mildly in favor of H/S bilingualism. Here again the potential complications of interpreting age cohort differences makes the total sample the most prudent data for generalization. Finally, income is clearly uncorrelated with H/S bilingualism in all three groups.

Bilingualism in the Context of Status Attainment

Looking at home/school bilingualism in the context of a path diagram allows one to distinguish its direct and indirect effects, and also to assess its importance in comparison with other factors. Figure I shows graphically what the pattern of correlations implied: H/S bilingualism has a definite depressing effect on educational attainment, but this is balanced by a mild *positive* direct effect on income. Table II summarizes the direct and indirect effects of language and class of upbringing for all three age groupings. For the older cohort there are two balancing positive effects and the stronger one is to occupation. Among younger men there is only one balancing direct effect, a strong .14 to income, and there is a definite negative direct effect to occupation—probably a life cycle rather than historical difference. The same negative aspects of home/school bilingualism that curtailed their schooling also hinder their early occupational attainment. The important point is that in either age group H/S bilingualism's negative effect on schooling is balanced by subsequent positive direct effects resulting in no net relation between it and income attainment, and even the net relation with occupational attainment is ambiguous. The long-run net insignificance of H/S bilingualism is supported in various other ways. Its inclusion or exclusion in

TABLE 2

Direct and Indirect Effects* of Home/School Bilingualism and Father's Occupation on Education, Occupation and Income for Los Angeles Chicano Men

	Education		Occupation		Income	
	direct	indirect	direct	indirect	direct	indirect
25–44 (N = 238)						
Home/School Bilingualism	−.23	—	.01	−.08	.08	−.07
Father's Occupation	.15	—	.33	.06	−.03	.18
25–34 (N = 138)						
HS	−.32	—	−.12	−.09	.14	−.14
Fa Occ	.04	—	.20	.01	−.07	.12
35–44 (N = 100)						
HS	−.08	—	.10	−.03	.04	−.02
Fa Occ	.28	—	.43	.10	.08	.18

Notes: *Only the forward (causal) indirect effects are considered. Total effects are the algebraic sum of direct and indirect effects and, since home/school bilingualism and father's occupation are essentially uncorrelated, they are nearly identical to the zero-order correlations in Table 1. For calculation of this table all coefficients, significant or not, were included.

the basic path model of attainments changes the other coefficients hardly at all; nor does it account for much additional variance after education. Table II shows that its total (direct plus indirect) effects on occupation and income are distinctly less than the lasting effects of father's status.[4]

Class Variation

That bilingualism might have different consequences in different class contexts was tested in two ways: mean attainments were compared by language *and class* of upbringing (tables omitted) and the path model of Figure I was replicated for separate class origin groups (summarized in Table III). Any reasonable definition of middle-class status produced groups too small for separate analysis of the ten-year cohorts, but for reasons already discussed the full sample is probably the best data. Using subgroup means or path coefficients, the hypothesis of varying effects is not only confirmed, it is clear that the pattern of effects actually *reverses* between lower-class and middle-class Chicanos. Within the lower class those Chicanos reared in English have a clear two-year schooling advantage. But among those raised in the middle-class the advantage shifts to those reared in Spanish, who average about a year more of schooling than English monolinguals. Table III shows that among lower-class Chicanos the basic model of Figure I is intensified, with direct home/school bilingualism effects of −.34 and +.17 to education and income, respectively. Among middle-class-raised Chicanos the same effects are +.17 and −.16. The total effect on income is mildly positive (+.08) for lower-class origins and mildly negative (−.06) for middle-class origins. The pattern among those with working-class origins is less clear; the only strong direct effect is the negative one on schooling (−.20) and the total effect on income is somewhat negative.

---

[4] For readers unfamiliar with path analysis I should point out that total effects are simply the sum of all paths leading from one variable to another, and each path is computed by multiplying the coefficients along the path. The term net effect is sometimes used as a synonym for direct effect, or standarized regression coefficient (beta). This partial relation sense of net applies to a single regression equation, but not to a path model, the point of which is to assess the total or net direct and indirect effects.

TABLE 3

Direct and Indirect Effects of Home/School Bilingualism and Father's Occupation by Class of Upbringing for Los Angeles Chicano Men, 25 – 44.

	Education		Occupation		Income	
	direct	indirect	direct	indirect	direct	indirect
Lower Class ** (N = 113)						
Home/School Bilingualism	−.34 *	—	−.05	−.07	.17	−.09
Father's Occupation	−.14	—	.08	−.03	−.05	.00
Working Class (N = 97)						
HS	−.20	—	.05	−.08	−.02	−.06
Fa Occ	−.03	—	.26	−.01	−.12	.08
Middle Class (N = 35)						
HS	.17	—	.02	.09	−.16	.10
Fa Occ	−.07	—	−.28	−.04	−.29	−.10

Notes: *Despite the truncated variance father's occupation was left in the equations to avoid inflating the effects of language. The simple correlations with education were virtually identical: −.34, −.20, .18.

** Lower Class = Duncan status scores 0– 12; Working Class = 13 – 50; Middle Class = 51 – 99.

DISCUSSION

Clearly the model of balanced effects is best supported, but in neither theoretical nor practical terms does this mean that H/S bilingualism makes no difference. For the Chicano majority (only about fifteen percent of the sample were brought up middle class, and two-thirds of the rest were raised primarily in Spanish) home/school bilingualism does have negative educational consequences, consequences possibly underestimated by our results for two reasons: the difference is often between finishing high school or not, and the quality of schooling received by H/S bilinguals is probably also worse. H/S bilingualism is as important as parental status in determining educational attainment among Chicanos. The mean difference between H/S bilinguals and English monolingual Chicanos is 1.3 years, about the same as the difference between lower-class and middle-class Chicanos (tables omitted); the effect on education in a regression (Figure I and Table II) is actually greater. Further analysis shows that the place of education in the status attainment cycles of English- and Spanish-raised Chicanos is quite different. Family status has no clear impact on years of schooling for the former, but makes a considerable difference (beta = .31) among the latter. This is direct support for the hypothesized importance of resources (class, individual or school, but we can vary only the first) in determining whether or not bilingualism will be a scholastic handicap. The greater subsequent effect of education for those raised in English (mentioned at the beginning of the presentation of results) indicates that education plays its usual key role in status attainment for English raised Chicanos, but not for the home/school bilinguals.

Home/school bilingualism does account for a considerable portion of the Chicano/Anglo schooling gap. The magnitude of that gap for native-born Chicanos 25-44 is not more than two years (U.S. Bureau of the Census, 1973b)–just about the advantage of English among lower-class Chicanos. The rather good showing of English-speaking lower-class Chicanos (who average over twelve years of schooling) shows that this is not just an additive "class effect" but rather a genuine interaction. What may be an advantage in the middle class is clearly a disadvantage among the poor. Whether the great gap between poor and middle-class bilingual Chicano children comes from actual cognitive disadvantages and advantages of bilingualism in the two circumstances, or to differential treatment by teachers and others cannot be convincingly answered here. But if status and wealth are regarded as extrinsic factors, then in this sense the disadvantage of Chicano H/S bilingualism is distinctly extrinsic.

I predicted that H/S bilingualism would have no direct negative effects after schooling for the blue-collar Chicano majority. But how could it have positive effects? It is tempting to speculate that the greater flexibility and nonverbal intelligence that some researchers (Darcy, 1946; Leopold, 1949; Balkan, 1970) have found in bilinguals really pays off on the job—not in schools with their emphasis on conformity rather than productivity and creativity. But speculation about the social consequences of psychological mechanisms must be left for bilingual social psychologists. A more mundane sociological explanation can be based on that attribute that most clearly sets bilinguals off from monolinguals, that they are able to function in two languages. Speaking Spanish does not help at school (including Spanish classes according to considerable impressionistic evidence); but then it does not in most jobs either, whether blue or white collar. But competence in two languages could increase one's access to job information and number of contacts. The business of getting jobs is often a question of personal contacts, both close and casual (Bott, 1957: 124-125; Granovetter, 1973). The close contacts, with family and good friends, would not seem affected by language. But the network of casual relations that may in fact be the more important (Granovetter, 1973) could be enriched for Chicanos who function well in Spanish.

Preliminary field investigation indicates that mutual aid among Chicanos is very real, if not so organized as among some European and Asian immigrant groups. An effective Chicano ethnic job network exists, not so much for jobs within the community, but rather knowledge about and connections to jobs (mostly manual and often well-paying "dirty work") in the general economy. Fogel argued, and partially demonstrated, that Chicano community-dependent jobs tend to produce lower incomes (in Grebler et al., 1970: 235-239) but this applies only to occupations that are actually within the community. On laborer and other manual occupational levels Fogel found that Chicanos do quite well in comparison to their competition and it is on these levels that the Chicano ethnic job network seems to function best. Access to this network cannot immediately alter occupational level, but it can guide one to better paying jobs within a particular level. That the direct positive effect goes to income rather than occupation supports this view. On the other hand, among older men only it goes more to occupation, suggesting that continuous access to the network does improve job status in the long run.

Why does it help to be bilingual? In part it might be the simple capacity to communicate with Spanish as well as English speakers. But Chicano bilingualism, in both its Spanish and its English style, is a badge of ethnic in-groupness, not just a stigma to outsiders. It is very much a bond that strengthens the ties of Chicano to Chicano. Indeed, Chicanos often test each other (not necessarily consciously) on lingual criteria, especially if the other is in some ways marginal in other aspects of ethnicity. I suggest, then, that H/S bilingualism provides positive direct effects because it is a sociometric resource, giving better access to an ethnic job network in which knowing Spanish widens and strengthens one's network of contact, without reducing the flow of help or information from other sources transmitted through English.

The reversals of effects for middle-class Chicanos can in each case be explained by aspects of the theory of extrinsic effects. Class resources explain how H/S bilinguals can overcome early learning difficulties and reach parity with English-speaking Chicanos. The scholastic advantage of a literate ethnic tradition explains how they might excel. The data indicating their superiority are far from conclusive.[5] But from even the most cautious perspective one

---

[5] Among women home/school bilingualism has a corresponding strong negative effect and that effect

can conclude that H/S bilingualism is not as great an educational disadvantage for Chicanos brought up middle-class. They may be subjected to discrimination in school, but school attainment is not just a question of discrimination. Conscious as well as unintended aspects of home environments also make some difference. The Los Angeles data, combined with impressionistic evidence for Chicanos and others, suggest that ethnic language maintenance may be an educational advantage under middle-class circumstances.

The subsequent negative class interaction is also best explained by two components, both part of the revised extrinsic theory. First, the ethnic job network does not serve middle-class Chicanos, both because middle-class job recruitment and requirements are more bureaucratic and, perhaps most important, there are so few Chicanos already on middle-class levels to provide contacts. This satisfactorily explains their lack of advantage. Their actual disadvantage in comparison to equally schooled English monolingual Chicanos is best explained by direct job discrimination against H/S bilinguals for their lack of language conformity and their persistent signs of inappropriate ethnicity. Seigel (1970: 739-741) demonstrated that middle-class blacks suffer from more direct income discrimination than lower-class ones. He offers no explanation, but surely at least part of it is the inappropriateness of their ethnicity in so much of the national middle class. Presumably very dark or otherwise very "ethnic" blacks suffer even more, though research along these lines is strangely undeveloped. Whether or not middle-class Chicanos as a whole suffer from the same relative disadvantage as middle-class blacks, it does seem true that among middle-class Chicanos the more ethnic are at a disadvantage.

CONCLUSIONS AND IMPLICATIONS

The fundamental hypothesis of this paper, that home/school bilingualism has no necessary positive or negative effects on attainments, is confirmed. Only when it interacts with group and individual status does bilingualism have any social consequences. Positive (in-group solidarity, access to speakers of two languages, a literate ethnic tradition, verbal flexibility) or negative (identification with a stigmatized ethnic group, non-conforming speech, early learning difficulties), these consequences are all only potentials, and their activation depends on circumstances. In the ordinary additive sense the effects of bilingualism are not "explained" by class variation, and yet they exist only in particular class and social context environments.

My predictions about where the negative effects occur are also confirmed, thereby lending support for the ethnic stigma hypothesis. The principal unexpected finding is the positive value of Spanish in the blue collar job market, accounted for by extending the group identification argument. Bilingual speech style conveys Chicano ethnicity to the in-group as well as the out-group and seems to support the existence of an effective ethnic job network among Chicanos.

On the practical level the findings have two implications. The negative economic value of language ethnicity for white collar Chicanos is evidence that direct job discrimination does indeed exist on this level against Chicanos. The salience of this discrimination has been minimal, but as more Chicanos qualify and seek to enter the middle class the importance of direct discrimination may actually increase. the negative effect on education has a much greater practical impact. Intergenerational language shift among Chicanos is more rapid than commonly supposed, particularly in urban areas, but a large proportion of the Chicano population will continue to grow up poor and speaking mostly Spanish at home. That their

---

intensifies among those raised lower class. However, H/S bilinguals show no educational superiority among middle-class women, although among those whose parents were also born in the United States they do as well as those raised in English.

bilingualism can be a positive resource after school, and that middle-class children can overcome bilingualism's scholastic disadvantage should not obscure the very real negative effect on educational attainment for the vast majority of bilingual Chicanos. We do not know the patterns of language effects for European and Asian immigrant groups, though impressionistic evidence suggests they are similar to the Chicano pattern. Language solidarity and ethnic solidarity generally are particularly valuable for Chicanos and other groups that cannot easily shed other indicators of their ethnicity. They can use ethnic solidarity to counteract the negative externally-imposed consequences of their ethnic stigma. But the Chicano climb out of poverty would be more rapid if schools and bilingual children got along better.

REFERENCES

Anastasi, Anne and Fernando Cordova
  1953   "Some effects of bilingualism upon the intellegence test performance of Puerto Rican children in New York." *Journal of Educational Psychology* 44(January):1-19.
Arizona State University College of Education
  1960   *Investigation of Mental Retardation and Pseudo Mental Retardation in Relation to Bilingual and Sub-cultural Factors.* Tempe: Arizona State University.
Arsenian, Seth
  1937   *Bilingualism and Mental Development.* New York: Teachers College.
Balkan, Lewis
  1970   *Les Effets du Bilinguisme Francais-Anglais sur les Aptitudes Intellectuelles.* Brussels: AIMAV.
Barker, George
  1947   "Social functions of language in a Mexican-American community." *Acta Americana* 5(July-September):185-202.
Blau, Peter and Otis D. Duncan
  1967   *The American Occupational Structure.* New York: Wiley.
Bossard, James H.
  1945   "The bilingual as a person." *American Sociological Review* 10(December):699-709.
Bott, Elizabeth
  1957   *Family and Social Network.* London: Tavistock.
Browing, Harley L., Sally C. Lopreato and Dudley L. Poston
  1973   "Income and veteran status: variations among Mexican Americans, blacks and anglos." *American Sociological Review* 38(February):74-84.
Carter, Thomas P.
  1970   *Mexican-Americans in School: A History of Neglect.* New York: CEEB.
Cicourel, Aaron
  1974   *Language Use and School Performance.* New York: Academic Press.
Cornejo, Richard
  1974   *A Synthesis of Theories and Research on the Effects of Teaching in First and Second Languages.* Austin: National Educational Laboratory.
Gumperz, John
  1972   "On the communication competence of bilinguals: some hypotheses and suggestion and further research." *Language in Society* 1(April):143-154.
Haugen, Einer
  1956   *Bilingualism in the Americas: A Bibliography and Research Guide.* Alabama: University of Alabama Press.
  1972   *The Ecology of Language.* Stanford: Stanford University Press.
Hickey, Tom
  1972   "Bilingualism and the measurement of intelligence and verbal learning ability." *Exceptional Children* 39(September):24-28.
Jencks, Christopher
  1972   *Inequality.* New York: Harper and Row.
Jones, W. R.
  1959   *Bilingualism and Intelligence.* Cardiff: University of Wales Press.
Kjolseth, Rolf
  1973   "Bilingual education programs in the United States: for assimilation or pluralism?" pp. 3-27 in Paul Turner (ed.), *Bilingualism in the Southwest.* Tuscon: University of Arizona Press.
Labov, W.
  1972   "The logic of nonstandard English," pp. 179-215 in Paolo Gigioli (ed.), *Language and Social Context.* Middlesex: Penguin.

Lambert, Wallace and Richard Tucker
  1972   *Bilingual Education of Children: The St. Lambert Experiment.* Rowley, Massachusetts: Newbury House.
Leopold, W. F.
  1949   *Speech Development of a Bilingual Child.* Evanston: Northwestern University Press.
Levinson, Boris
  1959   "A comparison of the performance of bilingual and monolingual native born Jewish preschool children of traditional parentage on four intelligence tests." *Journal of Clinical Psychology* 15(January):74-76.
Lopez, David E.
  1975   Home/School bilingualism and status attainment: a review of the literature and a fresh look at the Chicano Case. University of California at Los Angeles, Department of Sociology, unpublished.
Mackey, W. F.
  1972   *Bilingual Education in a Binational School.* Rowley, Massachusetts: Newbury House.
MacNamara, John
  1966   *Bilingualism and Primary Education: A Study of the Irish Experience.* Edinburgh: Edinburgh University Press.
Mittlebach, Frank and Joan Moore
  1968   "Ethnic endogamy—the case of the Mexican-Americans." *American Journal of Sociology* 74(July):50-62.
Peal, Elizabeth and Wallace Lambert
  1962   "The relation of bilingualism to intelligence." *Psychological Monographs: General and Applied* 76 (27, No. 546):1-23.
Penalosa, Fernando and Edward McDonagh
  1966   "Social mobility in a Mexican-American community." *Social Forces* 44(June):498-505.
Pinkney, Alphonso
  1963   "Prejudice toward Mexican and Negro Americans: a comparison." *Phylon* 24(Winter):353-359.
Poston, Dudley and David Alvirez
  1973   "On the cost of being a Mexican-American worker." *Social Science Quarterly* 53(March):697-709.
Saer, D. J.
  1923   "The effects of bilingualism on intelligence." *British Journal of Psychology* 14(July):25-38.
Siegel, Paul
  1970   "On the cost of being a Negro," pp. 727-743 in Edward Laumann, Paul Siegel and Robert Hodge (eds.), *The Logic of Social Hierarchies.* Chicago: Markham.
Tireman, L. S.
  1951   *Teaching Spanish-Speaking Children.* Albuquerque: University of New Mexico Press.
U.S. Bureau of the Census
  1971   *Current Population Reports. Series P-20, no. 312.* "Persons of Spanish origin in the United States: November 1969." Washington, D.C.: U.S. Government Printing Office.
  1973a   *Current Population Reports. Series P-20, no. 250.* "Persons of Spanish origin in the United States: March 1972 and 1971." Washington, D.C.: U.S. Government Printing Office.
  1973b   *1970 Census of Population. PC(2)-1D. Subject Reports:* "Persons of Spanish surname." Washington, D.C.: U.S. Government Printing Office.
U.S. Department of Health, Education, and Welfare
  1974   *A Study of Selected Socio-Economic Characteristics of Ethnic Minorities Based on the 1970 Census.* Volume I: Americans of Spanish Origin. HEW Pub. No. (OS) 75-120. Washington, D.C.
Vasquez, Jo Ann
  1974   "Will bilingual curricula solve the problem of the low achieving Mexican-American student?" *The Bilingual Review* 1(September-December):237-243.
Weinreich, Uriel
  1953   *Languages in Contact: Findings and Problems.* The Hague: Mouton.
  (1966)
Williams, J. Allen, Peter Beeson and David Johnson
  1973   "Some factors associated with income among Mexican Americans." *Social Science Quarterly* 53(March):710-715.

HARVESTING THE MONEY TREE: EDUCATIONAL
INNOVATION AS REVENUE SHARING *

TERRELL L. DONICHT
Challis (Idaho) School District

ROBERT B. EVERHART
Washington Department of Social Health Services

Considerable rhetoric exists about returning decision making prerogatives to local agencies rather than centralizing them in Washington. This rhetoric is found in education as well and was operationalized in the Experimental Schools Program (ESP) whereby local school districts were to propose, implement, and evaluate their own programs with minimal interference from the federal agency. This paper reports on one such ESP by examining expenditures of ESP funds.

A theme of political life for the past five years is that of the disengagement of the federal government from local affairs. This philosophy, eventually operationalized through the thirty billion dollar revenue sharing program, has affected most directly the fields of public safety, transportation, and general governmental services. Yet the spirit of revenue sharing —for local agencies to propose, implement, and evaluate their own programs with minimal federal constraint or guidance—has not been lost on education, even though school districts themselves generally do not directly participate in the revenue sharing program.

The federal government has proposed that, in the operation of schools as well, local school districts should have a greater determination in their own expediture of federal funds. Some recent federal programs indicate a departure from the practice of categorical or targeted funding (such as Title I and III, early childhood, vocational and career education) and a movement towards school districts proposing their own uses for federal funds and implementing programs with minimal direction from the federal donor. This paper reports on one such program, the Experimental Schools Program (ESP), funded by the National Institute of Education (NIE), and initiated under auspices of the U.S. office of Education (OE) before NIE was founded.

In this paper we will examine the operation of a change effort in a school district where the donor supplied the money but gave the school district the authority and responsibility for the design, implementation, and evaluation of its own change effort. We will examine the policy whereby the federal government provides local school districts control of federal aid for innovation. After briefly reviewing our techniques and the background of the ESP, we will discuss the ESP in fiscal terms—how money was allocated internally, how money was expended and for what purposes, and the relationship between federal funds and local funds. We conclude by discussing the ESP as an innovation resulting in dispersed expenditures, much like the use of federal revenue sharing funds.

Our case for examination is the Jefferson School District, a district of 7,500 students in a working class fringe area adjacent to a manufacturing and shipping center of 150,000 people. Even though we have only a single case, we believe the results described and our analysis of those results have definite transferability to other settings wherein the slogan of local implementation of programs by local people to solve locally identified problems is heralded.

*This paper was developed from research completed under Contract No. OCE-O-71-4751 with the National Institute of Education, Department of Health, Education, and Welfare. The authors acknowledge the assistance of Richard O. Carlson in commenting on earlier versions.

The authors were members of an evaluation team contracted by NIE to provide an external, summative evaluation of Jefferson's ESP for its five-year duration. The team was on site for the five years. Various team members did field work in the district and had access to district records in which ESP expenditures were listed. By examining these records, and by noting the source of income, expenditure and purpose of expenditures, and the budgetary category charged, we were able to determine for what purpose ESP monies were spent. Fieldwork on site (observations and interviews) provided additional and illuminative information.

THE EXPERIMENTAL SCHOOLS PROGRAM

The ESP is a five-year program with some 18 sites nationwide, three of which (among them, Jefferson) were funded in 1971. The ESP was based on the premise that, heretofor, many attempts at educational change had failed because they took into account only one of the myriad of factors said to affect the success of innovations. ESP proposed "comprehensive change"—changes that were mutally reinforcing or "synergistic"—as a counteraction to fragmentation. The simultaneous focus upon school governance, community participation, and curricular and instructional change were seen to be the three main mutually reinforcing areas, and formed the basic criteria upon which school districts were asked to submit letters of interest and eventual proposals.

Through ESP grants, school districts were given considerable latitude in the design and operation of their programs. The main stipulations were that proposed changes were to be "comprehensive,"—that is to involve simultaneous and interactive activity in the areas of governance, community, and instruction. School districts were also to establish their own internal evaluation unit to provide a formative evaluation function. School districts that evidenced the incorporation of successful "past practices" into a thematic framework were to be given preference in the receipt of grants. NIE pledged a non-interventionist stance, and encouraged the districts to identify their own problems and the solutions of those problems.

Jefferson School District proposed a number of changes. Community members were to be involved in policy making through participation in district-wide "charrettes" wherein goals, objectives, and programs were to be discussed. While not originally proposed, Jefferson created, in the second year of the project, an "ESP Cabinet" consisting of all 13 building principals. This body was given the responsibility of overseeing all ESP operations, and was created to insure that program adoptions were "integrated." Instructional programs were the main focus of the Jefferson proposal. Organized around the theme of "creating an optimal learning environment for each child," these proposed programs emphasized diversity and flexibility through differentiated staffing, an extended school day and year, individualized instruction, and diagnostic teaching. The instructional programs would, if implemented, require extensive coordination and interdependence within and between schools—a radical departure from previous district procedures. Finally, the worth of any program was to be determined partially by the results of a Planned Program and Budgeting (PPB) system, designed by the district's evaluation component to tie student outcome measures with program objectives, costs, and priorities.

THE ESP—INCOME AND EXPENDITURES

The OE/NIE provided Jefferson 4.76 million dollars, awarded in two installments.[1] Over 2.46 million dollars was provided the first 30 months to implement and operate the 10

---

[1] This amount constituted 11 percent of the district's total revenues for five years of the project and was meant to supplement other revenues.

instructional programs proposed by Jefferson for half (6) of its school sites. These sites were to fieldtest innovative programs, determine which were most successful, and then export the best programs to the remaining half of the district's sites during the second 30 months funding period. The latter installment, approximately 2.3 million dollars, would provide the fiscal impetus necessary to maintain previously implemented programs in the original half of the district and initiate and maintain the validated programs in the newly entering half.

Allocation Process

The allocation of almost five million dollars over a five-year period can be described as dualistic, inasmuch as budget decision making primarily occurred at two levels. Prior to the beginning of each 30 month funding period, the superintendent determined the total amount of funds needed for the period in those categories encompassing districtwide activities. The first category, *Pro Rata* account, was comprised of five sub-accounts: superintendent's office, maintenance of plant, operation of plant, transportation, and student health services. Monies budgeted for the Pro Rata accounts totaled almost $618,000, of which $389,000 was to cover the first funding period and almost $229,000 for the second. Monies allocated here were seen as ESP's contribution to district ongoing expenses.

The second major budget category, *Direct Support Services*, contained four sub-accounts: evaluation, training, dissemination, and administration of instruction. Money in these accounts provided districtwide services as indicated by their titles, and totaled $1,329,276 over the five-year period, $576,714 for the first 30 months and $752,562 for the second.[2]

After money for the districtwide services was allocated, the remaining funds were allocated to the project school sites on an equitable per pupil enrolled basis. Six schools received approximately $1,314,000 for the first 30 months, while 13 schools received slightly over $1,323,000 for the second 30 months. Once the allocation was made at the central office level, instructional program budget administrators (principals) at each school site devised instructional programs to fit the parameters set by the budget allocation for their school. Each principal budgeted his own 30 months funds in the manner which he saw fit, independently from other principals and independently from the districtwide administrators. Some of the principals constructed relatively detailed allocation procedures, identifying specific expenditures for the entire 30 month period, while others budgeted their 30 months funds on other rationales, such as a ratio of 50-35-15 percent for each of the last three years of the project.

Expenditure Processes

The expenditure of ESP funds, like their allocation, was dualistic. Funds within the pro rata accounts and direct support services accounts were spent by central office personnel; namely, the superintendent (pro rata and IGE accounts), and the directors of training and programs (direct support services accounts). School site expenditures were not centralized, and each principal was relatively free to exercise his own discretion once that allocation was received. There were few criteria restricting expenditures, and those existing were limited mainly to requests by the superintendent that principals stay within the general limits of the total budget allocation for their school, and that purchases be related to broadly stated objectives of the ESP. Each administrator purchased the goods and services which he (and/or

---

[2] During the first 30 months, a special account existed for the Jefferson ESP. This account, called the IGE account, was budgeted at $182,000 for the first funding period, also at the central office level. The "special" nature of this account will be described in more detail later in this section.

his staff) determined were necessary for operating the instructional program at his school site. Any money unspent at the end of each year was placed in an "undesignated fund" controlled by the ESP Cabinet. Money from this fund was usually allocated to school site administrators without reference to any formal criteria. One needed only to request an allocation and the request was granted almost automatically if a balance existed in the account.

While an attempt was made (and quickly abandoned) early in the project to keep track of expenditures by instructional program, expenditures were tracked by school site and by the individual pro rata and direct service accounts within which expenditures accrued. The tracking function became the responsibility of the ESP fiscal secretary, the only individual in the district who consistently had access to information on the fiscal characteristics of all project components and school sites. She published quarterly reports reflecting monies expended and monies remaining in each account, and functioned as an alarm system to warn budget administrators that spending in a particular budget category was reaching its limits and must either be curtailed or replaced with money from another budget category. Since principals kept few or no records of ESP related spending, they relied heavily upon the fiscal secretary to inform them about how much money remained in their school's account.

As a result, actual spending in the Jefferson ESP looked little like the original budget estimates, and budget expenditure discrepancies characterized almost all school and component accounts. The first 30 months expeditures were so far afield from estimates that the funding agency, with six months remaining in the funding period, required the superintendent to develop a completely new budget for that time period more accurately to reflect actual spending levels.

Substance of Spending—Where Did the Money Go?

Since the project was in its fifth and final year as this study was conducted, actual expenditures accrued were available for the first four project years only. By the end of this period, however, over 4.1 million dollars (86 percent) of the total money available had been consumed, and an examination of these expenditures yields a relatively accurate picture of the total project spending. The amounts expended for Jefferson's ESP through June 30, 1975 appear in Table 1.

Pro Rata Accounts. Over the first four years of the project, monies spent for pro rata services (or indirect support services as they were later called) were dispersed through five accounts during the first funding period and four during the second: superintendent's office, pupil personnel health services (later dropped), operation of plant, maintenance of plant, and transportation. These funds provided payments to numerous permanent personnel who, by and large, were already employed by the district and most of whose responsibilities were not significantly changed by the ESP. Pro rata funds also facilitated the purchase of supplies, materials, and equipment, most of which were only peripherally related to the ESP.

Direct Support Services Accounts. Spending for direct support services amounted to almost a million dollars, and supported operations within four components: administration of instruction, training, dissemination, and evaluation. Two of these components, dissemination and evaluation, were new to the district and directly resulted from the project proposal.

Nearly three fourths of the fiscal outlays for administration of instruction were for salaries and benefits, providing the full time support of two district level administrators (and their secretaries), one of whom continued to function in his original role as the director of secondary education and the other who was, in effect, an administrator without a funded program to administer. These funds also supported a host of previously employed officials, technicians, clerks, and secretarial personnel for short term services provided. Non-salaried expenses were

TABLE 1
ESP Accounts, In Dollars

Account	July 1, 1971– December 31, 1973	January 1, 1974– June 30, 1975	Total
Pro Rata Services			
Superintendent Office	$61,470	$17,854	$79,324
Pupil Personnel & Health	25,701	-0-	25,701
Operation of Plant	139,033	49,306	188,339
Maintenance-Plant	72,373	64,386	136,759
Transportation	82,351	58,210	140,561
Total Pro Rata	$380,928	$189,756	$570,684
Direct Support Services			
Administration of Instruction	$147,593	$31,251	$178,844
Training	92,335	86,867	179,202
Dissemination	63,737	27,647	91,384
Evaluation	258,703	287,372	546,075
Total Direct Support Services	$562,368	$433,137	$995,505
Individually Guided Education	$186,290	-0-	$186,290
Instructional			
School A (HS)	$297,307	$106,293	$403,600
School B (JHS)	315,902	129,180	445,082
School C (Elem)	167,129	69,679	236,808
School D (Elem)	161,782	60,793	222,575
School E (Elem)	173,624	65,844	239,468
School F (Elem)	212,180	63,057	275,237
School G (HS)	-0-	132,080	132,080
School H (JHS)	-0-	110,284	110,284
School I (Elem)	-0-	64,379	64,379
School J (Elem)	-0-	57,203	57,203
School K (Elem)	-0-	58,650	58,650
School L (Elem)	-0-	56,783	56,783
School M (Elem)	-0-	55,593	55,593
Total Instructional	$1,327,924	$1,029,818	$2,357,742
TOTAL ESP	$2,457,510	$1,652,711	$4,110,221

largely for general operating supplies, materials for the training component, furniture, and audio-visual equipment. The fund was cut in the second 30 months and was almost totally used for salaries of the disseminator and his secretary.

The district's training component expended $179,102 during the 1971-75 period for training and curriculum development in addition to and independent from training and curriculum development offered at the individual school sites. About one third of the funds were spent for a myriad of training endeavors for teachers, counselors, librarians, and para-professional personnel, while another third was spent to develop a social studies course and mathematics management system. The remaining third supported two administrative personnel, (neither of whose duties were greatly altered by the ESP), substitutes, and provided district printed materials, photocopying, consultant services, instructional assistants, and music equipment, much of which would have been necessary without the ESP.

Dissemination was the smallest of the four direct support components. More than half the funds for dissemination was used to provide salaries and benefits for the disseminator (who drew funds from "administration of instruction" as well) and his secretary. The other half of the funds provided office supplies and printing materials, and audio-visual equipment such as video cassette recorders, receivers, and television sets.

The evaluation component, largest of the direct support components in terms of money spent, was unlike the others discussed inasmuch as evaluation expenditures increased during the latter funding period compared to its funding level in the first period. Salaries consumed most of the evaluation funds (67 percent and 73 percent each funding period), as many personnel were hired to staff the new evaluation component. Remaining funds were utilized to purchase and lease considerable clerical and data processing supplies, materials, and equipment, including the lease of a new computer system during the latter funding period.

The Special Account—IGE. The $186,000 IGE (Individually Guided Education) account was a special account inasmuch as its purpose was not indicated by its title. On paper, this account was to provide fiscal support for those schools adopting the IGE organizational structure by paying the salaries of the lead teachers within them. Indeed, the salaries of the lead teachers in IGE schools (and the arts and crafts teacher in a non-IGE school) were paid through this account until all funds budgeted were consumed. However, the purpose of the account was more covert: ESP monies were channeled through the account to pay these salaries, thereby freeing district funds for remodeling that otherwise would have been commited to those salaried positions (this was done because project monies could not be used directly for remodeling expenses). This arrangement provided the funding agency little opportunity to monitor expenditures for district remodeling, and thus remodeling projects completed via these freed funds ranged from changing classrooms and resource centers to renovating the junior high school principal's office.

Instructional Accounts. By the end of the 1974-75 fiscal year, over 2.3 million dollars had been spent in the 13 school sites which comprise the Jefferson School District. During the first 30 months, six sites consumed over 1.3 million dollars in an experimental/control situation where one-half the district was to serve as the experimental setting and the other half the control setting.[3] During the second funding period, when all 13 schools were part of the experimental project, approximately one million dollars had been expended by the end of the first 18 months.

One high school, one junior high school, and four elementary schools were included in the ESP for the first 30 months of the project. These full-time vice principal level positions were funded by ESP for two secondary schools. Much of the remaining secondary school money was used to operate the schools' "interim" sessions (mini sessions largely comprised of non-academic courses), which required the purchase of electronic equipment, office furniture, audio-visual equipment, a 12-passenger van, and lease of facilities for swimming, bowling, skiing, and golf.

The four elementary schools—C, D, E, and F—spent their ESP funds to operate separate ESP programs which emphasized different curricular areas. Three of the schools adopted an IGE format as part of their ESP, while one did not. All of the schools utilized teacher aids under the auspices of the ESP, though number of aides per school and the subject area and grade level in which they were employed differed at each school. One school implemented an arts and crafts program, another a fifth day (part of every fifth school day devoted to

---

[3] The notion of "control" schools was in name only. During the first year of the project, the six ESP schools provided over $70,000 to the "control" schools for implementation of projects and services in those schools. This was done under the guise that the "control" schools needed to prepare for their entrance into the ESP during the last half of the project.

Other occasions arose during the first half of the project wherein the disparities between project and non-project fiscal resources were narrowed. Non-project schools formed a group for which the district's various non-ESP federal categorical programs were consolidated. Funds for these programs were subsequently limited to members of the non-ESP schools and were expended by those schools for programs often identical to those carried out in the ESP schools. In addition, monies spent for remodeling through the district building fund were limited to non-project schools, since much of the remodeling in ESP schools was handled via ESP funds.

student option activities) and another an interim period similar to the junior high school, as alternatives to regular school year activity. Each school adopted its own blend of commercially prepared curriculum packages; curriculum packages common to all four schools were a rarity.

The school sites' ESP funds were expended in much the same manner during the second 30 months as they had been the first 30 months, though there were more schools competing for the same amount of funds and thus less funds were spent per school. Secondary schools supported administrative positions which consumed considerable funds (and which often involved tasks not related to ESP), and continued to emphasize the interim endeavor. Both secondary and elementary schools spent funds for their own unique ESP programs, as each individual school's expenditures were characterized by the school's own mixture of teacher aides, clerks, secretaries (some newly employed and others long employed though paid with new sources of money), teacher-developed curriculum, supplies, materials, and equipment. Newly entering schools emphasized supplies and equipment rather than providing personnel positions, while the "veteran" schools exhibited just the opposite characteristic. To describe accurately the ESP expenditures during the second 30 months would require 13 separate descriptions, as each school site consumed ESP money according to its own principal and staff's perception of the ESP, a characteristic which, in itself, is descriptive.

The Other Money–Non-ESP Spending

The district was, in the superintendent's words, "able to remain solvent" with the federal money. The ESP contributed to the normal operating expenses of the district to such an extent that the established pattern of locally derived annually increased expenditures was reduced or less pronounced. The trend is illustrated in Table 2, which depicts the percentage change in non-ESP derived expenditures during the first three ESP years compared to average expenditure changes during the three years prior to the ESP.

TABLE 2

Non-ESP Expenditures, Three Years Immediately Prior to
Project Compared to First Three Years of Project, By Percent Change

Category	Average Expenditure Change for First Three Years of Project Compared to 1970–71	Average Expenditure Change for Three Years Immediately Prior to Project Compared to 1967–68
Principal's Salaries	5.2%	29.0%
Teacher's Salaries	3.5	10.7
Textbooks	−8.6	16.0
Student Health	−19.0	2.1
Transportation	−20.8	9.4
Plant Operation	−1.8	18.4
Administration of Instruction	−25.8	−10.8
Superintendent's Office	17.9	5.8
Maintenance of Plant	72.0	4.7
Overall	3.1%	12.5%

Table 2 indicates that the "value" of spending in all these accounts averaged only 3.1 percent ($18.62 per pupil) more in the first three ESP years compared to the 1970-71 baseline, while pre-ESP expenditures averaged 12.5 percent ($64.22 per pupil) more compared to the 1967-68 baseline.[4] In most instances, the value of non-ESP derived expenditures either declined or increased at a slower rate than existed in the three years before the ESP. When one considers the use of ESP funds in pro rata and direct support services for such items as transportation, student health, and plant operation, and when one notes the use of instructional account monies to pay for administrator's salaries in schools (administrators who, in most instances, spent only a fraction of their time in "ESP related" activities), the figures in Table 2 should not be surprising. Only in two categories (superintendent's office and maintenance of plant) was the value of expenditure greater during the ESP than for the years immediately preceding.

While spending less of its non-ESP funds, the district was also able to require less revenue from local sources. Every year the Jefferson district, like other districts in the state, had to secure voter approval of tax levies necessary for the normal maintenance and operation of the system. Jefferson asked voters for increasing amounts each year from 1967-74, but the size of the increases, relative to pre-ESP years, decreased the first three years of the ESP. In 1967-68, the levy amount was $548,032, a sum which increased each of three years prior to the ESP by an average of $158,952 or 29 percent over the base 1967-68 amount. During the first three ESP years, levies increased from $1,024,889 (requested in 1970-71) by an average of $123,270 per year, a 12 percent increase over the 1970-71 base. Expressed in 1967 dollars, the "value" of the increase in funds levied during each year of the three year pre-ESP period averaged $108,644 (20.2 percent over 1967-68), while the value of the increase during each of the first three ESP years averaged $43,630 (5.1 percent over 1970-71). Clearly, the district required a smaller increase in money (in both percentage and absolute terms) from local sources after the ESP grant had been awarded than it had before the ESP.

ANALYSIS

The ESP was envisioned as a program that would transform the school district from its traditional patterns to one where simultaneous activity was occurring in community, governance, and instruction—all focusing on an integrated and interdependent learning environment. Original models proposed that a student could transfer between any district school and be phased into a program so that there would be no disruption in the specific learning activities. While this expansive network did not develop, a number of constructive activities were developed. Individual teachers did receive money for a variety of curriculum development activities, the Interim activities were enthusiastically received, and the curriculum in many areas and in a number of schools was modernized. In the end, the superintendent and many administrators felt the project to be a success, although not for the reasons outlined in the original proposal.

Despite these perceived advantages, the examination of ESP expenditures indicates that the program became a potpourri of activities in the schools rather than the "synergistic" program originally conceived. The ESP cabinet created to facilitate program integration across the district, had little to do with fiscal matters as most monies were allocated to districtwide accounts or to schools on a per pupil formula. The members of the cabinet (principals of the 13 schools) were not interested in allocating money on the basis of need, and supported the equality formulas devised by the superintendent. Equitable allocation and independent spending characteristics thus led to the varied programs and services evidenced

---

[4] "Value" refers to the actual purchasing power of money expended over a multi-year period in an inflationary economy. In this situation, value signifies the 1967 dollar equivalence of post-1967 expenditures.

at each school with little regard for coordination with district objectives, as admittedly vague as they were. At the school level, ESP funds supported many instructional programs of an unrelated nature or part of the salaries of personnel whose duties were only minimally changed by the ESP effort. Because of this system of allocation and expenditure on a school rather than programmatic basis, the envisioned PPBES never became implemented.

There are some basic reasons why program funds were dispersed rather than focused. First, the ESP in Jefferson began more as an opportunity to be grasped than it did as a program meant to solve certain definable problems; in this sense it was based on an opportunity rather than a problem orientation, a common phenomenon in many federal programs (Berman and McLaughlin, 1975). Few principals or teachers knew what the ESP was or why it had come to Jefferson. Most defined it in terms of the educational hardware or curriculum packages that ESP funds had bought. Those who did not use such materials or who were unsure as to which source had funded the materials indicated that they were not involved in the ESP. The ESP's main effect was as a new source of funding at a time when general budget cuts were being considered. One district administrator said it very directly: "ESP is such a large grant that it helps us keep things we were going to cut back."

This opportunity orientation was congruent with Jefferson's long tradition of building autonomy whereby buildings operated inclusive instructional programs. Autonomy had gradually increased through the allocation of lump sum budgets to schools on a per pupil basis, a practice begun by the superintendent five years before the ESP and accelerated by the large amounts of ESP funds. This degree of fiscal autonomy gave principals considerable veto power over programs originating in the central office with which the principal and/or his staff disagreed. These forces facilitated the cabinet's emergence into a protectionist body wherein the individual choices of schools were legitimated and within which incursions from outside (such as by the superintendent or OE/NIE) were collectively averted.

Finally, and related to the patterns of autonomy, a pervasive norm of equality that influenced district operations became translated into the expenditure patterns reviewed earlier, a pattern dramatically illustrated in footnote 3. Early in the project, some schools had been granted more money than others on the basis of the materials and programs they desired. This practice led to considerable controversy among the schools and, by the second year of the project, the allocation of project monies was changed to a "per pupil basis." In the absence of clear standards as to what was to be valued, and in the void left by the lack of articulation as to what the project was to accomplish, a formula based upon equal distribution was the only defensible position. As the superintendent himself commented, "as an administrator, it's (the equality formula) the only way I can survive."

Throughout, the stance of the OE/NIE remained one of minimal involvement, so much so that one district official said, "you expect some greater sophistication in the grantor; they control an awful lot of money and we're probably doing some things that are pretty far off; but they've never stopped anything." While, OE/NIE officials sometimes pleaded for clarity during their occasional visits to the district, they remained faithful to their pledge as noted by one project official—that of simply "to give schools money for comprehensive change and then sit back and watch." Even during the early years of the project, while the district was being assailed for not having a truly "comprehensive program," OE/NIE's response was that it was the district's responsibility to decide what was comprehensive and that the federal government did not want to dictate what the change effort should be.

The end result was that ESP funds filtered down through the system much like any other funds, and were used, in part, to support various previously existing administrative positions, programs, and to support pro-rata expenses. While ESP funds were meant to *supplement* local revenues (and indeed were used for this purpose in some instances) Table 2 indicates that ESP, in part, *supplanted* local revenues, thereby permitting the school district to ask voters for proportionally smaller levies than had been requested before the ESP. In this sense, ESP funds warded off the need for substantially increased property taxes while maintaining most of the essential services provided before the ESP.

ESP as a program was very similar in philosophy, and its operation in Jefferson followed closely the practices of federal revenue sharing. Philosophically, the ESP fit the basic criteria of revenue sharing—fiscal need, an attempt to integrate program fragmentation into a "comprehensive" program, an allocation of resources based upon local rather than national need, and the general ideology of grass roots power (Byer, 1974). In terms of practice, we only have preliminary information on the nationwide uses of federal revenue sharing funds. However, these early returns indicate that the majority of revenue sharing funds, orginally meant to fund items or services local units normally could not afford, have served largely a substitutional function, thereby eliminating or reducing the need to raise monies locally in order to maintain basic services (Caputo and Cole, 1975; Murphy, 1975). Jefferson's use of monies appears to have followed a similar pattern. There is also every indication that the unarticulated spending patterns as evidenced in Jefferson's ESP are common in the use of federal revenue sharing monies (Reagan, 1972).

Unlike revenue sharing, however, the ESP was not intended as a cornucopia to be used for unlimited and unspecified purposes. There were some broadly stated objectives, and a variety of programs were to be operative as a result of the almost five million dollar investment. While some of these programs were implemented, the preceding analysis of expenditures suggests that many were not.

While the use of federal ESP funds had a revenue sharing effect in Jefferson, one might ask to what extent such results were atypical—perhaps a function of the district being responsible for program implementation with little direction or monitoring from the grantor. Though we have encountered only one study on the uses of external funds in relation to local funds, (Martin and McClure, 1969), the literature suggests that the ESP typified expenditure patterns in many innovative projects. House (1974), for example, indicates that most federal monies are spent with little concern for an agreed upon purpose, and that local school districts often "divert" federal funds to items in their own budget. Additionally, these finds are expended so that minimal financial commitment from local funds exists after termination of the project (Berke & Kirst, 1972). Murphy (1971), reporting on the use of Title I funds, notes that federal agencies have little effective direction and only a superficial knowledge of how monies are being spent, and that outside monies are usually absorbed into the system with little effect. More recently, McLaughlin (1976:409) has noted how Title I funds are used as general aid or "by stretching the categorical terms of the Act to its broadest interpretation." To this extent, Jefferson's use of federal funds for unarticulated purposes, which served to supplant local funds and thereby require a smaller demand on local tax sources, should not be seen as unusual.

CONCLUSIONS

Our data suggest that the rhetoric about how local people can solve their own problems through gifts of relatively unrestricted money is open to question. This method is not necessarily any more reasonable or efficient than is that of the federal government tightly controlling the uses of federal funds for education. The findings in this paper illustrate how ill-defined were the purposes for which the money was to be spent, thus permitting it to be spent for virtually anything. Additionally, the use of such funds without continual dialogue between the funding agency and the school district encouraged a loss of perspective on viable purposes for the use of funds, resulting in using monies to solve immediate problems (keeping the demand for local funds at a minimum) rather than to fund long-range programs tied to some explicit purpose. With the federal agencies' posture of benign neglect, there were neither the incentives for Jefferson to deal with programmatic objectives nor sufficient sanctions against use of monies to supplant local funds.

Policy makers will have to focus on a number of inter-related factors that influenced the Jefferson project (and other projects as well) in order to combat the natural tendency to use external funds in a revenue sharing fashion. First, before projects are funded and while they are in process, there must be a more consistent, uniform, and understood notion of purpose. Without this uniform understanding on the part of participants in the schools, then opportunism will influence strongly expenditure patterns. In this respect, the greater degree of clarity of goals associated with the proposed innovation, the greater the propensity to engage in the innovation (March & Simon, 1958).

More effort must be concentrated in the initiation phase (Rogers, 1962) of an innovation in order to reach a clear understanding of purpose. Currently, projects are conceived of and funded in rapid fashion (usually under the deadlines of terminating fiscal years) with insufficient consideration of the proposal, expectations for the grantor and grantee, the resources of the host institution to carry out what is proposed, or alternative plans that might better fit the exigencies of the situation. The Jefferson ESP was funded in this haphazard manner, and the resultant confusion in direction influenced the program for the next five years.

Third, funding agencies cannot absolve themselves from involvement in the local setting and expect events to work themselves out. A regular monitoring program, tied to pre-existing and ongoing expectations, must be in effect. Such monitoring need not mean control, but rather encouragement of the district's attempts to implement the change effort.

Finally, monitoring should be tied to a system of incentives used to encourage the proper expenditure of monies and to a system of sanctions if such proprieties are not evident. Yet a clear understanding of purpose in the beginning can assist in the establishment of incentives and make the administration of sanctions more defensible. Additionally, funding could be tied to stages in the program's development (Berman & McLaughlin, 1976) so that money for development of a complete program is dependent upon its successful development on an experimental basis. Therein would lie both the incentive for attempting the change as well as the sanction for not developing it, with the understanding that the funds might not necessarily be lost but rather placed into areas where success was more probable.

Without consideration of these factors, the federal system with its dispersion of power and control, will not only permit but encourage revenue sharing effects in the use of federal educational monies.

BIBLIOGRAPHY

Berke, Joel S. and Michael W. Kirst
    1972 "Intergovermental relations: Conclusions and recommendations." in Berke & Kirst (eds), Federal Aid to Education, Lexington: D. C. Heath, 377-408.
Berman, Paul and Milbrey Wallin McLaughlin
    1976 "Implementation of educational innovation." Educational Forum 40:345-370.
Berman, Paul and Milbrey Wallin McLaughlin
    1975 Federal Programs Supporting Educational Change. Santa Monica: Rand.
Byer, Greg
    1974 "Revenue sharing and the new federalism." Society, 58-61.
Caputo, David and Richard L. Cole
    1975 "General revenue sharing in cities over 50,000." Public Administration Review 35:136-42.
House, Ernest R.
    1974 The Politics of Educational Innovation. Berkeley: McCutchan.

March, James G. and Herbert A. Simon
  1958 Organizations. New York: John Wiley & Sons.
Martin, Ruby and Phyllis McClure
  1969 Title I of ESEA: Is It Helping Poor Children? Washington: Washington Research Project and NAACP Legal Defense and Educational Fund.
Murphy, Jerome T.
  1971 "Title I of ESEA: The politics of implementing federal educational reform." Harvard Educational Review 41:35-63.
Murphy, John C.
  1975 "General revenue sharing's impact on county governments." Public Administration Review 35:131-35.
Reagan, Michael D.
  1972 The New Federalism. New York: Oxford University Press.
Rogers, Everett
  1962 Diffusion of Innovations. New York: Free Press.

THE ORGANIZATIONAL TRANSFORMATION OF A FEDERAL EDUCATION PROGRAM: REFLECTIONS ON LEEP*

LINCOLN J. FRY
Ventura Region Criminal Justice Planning Board

JON MILLER
Laboratory for Organizational Research
University of Southern California

This paper describes the history of a law enforcement educational program (LEEP) in a small private college. This venture was characterized by conflicts over the educational mission of the program, intense rivalries between program factions, and student alienation. These problems, and the decision of the college finally to implement a competing program in order to divert students and their funding away from the original law enforcement educational program, were at least partially accounted for by the competing interests given surface expression in the imprecise goals guiding the federal funding effort. The dissatisfaction of LEEP funded students with the type of educational services received and the reaction their presence created in the college community were factors contributing to the conflict surrounding the program. One important implication of the study is that educational policy goals must more closely reflect the students' perceptions of what they want if such ambitious programs are to succeed.

This account describes the checkered history of an Administration of Justice (AJ) program, funded by the Law Enforcement Educational Program (LEEP), that struggled to survive in a small private college. The LEEP approach to law enforcement education took its objectives from the Task Force Report on the Police (1967) prepared for the President's Commission on Law Enforcement and the Administration of Justice. The guiding philosophy of this report was expressed in the strong, if not particularly well-supported, assumption that higher education is the only reliable way to provide the sophistication and skill that modern law enforcement requires. In this case study we describe the AJ program perceived as a vehicle for providing college training to be administered by and therefore largely controlled by people with strong direct ties to the criminal justice community. This program was attractive to the college, at least in part, because it served as a channel for federal money to solve some pressing financial problems.

Our study is based on four years of direct observation, supplemented by interviews with program personnel and with representatives of the federal funding source. By the time our observational period ended, the college had actually started a more traditional academic public administration program for criminal justice personnel to attract students and their LEEP money away from the federally funded AJ program. This was far removed indeed from the results envisioned by the federal funding agency and by the law enforcement personnel participating in the administration of the AJ program. Our purpose here is to show the implications of this anomaly for the implementation stage of educational policy formation. To this end we have attempted to document the factors appearing to transcend the immediate situation in order to shed some light on the problems plaguing large scale

*This paper was written while the senior author was supported by a grant from the National Institute of Law Enforcement and Criminal Justice 75-N1-99-0108. Interpretations and conclusions are those of the authors and are not to be construed as official or representing the policy of the National Institute of Law Enforcement and Criminal Justice.

educational programs in general and to suggest how programs such as LEEP might be redirected to reflect their original intent.

We have assumed that most public policy ventures are designed to produce innovation in existing organizational networks. Support for this position comes through clearly in the educational research conducted by Corwin (1975), who concluded that federal programs represented a critical ingredient in school innovation, more important than sociologists have previously acknowledged. It is also important to explore how organizational realities influence the likelihood that public policies can be successfully implemented. Whichever approach is taken, it is clear that social scientists can make a contribution to policy formation and implementation by stressing what is known about the environments of organizations.

Organizations have generally been conceptualized as goal attaining structures, and much discussion is devoted to the problems of goal identification and measurement (Etzioni, 1964; Perrow, 1961) as well as to how goals are displaced (Sills, 1957; Merton, 1957). In other research in law enforcement settings and elsewhere (Fry and Miller, 1975; Miller and Fry, 1976) we argued that when program goals are imprecisely defined, this factor by itself prevents organizational participants from moving in any consistent direction. We also recognize that this may be a reversible proposition, that competing directions and conflicting vested interests may make it inadvisable, if not impossible, to formulate precise and unambiguous goals. Whatever the interpretation, the correlation seems clear; vague goals and internal conflicts seem to be wedded to each other in many areas of public policy.

Few programs involve more such organizational inconsistencies for policy formulators than those educational programs designed for criminal justice system personnel. In particular, the programs LEEP has funded are characterized by a lack of clearly defined goals, by philosophical conflicts, shortsighted administrative decisions, intensive rivalries and student alienation. Many of these programs perform as if they were designed for failure rather than success. We can document these problems in some detail because our involvement was with an especially confused law enforcement educational program on a small religious liberal arts college campus. The relationship between law enforcement and academia has always been a grudging one, and in this AJ program all the latent antagonisms between the two surfaced. Before we describe the case a little background on LEEP will probably be helpful.

The Law Enforcement Educational Program (LEEP)

As we noted, the policy statements resulting in the establishment of the Law Enforcement Educational Program may be traced to the recommendations of the Task Force on the Police of the President's Commission on Law Enforcement and the Administration of Justice (1967). Implementation was established by the Omnibus Crime Control and Safe Streets Act of 1968 and continued with the Crime Control Act of 1973. The Task Force Report firmly stated that the quality of police services would not significantly improve until higher education requirements for personnel were established. Academic education was seen as instilling the ability to judge the quality of human behavior while specialized training in a college setting was seen as providing the needed technical skills and attitudes to complete complex tasks (1967:126-127).

Carter and Nelson (1973) note that LEEP students are not required to pursue degrees or certificates in criminal justice, criminology or police science. They may enroll in programs such as public or business administration, computer science, urban planning, psychology or sociology. At the same time, LEEP guidelines (1973:7) specify that educational institutions

shall exercise conscientious judgment in ascertaining that the LEEP recipients' academic program relates to the employee's duties and/or those job functions that reasonably can be anticipated by the student.

In short, while education has been seen as the means to enhance the professional qualifications of criminal justice personnel, how this educational mission was to be accomplished was not clearly specified for organizations dispensing the educational services nor for the direct recipients of the funds, LEEP students.

LEEP has become a major source for debate in the professional law enforcement literature[1] prompting the *Police Chief* (1975:8) to devote an entire issue to education and training, giving special attention to LEEP.[2] Misner (1975) provides an overview of the problems plaguing these programs, including imprecise program goals, reliance on external (federal) funding and a lack of commitment from educational institutions to law enforcement related programs. Indicating that LEEP funding provides $40,000,000 a year to about 100,000 students enrolled in around 1,000 institutions, he argues that too many criminal justice educational programs have begun merely for the money and cites the heavy reliance on part-time instruction in these programs as an indication that institutions are not committed to them; the fact that the majority are supported almost exclusively by federal funding is seen as a further support for both contentions. As we will show, we found these issues directly relevant to the program we observed.

THE SETTING

Our connection to LEEP began in a small private liberal arts college in California in fall, 1971. Like many others, this one was on the verge of closing its doors. To illustrate, only two faculty members had contracts when school began in the fall of 1971 while the remainder were forced to wait to complete their arrangements until the college received a large church-secured loan. The loan was received and at about the same time the college made some major administrative changes, including hiring a new president.

The school had hired a consultant in 1970, the director of a junior college Administration of Justice program, to explore the feasibility of entering the law enforcement educational field by establishing a police science program. He suggested that the program be expanded to an "administration of justice" perspective, more in tune with federal educational policy specified by LEEP. This suggestion was adopted and the first undergraduate courses were offered in the spring of 1971. The school received federal money then for the first time. The program grew and the college attempted to secure expanded LEEP funds during the 1972-73 academic year.

The program recruited its first core faculty early in 1972, one full-time instructor and one half-time full professor. The instructor was a retired federal law enforcement officer and the professor was a retired academic of some distinction. At the beginning of the summer of 1972, the consultant and the new faculty members received pressure from the administration to develop a Master's Degree program by the fall. Accordingly, the summer was spent developing grant applications and recruiting students. A program was developed and there were over 100 students when school began, of which about 60 were graduate students. The program also added a part-time coordinator who taught some classes. The remainder of the instruction was delivered by part-time personnel.

The influx of students, especially the large number of graduate students, was explained by several factors. This was the only four year, degree-granting institution within the area

---

[1] Some favorable assessments of the impact of education on law enforcement personnel have appeared in the academic literature (Senna, 1974). Those which have not been favorable have stressed the negligible effect of education on performance (Smith and Ostrum, 1974).

[2] The majority of the contributors to this issue were associated with academic institutions offering degrees in law enforcement. As a result, academic concerns accounted for the major issues raised, including accreditation (Misner, 1975), admission procedures (Kuldau, 1975), curriculum (Kuykendall and Hernandez, 1975) and the impact of education on professionalism (Moore, 1975).

served by the surrounding county's criminal justice system. The educational levels of the personnnel within this system were extraordinarily high; for example, most agencies encouraged college education and one police department had an entry level B.A. degree requirement for patrolmen. Further, the number of law enforcement personnel who lived in the immediate area was also very high. One community of 70,000 had 1,500 residents who were members of a large metropolitan police department located in an adjacent county.

The First Hints of Conflict

Relationships between the Law Enforcement Educational Program and the school administration had been very cordial when full operation began in the fall of 1972. Everyone concerned was aware that it had started on very short notice, especially the graduate component. As a result, discussions about the new program tended to focus primarily upon the improvement of the curriculum. However, the first conflict developed quickly over keeping the federal law enforcement money ($68,000 in the 1972-73 year) separate from the rest of the college's funds. Upon returning from a seminar held by LEEP, the one full-time member of the AJ department requested to know whether the monies allocated to the college were kept in a separate fund, a requirement he had learned was mandatory under the LEEP guidelines. He was informed that this was really not his business; but that the money was to go into the general college fund. The school financial officer indicated this arrangement was not a problem because these funds were disbursed to individuals under the LEEP program, making record-keeping a simple matter.

Student unrest over class scheduling, the student-faculty ratio and graduation requirements also began to appear shortly after school opened and considerable time was spent reassuring the students, primarily police officers, that changes would be made and faculty expanded. Graduation requirements at the Master's level were a major issue; some students had transferred with credit from other colleges and expected to complete their degrees at the end of the first full year of the operation of the graduate program. It was unclear whether they had to take comprehensive exams or the Graduate Record Examination, even though the GRE was listed as an admission requirement. The only admission standard actually applied at the graduate level was a Bachelor's degree. The GRE was never used as an admission standard; students merely took it to fulfill graduation requirements.

At this time, the faculty of the larger institution were generally silent regarding the AJ program. It was difficult to get faculty members from different traditional disciplines to offer evening courses for the program, especially at the undergraduate level, so that it would be possible for students to meet general education requirements for graduation. Yet the classes were predominantly night classes because of the clientele served.

A new academic dean joined the college administration during the summer of 1973 and this event precipitated another conflict between the larger institution and the Administration of Justice Program. The new dean's role had been defined by the college administration as one of improving the academic quality of all of the institution's departments and programs. Conflict immediately developed between the law enforcement-oriented members of the AJ program and the dean on the basis of their perceptions of his attitudes toward law enforcement education. He had expressed concern over the adequacy of the instruction students received and questioned whether the majority of those teaching in the program were qualified, making it clear that law enforcement experience in combination with either a B.A. or M.A. degree was not consistent with his perceptions of what constituted adequate faculty. Other statements that the dean made were interpreted to mean he felt the program was of questionable merit and his general position came to be defined as one philosophically opposed to grant programs and law enforcement personnel on campus, while his vision of the only realistic goal of such a program was perceived to "humanize cops."

These debates over accounting, staffing, curriculum requirements and matters of philosophy formed the background for the divisive issues that eventually seriously compromised the LEEP program's ability to function.

Issues in the Open

The 1973-74 academic year was crucial for a number of reasons. The LEEP sponsored AJ program became a major source of concern to the college's administration as open conflict began to develop between them and the program's personnel. Those teaching in the program were also divided among themselves. In fact, as the year progressed, the members of the program increasingly began to turn on each other because of differences in opinion over "academic" versus "law enforcement" objectives. The academically-based personnel stressed a "broadened outlook on the world," stressing the impact of education upon professionalism that others saw as opposed in important ways to the stress in the LEEP Guidelines (1973) upon technical preparation as a basis for more adequate performance on the job. Each faction in this argument blamed the other for the problems the program experienced in delivering adequate educational services to the students, attributing program failure to the other's mistaken beliefs about the educational mission of LEEP.

The administration's position on this conflict, as well as on the service delivery problems the program was experiencing, was unclear. Officially, all administrators stressed their desire to improve the academic content of the program. Yet they also indicated that they were not responsible for the state of the program and were reluctant to intervene. The college president tried to play a facilitator role, while the new dean was definitely seen as the enemy by the law enforcement-oriented members of the program, and as a supporter by the academics.

While the conflict continued visibly unresolved, one result was that the faculty of the rest of the college began to question whether the program should be on campus at all. Echoing the dean's position, they noted the lack of academic qualification of the majority of those engaged in LEEP instruction. As would be expected, the academic element in the AJ program looked to the college administration and faculty for support in their internal struggle with the law enforcement element. The latter, in turn, looked primarily to the funding source, LEEP, stressing mandates outlined in the LEEP manual which theoretically guided the program's operation. The sides were not completely drawn along law enforcement versus college lines. The law enforcement faction did receive some support from a small minority of the faculty. At the same time, another faction in the college environment was drawn into the fray, namely, those concerned with the finances of the college. They were defined as "friends" by the law enforcement faction. These two groups worked closely to secure increased funding. They accomplished their aim; and with supplemental LEEP funding, over $150,000 was received as the AJ program limped into the 1973-74 academic year.

Money became more and more the major issue in the relationship between the college and the program. Concomitant with questioning by the faculty of the existence of the Administration of Justice Program on campus, the college announced that it now had a much improved financial position. It stressed the efficiency of its new administrative component but beyond this the source of the improvement was not identified. The law enforcement faction of the AJ program was quick to point out the amount the college reported itself to be in the "black" was equal to the size of the funds LEEP students received to pay their tuition. Program members interpreted the questioning of whether they should continue on campus to mean that the college believed it had recovered financially to the point where the AJ people and their funds soon might not be needed. Program members were quick to note that the amount of grant funds the college received was a poor indicator of the amount of money actually received from the AJ program. Some students who were not eligible for LEEP funds paid their own tuition. In particular, federal law enforcement personnel and some students not employed in criminal justice related fields were excluded from receiving LEEP funds, and they did represent a sizeable number of students.

In fact, the number of non-LEEP funded AJ students began to grow even more in the 1974-75 academic year when the college started an extension program for federal officers. One federal agency assisted by providing classroom space free of charge. The extension program, taught by part-time instructors, was primarily attended by graduate students who paid a somewhat reduced tuition.

Issues Behind the Scenes

For a time, the law enforcement faction appeared to win in their struggle to have the program develop in the manner they thought to be consistent with the goals of LEEP. They achieved this edge by stressing the LEEP requirements, by pointing to the amount of money the program was bringing into the college, and by attempting to involve the program's advisory board, comprised of the heads of the major law enforcement agencies of the encompassing criminal justice system, to a much greater extent in program policy-making procedures. The search for a full-time director, one consistent with their perceptions of the program's objectives, was their major demand, along with more faculty. A full-time director was appointed at the beginning of the summer of 1974 who was an academic but one whose alliances were much stronger with the law enforcement community than with the college.

However, the optimism about improvement in the relationship between the program and the college was short lived as conflict developed more or less out of public view between the new director and the school administration. This new director had yet a third orientation for the program, namely, to turn it into a criminal justice research center, stressing the need to improve the quality of graduate education in particular.[3] The administration's position was that the academic quality of the undergraduate program was most in trouble. To further his objectives, the new director attempted to integrate the graduate AJ curriculum with the offerings of a nearby large urban university with considerable experience in criminal justice education, primarily through its School of Public Administration. He also began to find grants. Two things followed: a preliminary grant proposal was received favorably by a federal funding agency, requesting a formal grant application be submitted; and the urban university professed interest in offering joint degrees with the local program. The dean and associate dean of its School of Public Administration visited the college to discuss possible arrangements. Severe conflict developed between the AJ director and the local college administration over both of these incidents.

In the first place, the college administration expressed disapproval over the grant application, indicating that it should not be submitted. The size of the LEEP money to be received during the 1974-75 academic year, $258,000, was by itself overwhelming to one administrator; the "tail was already in danger of wagging the dog." The number of students projected

---

[3] Graduate education was a source of conflict in this college. Some administrators did not believe that the college should have entered the graduate degree market at all, emphasizing the point that the school should be strictly a four year teaching-oriented institution. In fact, the support the law enforcement-oriented element received came primarily from those members of the regular faculty who were also forced to deliver graduate education without adequate institutional support, especially in terms of faculty. At the same time, only a limited number of LEEP funded graduate students endorsed the new director's emphasis on improved graduate education, mainly students whom we will describe later as those wishing to escape the "system."

(approaching 200), which had always been at least ten percent of the student body since the program had become fully operational, threatened to rise even further, destroying the small liberal arts atmosphere the administration wanted to preserve. Further, a basic question was still whether cops really belonged on campus, at least in such large numbers.

An even more critical issue emerged over the alliance with the urban university. This became clear when, after meeting with the representatives of institution, the administration revealed for the first time that their own School of Public Administration was in the final planning stages, indicating that it would open in the 1975-76 academic year. The new Public Administration Program was to have a degree option for criminal justice majors who would be offered degrees in public administration and who, crucially, would remain eligible for LEEP funds. Faculty for this new program would consist of the college's regular faculty members while the Administration of Justice degree would continue to exist as a separate program.[4] In short, the Law Enforcement Educational Program's efforts to improve its educational product by an outside alliance had infringed upon the college's long-range planning and the possibility of such an outside alliance had to be abandoned. It is no surprise that the AJ program personnel felt they had been exploited as a conduit for federal money and then pushed aside when the college found another way to preserve the flow of money.

Several factors accounted for the course of action taken by the college's administration. First, it was argued that the college's traditional faculty could be used more effectively in their own public administration program, especially if various departments integrated some of their upper division course offerings into this new program. Some faculty were forced to meet with classes containing only three or four students merely to maintain their required teaching load. Some departments had very few majors while the AJ program was one of the largest on campus, second only to education. The LEEP classes were very large; forty or more students were not uncommon, including courses at the graduate level. Furthermore, it had become common knowledge that the future of LEEP funding was in question and that the program was likely to end, possibly as early as 1977. Reduced funding was the forecast for the 1975-76 academic year.[5] And so an effort to launch the new Public Administration Department with students diverted from a program with an uncertain future while the money from their LEEP support was still available appeared to be a logical course of action.

This major decision was the watershed, and after it was made other problems became more severe in the AJ program during the summer of 1974. Especially troublesome were the interpersonal relationships between the college administration and the retired law enforcement member who repeatedly threatened to resign, while the administration continually indicated they wanted to fire him.[6] A major confrontation occurred, one which embroiled the new AJ director and he resigned, indicating that his loyalties were completely with the member of the AJ program and opposed to the administration. A part-time director was appointed to replace him.

Another issue exacerbating the confrontation between the college administration and the full-time participants in the LEEP program had been the scheduling of a meeting with representatives from LEEP for the purpose of clarifying LEEP program requirements. The

---

[4] A major source of irritation to the members of the program was the inability to receive departmental status.

[5] LEEP funds the college received were reduced to $183,000 in the 1975-76 academic year. However, the amount of funds is not certain. Colleges apply for supplemental funds, depending upon surpluses available in the district office.

[6] The retired law enforcement person signed a contract for the 1975-76 academic year; however, he was dismissed at the end of the fall semester and the remainder of his contract was bought back by the college. The half-time professor had previously left the program at the end of the spring semester, 1974.

administration opposed this meeting on the grounds that they were simply not ready for it, while the AJ member's position was that they were responsible for the quality of the LEEP venture and for seeing that the funds were used properly. Inherent in such a meeting was the implication that LEEP personnel might audit the funds, dictate policy on the courses students should be required to take, and policy on the administration of the program, especially the number of faculty the college would have to employ because of the student-faculty ratio.

The meeting was held and the college administration scored a major victory. It became clear to them that there *were* no specific curriculum guidelines or enforceable student-faculty ratios and based upon this knowledge, they acted quickly. An announcement was immediately sent out that the college would no longer accept four-unit graduate courses meeting once a week in future class schedules. Since the AJ program was the only one offering four-unit graduate courses on campus, which met on a single night, it was clear to whom this dictate was directed. The LEEP requirement for full-time graduate student status was nine units a semester, which meant graduate students had to take two four-unit seminars, meeting once a week, plus a one-unit "independent study" to remain eligible, attending school at least two and sometimes three times a week. The rationale given for the new policy was that graduate students could not absorb four units of learning in one sitting and all graduate courses would have to meet on two different nights in the future. As a result, the students were faced with the prospect of having to attend school at least four and possibly five nights a week to remain eligible for LEEP. This was a major hardship for law enforcement personnel whose full-time jobs already averaged over 40 hours per week. However, there was the possibility that the "new" public administration program would offer three-unit graduate courses which would meet on a single night. This appeared to be a clear indication that students could enroll in the public administration program, attend three classes (each worth three units) per week and remain eligible for LEEP. This was an ingenious organizational play but not one designed to promote harmony between the AJ program and the rest of the college.

Student Reactions

Student discontent with the college throughout these struggles grew continually over the period of observation. They had been the most vocal group at the meeting with LEEP, and their representatives gave interviews to the local press afterward. This expression resulted in unfavorable publicity, especially the statement that the college was not reinvesting the LEEP funds into the educational program as mandated, supported by the information that the college had not hired any new faculty despite the rise in the number of students.

The administration countered that the faculty of the program, especially the full-time law enforcement member, "agitated" the students and had in fact "turned them against the college." The administration held this view even when a survey of the LEEP students was conducted after the proposed class schedule change had been announced. Overwhelmingly, the students indicated dissatisfaction with the program as a whole and a large number said they would leave college if the class schedule change became institutional policy. The dean's reaction to these results was firm; the change was not a negotiable item. However, after the intervention of the members of the LEEP advisory board, and after many student interviews held with major administrators, a notice was publicized indicating a moratorium on the class schedule change until the following year. This issue was not raised again during our involvement but the Public Administration Program did begin as scheduled in the fall of 1975.

The reaction of the students to the program and the college's reaction to them are important considerations in unraveling the problems associated with LEEP. This campus had never experienced any student or faculty unrest. Professors' complaints about the regular students usually involved their silence, especially in lower division classes, where the major instructional problem was to generate class discussion or student interaction. By way of contrast, LEEP students were older, aggressive and definitely political in their perceptions of the College LEEP program. They quickly reached the conclusion they were not wanted on campus, and only tolerated for the money their program brought in. They believed they were exploited by the college, especially in terms of the type and quality of the educational instruction and student services the college gave them.

Students complained that their perceptions of the goals of LEEP were in contrast to the type of educational program they encountered in this college. They spent a considerable time trying to petition out of what they considered unrealistic requirements. The required religious courses at the undergraduate level, for example, were a constant source of discontent. Students expressed resentment that they were expected to take these courses irrelevant to their jobs. Students saw these requirements as a way for the college to fill courses with LEEP funded students.

Another source of trouble was the unusual roles played by some individuals who were students or part-time instructors but also members of the LEEP program's advisory board; that is, they were either the heads of the local law enforcement agencies or high-ranking officers assigned to the advisory board. These individuals were vocal and put great pressure on the administration at the time of the proposed class change. As a result, those who played important non-student roles in the structure of LEEP within this college—as well as the vocal majority of the LEEP students who complained openly when they felt treated unfairly— created a major problem for the college administration. Despite the money LEEP brought in, some administrators openly questioned whether this benefit was worth the constant student problems they experienced. The irritation was a large contributor to the college's plan to develop a competing program, one which would eventually rid them of the LEEP-AJ alliance and the sounding board it offered malcontents.

DISCUSSION

Evidence of program failure does not always coincide with program termination. Despite all the problems this LEEP program has experienced, and which seriously compromised its educational mission, it now has over 230 students. This expansion has come primarily from the enrollment of federal law enforcement officers in the extension program that was added. At the same time, the program has only one full-time member, hired at the instructor level, in addition to the acting director who does not teach. Although the educational program never had more than two full-time faculty members and now has only one full-time member for over 200 students, more than half of them graduate students, there is no evidence that the college has ever violated any LEEP rules or regulations. It is not clear which ones, if any, of the many vague and imprecise goals we mentioned at the onset are served by this arrangement, but quality education to improve the delivery of law enforcement service is certainly not among them. Those connected with the funding source who agreed to comment have stated that this college is no worse than a number of other schools receiving LEEP money, especially in terms of the quality of educational services they deliver, or in terms of their reliance on part-time faculty. They have indicated that some schools in their jurisdiction are worse.

It is our interpretation that the origin of the problems plaguing LEEP in this small college and elsewhere can be found in the badly articulated and incompatible interests and the resulting imprecise goals which have always guided the federal funding effort. Education is good for almost everyone in law enforcement, the Task Force (1967) argued, but what kind of education with what kind of delivery system has remained only vaguely defined. This vagueness has left room for the kinds of manipulations we have described. Not only did this absence of direction allow the college, itself beset by financial problems and conflicts with deep strutural roots, to transform the LEEP funding to conform to its own particular needs, but ambiguities at the policy level at least partially accounted for the philosophical conflicts, intense rivalries and the student alienation characterizing the program. The group most adversely affected were the students funded by LEEP, the majority of whom did not receive anything even close to the kind of educational experiences they wanted or expected. In fact, one of the most important policy considerations affecting the future of LEEP, the issue that most clearly transcends this casestudy, is the problem of redirecting the kinds of educational services offered to take into account the wishes of the personnel in the criminal justice system.

Elsewhere (Fry and Miller, 1975; Miller and Fry, 1976) we have stressed that the kind of services clients want or think they need should be a primary concern of any policy ultimately generating the programs to deliver services. This is not to say that policemen are curriculum experts or that there was a single orientation emerging among LEEP students regarding the type of educational services that would most clearly meet their needs. Some students said they wanted an academic curriculum, especially a management-oriented one. These students tended to be either more advanced in rank and/or those who believed they would have a second career teaching in a criminal justice program after they had retired. However, the majority of students were lower-level personnel (especially patrolmen) and they had expected LEEP to provide educational experiences to improve their own particular job performances, opting primarily for a police science orientation. This group clearly saw the value of college training in terms of thier own promotability within their specific organizations. Becoming too academic could, in their view, actually hinder their chance for advancement given the practical orientation they saw to pervade criminal justice agencies. Those who wanted "academic" training were those most likely to leave the criminal justice system, either through retirement or to engage in another career. While possibly beneficial to them, this aim is self-defeating to one of the goals most salient to LEEP, namely, to improve the quality of the personnel in the system through advanced education. Knowing how many students saw the program as a means of escape from the system would also have been useful information from the point of view of policy formation. Again, the point is not that student participation in planning guarantees success but rather that when no attempt is made to gauge these opinions and take them into account at the planning stages, the resulting program will be more predisposed to failure by the ignorance this reflects and by the alienation it creates.

Imprecise goals and competing interests further contributed to the detrimental effect the college atmosphere had upon students. All the factions tried to impose their particular view of the world on LEEP students, especially their perceptions of the mission of the program. It was clear that some felt that cops needed to be "humanized" and were adamant about imposing a liberalizing effect into the curriculum, especially in terms of a heavy emphasis upon sociology and psychology courses. Along with this orientation was the assumption that LEEP students were academically inferior to the regular students and that something had to improve their performance. These attitudes were transmitted to LEEP students, suggesting to them that they were only tolerated on campus. This general reaction to LEEP students was perhaps the most damaging learning experience they encountered.

Looking at the other side, there is an "environmental impact" interpretation inherent in the relationship between the LEEP program and the college that raises the question of the role of the funding source in determining the probable impact of LEEP students on a small college. Those charged with fiscal responsibility and for assessing the functioning of these programs have been handicapped by the same ambiguous LEEP guidelines. Further, in the local area we studied, employees operating from a single office were responsible for many colleges spread throughout the western part of the United States. Because of a reduction in the amount of funding for this office, a single employee now monitors over $5,000,000 in funds dispersed to 100 colleges located in California, Arizona, Nevada and Hawaii. While this single employee may be able successfully to monitor the fiscal and administrative relationships between LEEP and these schools, it is not possible to see how any one person could have more than a fleeting notion of the kinds of internal problems we have described here.

LEEP officials report that the guidelines are being improved and the program is beginning to function in a much more satisfactory manner. At the same time, there is the distinct possibility that LEEP will simply end in 1977. The guidelines necessary for success are only now being imposed when the program has been slated for extinction. One result is that there is a danger of sacrificing the educational momentum that some people in the criminal justice system have worked for years to generate. The program is relatively new and there is an opportunity to make it successful even at a reduced funding level. Some criminal justice personnel do report personal benefit from their LEEP experiences and some agency heads report that increased education has improved the quality of their personnel. To abandon the LEEP venture and still impose increased educational requirements, as many jurisdictions are likely to do, will only cause further problems.

In summary, we have described the history of LEEP in one small private college. It is our impression that the problems we have described can be accounted for by too many interest groups pulling in too many directions at the federal level, with this conflict superimposed on an organizational climate in the small college itself so beset by crisis that it was ill-suited to implement such a delicate program. Put another way, the educational innovation hoped for from this program was seriously compromised by organizational problems at the level of the funding agency and by organizational inadequacies at the level of the college. None of the problems we have described were trivial and it would be naive to think they would have been wished away by a mere spirit of greater cooperation. However, even something as mundane as a survey of the interests of program participants would have made it possible to anticipate the major sources of tension and to devise workable organizational strategies to manage them. As the program stands—and we believe this applies to most of the similar programs funded from the same source—the organizational climate is the greatest obstacle to adequate service delivery.

REFERENCES

Carter, Robert and E. K. Nelson
1973 "The law enforcement education program—one university's experience." Journal of Police Science and Administration 1: 491-494.
Corwin, Ronald
1975 "Innovation in organizations: the case of schools." Sociology of Education 48: 1-37.
Etzioni, Amitai
1964 Modern Organizations. Englewood Cliffs, New Jersey: Prentice-Hall.
Fry, Lincoln J. and Jon Miller
1975 "Responding to skid row alcoholism: self-defeating arrangements in an innovative treatment program". Social Problems 22: 675-688.
Kuldau, Von
1975 "Criminal justice education: myths or reality." The Police Chief 42: 18-19.
Kuykendall, Jack and Armand Hernandez
1975 "A curriculum development model: quality control programming in justice education." The Police Chief 42: 20-25.

Merton, Robert K.
   1957   Social Theory and Social Structure. Glencoe, Illinois: Free Press.
Miller, Jon and Lincoln J. Fry
   1976   "Re-examining assumptions about education and professionalism in law enforcement." Journal
          of Police Science and Administration 4: 187-196.
Misner, Gordon
   1975   "Accreditation of criminal justice education programs." The Police Chief 42:14-16, 78.
Moore, Merlyn
   1975   "The field and academia: a message." The Police Chief 42: 66-69.
Perrow, C.
   1961   "The analysis of goals in complex organizations." American Sociological Review 26: 854-866.
Senna, Joseph
   1974   "Criminal justice higher education—its growth and directions." Crime and Delinquency: 389-
          404.
Sills, D. L.
   1957   The Volunteers. Glencoe, Illinois: The Free Press.
Smith, Dennis and Elinor Ostrom
   1974   "The effects of training and education on police attitudes and performance: a preliminary
          analysis." Workshop in Political Theory and Policy Analysis: Indiana University.
Task Force Report: The Police
   1976   Task Force on the Police, the President's Commission on Law Enforcement and the Administra-
          tion of Justice. Washington, D.C.: U.S. Government Printing Office.

EDUCATIONAL POLICY FOR THE LARGE CITIES

ROBERT J. HAVIGHURST
University of Chicago

In order to rebuild the inner city, we must solve the problem of educating children in the inner city schools. Bloom's findings suggest a solution to this problem: all children can master ordinary school curriculum and therefore a strategy of equal end products is viable.

The Crisis of Public Education lies in the big cities. All of the big cities show below average scores on tests of school achievement, with little or no improvement since 1965, when Congress passed the Elementary and Secondary Education Act aimed to raise the school achievement of students in the low-income areas of the great cities.

There has been more or less continuous flight of white middle-income parents of school-age children to the suburbs of the large cities. This, together with continuous migration of black and Spanish-speaking families to the cities has produced more and more ethnic segregation in the public schools. Decreasing school enrollments, due mainly to lower birth rates but also partly to decreasing population of some big cities, creates actual or theatened reduction of school system expenditures, resulting in unrest among teachers.

With this situation, worsened rather than bettered during the past five years, questions about educational policy and practice in the big cities are inevitable, as are demands for changed and presumably better educational policy. I think much of the analysis underlying these demands is over-simplified and often incorrect. However, there is a need for analysis of the problem, and for some useful indication of its basic causes, and of the directions improved educational policy and practice should take.

SOME FAULTY ANALYSES AND PRESCRIPTIONS

There are five groups of critics and analysts of education at the elementary and secondary levels who have had more attention and more influence over educational policy than was good for the cause of education. They are:

1. *Proponents of local community control of public schools and of political decentralization of school government in the big cities.* There was a period of three or four years when this kind of reform of big city education seemed promising to many thoughtful and well-informed people. The drama played out in New York City from 1967 to 1970 will at least help us to avoid some major mistakes. In 1967, the New York City Board of Education set aside three areas of the city for an experiment in local community participation in the operation of the schools. Two of the "demonstration areas" were black and Puerto Rican in composition, and the other was Chinese and Puerto Rican. The Ford Foundation provided funds for Professor Marilyn Gittell, a social scientist at Queens College, to advise and assist these projects. At the same time, Mayor Lindsay appointed an Advisory Panel, chaired by President McGeorge Bundy of the Ford Foundation, to advise on the problems of the New York City School System. This Panel reported in Autumn of 1967, under the title, *Reconnection for Learning*, and proposed the school system be subdivided into at least 30 community school districts with elementary school boards largely independent of the New York City School Board. Ultimately the New York State Legislature in 1969 directed the New York City Board of Education to create 30 to 33 community districts, each having an elected community board with substantial powers over the elementary schools, but not the high schools. The *New York Times*, in an editorial on November 9, 1967, welcomed the

145

report of the McGeorge Bundy citizens' panel recommending decentralization of the city school system with the following words:

> If this proposal is radical, it is justified by the fact that the situation is desperate. If the cure is drastic, it is necessary because a long succession of moderate reform efforts has failed to halt the deterioration of New York City's gigantic school system. . . .

During the period from 1967 to 1969, a heated controversy arose in the Ocean Hill-Brownsville area of Brooklyn over the action of the local "people's school board" in discharging certain teachers, and there was an extended teachers' strike called by the New York City United Federation of Teachers to support the teachers. The Federation claimed they had been unfairly treated. After the New York City Board of Education followed the State Legislature's order to create autonomous elementary school districts with locally elected school boards, the community districts were created with boundaries that tended to preserve racial and ethnic segregation, and it was no longer possible for the City Board of Education to work effectively for racial integration in the elementary schools. The performance of school children on standardized tests did not improve. A 1976 publication on Children in New York City, made by the Foundation for Child Development, documents the contemporary pathology of children and youth in the City of New York.

The movement for local community control grew powerfully in many of the large cities, after 1965. Detroit went through a period of local dissension over problems of racial segregation, and eventually the Michigan State Legislature in 1969 passed a law dividing the Detroit School District into eight regions, each with an elected regional school board. The Central School Board is composed of thirteen persons, one each from the eight regional boards, and five elected from the city at large.

These two areas, New York City and Detroit, are examples of *political decentralization*, with a maximum of local community control. They are somewhat contrasted with a program of *administrative decentralization,* occuring during the same period in a number of large cities. In the latter type of decentralization, the central school board retains authority over the entire school system, but establishes a number of *local advisory councils* chosen by local communities to work with the staff of the school and then often with the district superintendent. Chicago and Los Angeles have taken this course. Some of the advisory councils have asserted themselves vigorously enough to cause the removal of school principals or the choice of new principals and teachers seen as more in harmony with the minority groups dominating the local schools.

The case of Detroit illustrates further the errors of breaking the big city into local or regional school districts with autonomy. Detroit schools cannot now cooperate effectively on a city-wide basis for such goals as racial integration, since the eight regional school districts have boundaries which favor segregation. Chicago and Los Angeles, which did not go beyond *administrative decentralization* have had better records of flexible and city-wide attack on school problems and issues.

2. *Upper middle-class domination and anglo racism are the seat of the problem.* This general view of the situation argues that, since the middle of the 19th century, the American upper-middle class has dominated the public school system, structuring it and administering it to favor the children of the middle class, severely limiting the educational opportunity of poor people, European ethnic minorities, and black and Spanish-origin minorities. As evidence for this conclusion, facts are given on the numbers of ethnic minority group children retarded a year or more in school, leaving school before reaching or finishing high school. Some leaders of the black minority argue that similar prejudice has operated in the school system, even after the 1954 Supreme Court Decision eliminated the dual school system of the South and some northern communities.

This general analysis of the problem certainly has some facts in its favor, but has been used uncritically by apologists for certain minority groups to avoid careful study of the problem in all its complexity, identifying what certainly are multiple causes. For instance, the considerable degree of upward economic mobility of the ethnic groups has not been reported carefully by those crities, nor how much it owes to public education. If mentioned, this essential fact has been dismissed with the statement that the Anglo upper middle-class has "permitted" a small amount of upward mobility through education as a means of rewarding a few people who then join the "conspiracy" on behalf of their children, while the mass of the minority groups are systematically excluded from educational opportunity.

3. *The American capitalist economic-political structure denies educational opportunity to the mass of the workers; we need a socialist society.* This ideological argument is used by a small group of critics with or without data on the educational and economic achievement of youth in the various economic classes. As a statement of ideology, it deserves attention from students of the socio-political structure of society and its relation to the educational system. There is evidence from other countries that a socialist society does more to provide educational opportunity for the youth of the manual working class than does a capitalist society. But serious students of the present educational problem in the USA must turn elsewhere to seek solutions, unless they believe enough unrest will arise in American society during the next 25 years to produce a revolution. Otherwise, the holders of this viewpoint will have to work for minor political changes to move gradually in the socialist direction.

4. *Advocates of "de-schooling society."* In terms of the amount of influence it has had upon educational policy and practice, the group that gathered around Ivan Illich and his writing hardly deserves mention. Illich has flitted on to other causes, always serving as a useful gadfly, but offering little or nothing substantial as basis for real improvement. The de-schoolers argue that the middle classes have kept the masses out of the pathway of progress leading through education, though their evidence is even less persuasive than that of the critics in the second group above. And proponents do not offer any solution that would really help poor people. For instance, Illich's proposal of a set of "learning exchanges" where people assemble to teach those who want to learn is an interesting middle-class idea now operating in several places serving middle-class people. But the de-schoolers have yet to tell us how the mother of five children living on Aid for Dependent Children can find ways to get education for her children wandering in the streets of the big city ghetto, after Illich's de-schooling proposal goes into effect. Public schools have more promise for poor children, and children of poor families have more need of public schools than any other group in this country.

5. *The "anarchist-individualist" group who argue that children should determine what kind of education they need.* This recurring theme of John Holt and others who have not taught the children of the poor in the big cities has found favor with many devoted and some gifted teachers who work in "open schools" or "free schools" in the big cities, nearly always serving children of middle-class parents. One looks in vain for any indication of a workable policy and practice coming from this group applicable to the school systems of the big cities.

WHAT, THEN, IS THE PROBLEM AND WHAT IS THE SOLUTION?

If these varied approaches to the problem of public education in the big cities do not work, what will? What analyses of the problem are most worth carrying through? What policies should be developed?

I believe that attention and action should focus on three institutions: the family, the school, and the big city; and effective action is now under way in all three areas.

HELPING THE FAMILY DO ITS PART

It has been well-known for 30 years that the school achievement of children and youth is closely correlated with the socioeconomic status of their families. James Coleman's (1966) study established for a national sample of public school students that the largest known share of the variation in school achievement test scores was predicted by the socioeconomic status of the family. This finding had been fully demonstrated in smaller samples and more intensive researches. The University of Wisconsin group centered around William Sewell and Robert Hauser have investigated this pattern for rural and urban youth in the state of Wisconsin. Although there are minor criticisms of the statistical methods and the sampling methods used by these and other researchers, no one seriously doubts that the family socioeconomic status is the most significant cause we know about in the school achievement of children and youth.

Since socioeconomic status is generally measured rather crudely by combining indices of parents' educational level, prestige of father's occupation, and family income, it is recognized that these are only indicators of processes occurring in the home to help or hinder a child's learning in school.

The nature of these processes was explored and demonstrated by some of Benjamin Bloom's students in the period from about 1963 to 1965. Dave, and Wolf, among others, interviewed samples of families whose socioeconomic status and children's school achievement varied over a wide range. These researchers knew that the correlation coefficient of school achievement and family SES was about .4 to .5 for these children. They produced a measure of "Family Press" or family environment, based on interviews with the parents, which counted such things as: frequency of parents reading with and to their children, presence of children's encyclopedias in the home; provision for children doing their home work; frequency of visits to museums; use of the public library. Their scores for Family Press showed a coefficient of correlation of .7 to .8 with achievement in school.

Other researchers have worked with mothers of young children, to help them learn to teach their children and to help their children do better in school. The work of Susan Gray and of Phyllis Levenstein shows that this procedure improves the school performance of young children.

In the most recent years the "Child-Parent Center" procedure has been developed in a number of big city school systems to help the children in areas of low income. For instance, in Chicago a total of ten Child-Parent Center programs were instituted in schools in low-income areas, bringing parents into contact with teachers when the children were four or five years old. These children have shown progress in reading at the level of national averages, though they come from families of low socioeconomic status.

Still, with all this cumulating evidence, some people, including some leaders of minority ethnic groups, continue to blame the public school system for what they call "racism," for prejudice against children of certain minority groups, for providing what they call "inferior" schooling to their children.

But the time seems to be at hand when at least some minority group leaders are placing the responsibility for school achievement of their children upon the parents and upon the minority groups. The black columnist, Carl Rowan, wrote a column entitled "Compensatory Education Helps," published in the *Chicago Daily News* on January 2, 1976. He commented on the findings of a report of the General Accounting Office of the federal government evaluating the use of Title 1 funds under the Elementary and Secondary Education Act. The GAO quoted state education officials as declaring Title 1 reading programs successful because: "more than 50 percent of the participants gained above the national average," and "35 percent of the deprived youngsters actually were closing the reading gap while six percent were holding even with the national norm." Rowan commented, "You must begin with an understanding that we are talking about seven million children who, with rare exceptions, have grown up in poverty, hunger, sickness and a stifling home environment, which is bereft of guidance or motivation."

This recognition that children from poverty-stricken homes, as a statistical group, are handicapped by their home experience has been dramatically stated more recently by the Reverend Jesse L. Jackson of Chicago. Writing in the *New York Times Magazine* for April 18, 1976, the leader and originator of PUSH (People United To Save Humanity) called on blacks to take positive responsibility for improving conditions in the big cities, and especially for improving the schools.

It is time, I think, for us to stand up, admit our failures and weaknesses and begin to strengthen ourselves. . . . What we must do for our young people is challenge them to put hope in their brains rather than dope in their veins. . . PUSH has begun a national program. . . to address urban problems, beginning with the public schools. . . Parents, teachers, superintendents, school boards have all failed to improve discipline and create a proper atmosphere for learning. And if our young people are not learning today, we will not have the doctors, engineers, lawyers, mechanics, nurses, clerks and accountants that we will need to manage the cities. . . The greatest potential for self-development is to be found in the public schools in our cities. Predominantly black schools in most urban areas with high concentrations of black people are largely out of control. Violence against students and teachers, perpetrated by students, is steadily and dangerously increasing. . . Discipline has broken down. We need to change this because it is necessary for our development, and because no one else is going to do it for us. . . Our program is simple. We want to get black men from the neighborhoods to replace the police in patrolling the school corridors and the street corners where the dope pushers operate. We want all parents to reserve the evening hours of 7 to 9 for their children's homework. We want student leaders and athletes to help identify and solve discipline problems before they get out of control. We want the black-oriented media to find ways to publicly reward achievers (72-73).

If the school system can come to terms with leaders of the minority groups where children do least well in school, both on the national and the local scene, that will become the basis for the next two major steps in educational policy and practices.

REVIVAL OF THE CENTRAL CITY

If present trends continue, the big cities of the United States will become increasingly Black or Hispanic. For example, the minority population of Atlanta was 38 percent in 1960 and 52 percent in 1970. The Atlanta public school system became 69 percent minority (almost all black) in 1970. Black student enrollment increased by 146,000 between 1970 and 1972 in the 100 largest school districts of the country, while total enrollment in the same districts decreased by 280,000 students.

It is always dangerous to put much faith in extrapolations of past trends, especially in the area of population change. Yet a variety of critical analyses based on current demographic data and on studies of central city and suburban population change in the larger metropolitan areas leave no doubt that these basic population changes will extend over the next 25 years, unless *major* economic and educational policies are created to arrest or reverse trends.

Such policy changes are already in the making, and educators are involved in them. The goal of these policies is to make the central or inner city part of the big metropolitan areas more attractive to middle-income people of all ethnic groups, so as to increase the inner city population and to make it economically and racially integrated.

HOW TO CREATE AN INTEGRATED INNER CITY

Harpers Magazine for January, 1975, contained an article by Arthur M. Louis entitled *The Worst American City*. He gave the "vital statistics" of the fifty largest American cities. A variety of indices were combined to give composite or global ratings, with the following cities at the top of the list from best on down: Seattle, Tulsa, San Diego, San Jose, Honolulu, Portland (Oregon), Denver, Minneapolis, Oklahoma City, Omaha. The author notes (p. 71) that several of those cities have expanded their boundaries by annexing suburbs, or they originally covered an extensive area of open land which became suburbs. "By absorbing suburbs, with their lower crime rates, greater affluence and better health and housing conditions, a city can dramatically improve its vital statistics." From the bottom and moving up, the order of cities is: Newark, St. Louis, Chicago, Detroit, Baltimore, Birmingham, Jacksonville, Cleveland, Norfolk, San Antonio. Examining these cities, one notes that the "better" cities are all well under a million in population, and they tend to have relatively small proportions of black or Hispanic population.

However, it is not the presence of the minorities in smaller or larger proportions that causes the city to be "good" or "bad," but health, housing quality, educational level, crime, income level, transportation facilities. City government, business, and educational leaders are working to make the cities "better." The inner city, or the "central city" of a Standard Metropolitan Statistical Area, must return to full vigor if the large city is to prosper. With its downtown offices, central library, museums, department stores, theaters, universities, and community colleges, the inner city cannot function effectively for the entire urban population unless it is integrated racially and economically. And these facilities cannot be dispersed among the suburbs and still serve the population of the metropolitan area efficiently.

Specific improvements for the inner city. Enough big city renovation activity is now occurring to enable us to review the range and variety of constructive contribution to a viable and healthy inner city. New or well-kept middle-income housing is essential. There must be some major supplementation to the subsidized public housing which came in the 1950s and did much to turn white residential areas into segregated ghettoes. The public housing funds were mistakenly allocated to the building of high-rise apartment blocks in areas of deteriorated housing, and these buildings were generally rented to low income families on a segregated basis.

Several cities are now encouraging private capital to build good middle-income housing on land (sometimes vacated by railroad yards and sometimes set free by light industry) but always within easy bus or subway rides from the downtown area. Areas already with these characteristics are in demand for rental housing and condominium sales. For instance, the Hyde Park-Kenwood area of Chicago is 15 minutes by frequent commuter trains from downtown Chicago. This area has become integrated mainly in the past 20 years. The public and private schools are varied and suit a variety of educational tastes. The University of Chicago is located in this area, and helps to stablize the integrated residential population.

There are generally stretches of vacant land near the downtown area of a big city, some of it from unused railway freight yards, some from housing that has deteriorated so badly that it has been taken over and torn down by city or federal authorities. These areas can be restored to middle-income occupancy by people who work in the downtown area. In effect, if rents are modest, these areas will represent bargains for families with young children, who have hitherto depended on automobile transportation to work. The growing cost of gasoline makes it necessary to seek cheaper transportation, by bus or subway in the inner city.

The two impediments to middle-income occupancy of these areas are crime on the streets and segregated minority schools. Both of these can be and are being changed by police work and by the maintenance of integrated neighborhood schools or magnet schools. The key which unlocks the door to these improvements is the collaboration of local city government with the local school board, and local business leadership.

Stabilization of population in existing middle-income areas. The big cities have in the past 20 years developed large areas of minority residential segregation where the minority groups have stable middle-level incomes. The minority groups are generally black or Hispanic, but they are similar in income level to the Polish, Italian, Greek and Slav groups established in areas of the big cities during the past 30 years.

These residential areas are not as tightly segregated as the low-income areas of the big city, and generally not so large (for any one ethnic group) as to fill up a high school area, though often they do fill up one or more elementary schools. Furthermore, these middle-income residential areas will not be subject to pressure for more housing by black and Hispanic families if some of the former low income ghetto areas are renovated with middle-income housing described in the preceding section.

For large cities with black or Hispanic populations up to 100,000, high schools can be integrated, but some elementary schools may be filled with minority pupils. On the edges of these residentially segregated areas, magnet schools can be located with free bus transportation for pupils, and with enrollment quotas.

However, for the cities with as many as half a million black or Hispanic population, the present pattern of residential segregation may persist for the next 25 years, and these areas will be large enough to maintain segregated high schools over that period of time. For the large cities with large minority populations steadily moving up the economic scale, such as Chicago, Cleveland, Detroit, St. Louis, Philadelphia, New York, Los Angeles, the most effective action to increase racial integration in the schools is to establish a number of very attractive magnet schools, with free bus transportation for students.

Magnet schools are crucial. The *magnet school* has proved a most valuable and essential innovation in the several large cities where the Board of Education has succeeded in moving toward racial integration. Cincinnati and Houston have made noteworthy progress in the most recent years, largely through the deliberate and carefully planned use of magnet schools. According to James N. Jacobs, of the Cincinnati school system, the potential market for alternative or magnet schools is 20 to 40 percent of the student population, depending on resources and promotion of the concept.

How rapidly can stable integrated education come in the large cities? A major contribution to my thinking about this question has been made by Gary Orfield in an article in the journal *Social Policy* for January-February, 1976. He proposes a two-fold strategy. First, inner-city redevelopment and revival, along the lines suggested here. Second, a program of metropolitan area-wide desegregation with some busing of pupils, and a vigorous policy of metro-wide open housing.

The broad strategy is based upon the assumption that municipal government, the public school system, and the business and professional leaders of the city can and do work together on a concerted plan to make the central city more attractive to middle-income people. Under these circumstances, the schools can move steadily toward a greater degree of integration, and the amount of residential integration will increase, especially when any family can count on gaining access to magnet schools for its children, if unsatisfied with the local neighborhood school.

I think the next 25 years will very probably succeed in establishing stable, integrated education in the big cities, based on a substantial degree of residential integration. This trend will require something like a Coordinating Council, consisting of representatives of government, education, business, labor and the professions, acting as the conscience of the city, and marshalling public opinion on local issues that favor or militate against integration.

SCHOOL SYSTEM POLICY AND PRACTICE

The third area of policy and practice leading toward basic and permanent improvement lies within the school system. No doubt the school system needs change in order to bear its appropriate and necessary share of the vast weight of the problem of education in the big cities. There certainly have been urban educators who tried to blame the poor school achievement of students in the big city public schools on conditions over which they say have little or no control—especially the inadequate help given many children by their parents, and the flight of middle-class and especially middle-class white families from the central cities of the big metropolitan areas.

But this fault of some educators has been belabored by enthusiastic bureaucracy-haters. The bureaucracy of the big city school system has been a favorite target. And there is some factual basis for the charge that the "experts" in the field of educational administration, who held sway over most big city school systems from about 1910 to 1970, supported by prestigious university schools of education, have been too slow to move where action was needed. I believe the most effective exponent of this view is Michael Katz, whose book, *Class, Bureaucracy and the Schools: The Illusion of Educational Change in America*, was published in 1971.

> Bureaucratization has lessened their sensitivity to their communities, to their students, and to the informed and constructive criticism that would make progress possible. . . . American education still lacks a real alternative model to hierarchical bureaucracy. . . . One consequence of bureaucratization, Amitai Etzioni has pointed out, is the separation of *consumption*, "those who are served by an organization, from *control*, those who *direct* it" (103).

But there has been positive and valuable change in the school system, especially with the aid of money from Title 1 of the Elementary and Secondary Education Act, and with money from the Bilingual Education Act. David Tyack closes his 1974 book on *The One Best System: The History of American Urban Education* with this sentence:

> To create urban schools which really teach students, which reflect the pluralism of the society, which serve the quest for social justice—this is a task which will take persistent imagination, wisdom, and will (291).

I thoroughly agree, and I believe it can only be achieved through a strong school administration, with power over a wide population area, preferably a metropolitan area, with a strong planning function, and with a bureaucracy.

Beyond this issue of the use of a bureaucracy to operate a large school system efficiently, lies the issue of *what and how much the schools can be expected to teach*. It just may be that we as educators have been misled by our doctrine of *individual differences in learning ability*. We may be on the verge of developing a new set of beliefs and practices about the learning ability of what in the past we have called "average" and "below average" students. This change will probably be fostered by a new book by Benjamin Bloom entitled *Human Characteristics and School Learning*.

Bloom's message is that the long-accepted doctrine of "individual differences" in a normal population of students has no factual basis in the abilities of the students to learn what the school attempts to teach. The book makes a basic distinction between "intelligence" as measured by an ordinary intelligence test and ability to learn the material in the school curriculum. The ordinary intelligence test does not measure "ability to learn," according to Bloom. The school can and should work for *equality of outcome* in school learning, rather than *equality of opportunity*. The latter goal implies there will be a range of outcomes due to a range of abilities of students, and this does not need to happen. If students are taught systematically and appropriately, individual differences in what they learn will approach the vanishing point. Some students require a slightly longer period of study, but not much longer, if their knowledge level is diagnosed accurately and they are taught the material they need at the level where they are now. Many students have difficulty in "keeping up" with the class in the ordinary school because they come with a variety of "entry skills" or "entry knowledge." For example, in the sixth grade of a school, the teacher treats students alike, giving the same lesson assignments, not because students are at the same level of previous knowledge, but because, according to the doctrine of individual differences, some are *better* and some are *poorer* learners than others. If they all have equal "opportunity," the knowledge they gain in this sixth grade will be distributed according to the "normal" distribution, from high to low. Bloom says teachers should not assume that some pupils are "good learners" and some are "poor learners." In this situation, the teacher's job is to discover who are the slower learners, where they stand with respect to the knowledge and skills expected of sixth graders, and then teach them systematically from the base of their present level of entry skills and knowledge. If the teacher does this, the slower learners will learn as much as the faster learners.

In effect, Bloom has set aside the concept of "intelligence," which he investigated so thoroughly in his book published in 1964—*Stability and Change in Human Characteristics*—arguing that the quality measured by an intelligence test need not control how much the student learns of the school curriculum. He says:

> Generalized characteristics of the learner—such as intelligence and aptitudes—are highly resistant to modification, while characteristics such as specific prerequirements and motivation for a particular learning task are modifiable to a greater degree at most stages in the individual's history. . . (15).
>
> But even more important are the notions (1) that the student's ability to learn as indicated by the time and effort required to learn a particular set of tasks is highly alterable and (2) that under ideal conditions there will be little variation in students' ability to learn when judged in terms of time and effort required to learn one or more learning tasks for which the students are adequately prepared and motivated and for which instruction is appropriate to the learners (15).
>
> The central thesis of this book is that variations in learning and the level of learning of students are determined by the students' learning history and the quality of instruction they receive (16).

ANALYZING BLOOM'S THEORY OF LEARNING

The *general theory of school learning* which is the substance of this book has grown out of Bloom's work on mastery learning, which he now regards as a special case of the more general theory. This theory consists of generalizations about schooling, learning, and human characteristics. The theory attempts to explain school learning in terms of three interdependent variables.

a. How far the student has already learned the basic prerequisites to the learning to be accomplished.

b. How far the student is (or can be) motivated to engage in the learning process.

c. How far the instruction to be given is appropriate to the learner.

These variables are all measurable, and this book shows how the three variables account for school learning and differences in school learning in any of a number of school systems studied. Furthermore, this theory has been tested in several countries, with similar results.

Bloom says that he was much influenced in the beginning of his work on mastery learning by John B. Carroll's *Model of School Learning* (1963). Carroll stated that if students have a normal distribution of *aptitude* for learning some subject and if they are all given exactly the *same instruction* (in terms of amount and quality of instruction and learning time allowed) then their achievement measured at the completion of instruction and study will be normally distributed. Under such conditions the relationship (coefficient of correlation) between students' aptitude measured at the beginning of the instruction and their achievement measured at the end of instruction will be relatively high (about +.70). Conversely, if students are normally distributed with respect to aptitude, but the kind and quality of instruction and the amount of time allowed for study are made appropriate to the characteristics and needs of *each* learner, the majority of students will achieve *mastery* of the subject. In this case, the correlation coefficient between aptitude measured at the beginning of instruction and achievement measured at the end of instruction should approach zero.

The student of mastery learning will recognize that Bloom and his associates did just this for several groups of students and several school learning subjects and proved that they could teach students to a mastery level, despite differences among students in "aptitude." Thus, the researchers pushed the correlation coefficient to zero between "aptitude" as measured by intelligence tests or previous achievement in this subject area and achievement under mastery learning programs. From this time on, Bloom ceases to be much concerned about measuring "aptitude" of students, and becomes concerned about diagnosing their needs and characteristics relevant to the subject matter to be learned. That is, he turns his attention to the three interdependent variables around which his general theory of learning is built.

The three major interdependent variables have been analyzed and studied by Bloom and others in enough detail to form the main body of this book, though Bloom says there is much yet to be done. Each of the three variables is treated at some length in a chapter, with the following titles:

Cognitive Entry Behaviors
Affective Entry Characteristics
Quality of Instruction

Bloom points out that attention to each of the three major interdependent variables alone produces improved school learning. The individual teacher or school principal can often do something to improve the class or the school by working with one or another of these variables. But it is more complex and more difficult to combine improvement of all three of the variables, or any two of them—Quality of Instruction, Cognitive Entry Behaviors, and Affective Entry Characteristics. The goal is to apply all three variables together, and thus to get a mastery level of achievement for nearly every student. Perhaps a practicable goal would be to reduce the variation of students' achievement to about ten percent of what is observed in a regular school program without mastery learning procedures. Actually, Bloom reports several studies which did reduce the achievement variation to about 20 percent of the variation in school classes without mastery learning programs.

All of this is to state that the interrelation of the variables in this theory is a problem that has only been touched at the surface. The separate contributions of the variables is relatively clear. However, the ways in which the variables in combination alter both the teaching and learning processes as well as the cognitive and affective outcomes of the learning is largely a problem of the future (20).

Bloom closes with some statements of values motivating him and his colleagues.

The distribution of school achievement is a direct consequence of student involvement in the learning process and of instructional processes used by teachers and others in the school situation. Each distribution (of school achievement by students) is causally related to the variables we have described, and ignorance about them does not free the teacher or the school from responsibility for them. We prefer distributions which are indicative that most students have mastered what the school has to teach (205).

The message will galvanize many vigorous and resourceful educators. The schools can make a difference, and a big difference in the case of students who would otherwise do poorly in school achievement. But if the schools are to make this kind of difference, there must be major changes in the methods of teaching, the methods of organizing a school for improved learning. And these changes must be brought about through improved teacher training and improved school administration.

What this book does for educational policy and practice is to re-distribute the weight of responsibility for low school achievement to a more even balance among the three factors discussed here—the home, the political and social leadership of the city, and the school. Bloom argues that the teacher, as "manager of the learning situation," can work with the students' cognitive and motivational status to permit the "slow" student to learn the material in the ordinary school to a "mastery criterion," with the slower students needing only ten to 20 percent more time than the fastest 20 percent of this group. But of course this kind of learning outcome depends on appropriate curriculum, materials of instruction, diagnostic materials, and methods of teaching.

CONCLUSION

With these three basic factors in a constructive program of educational policy and practice, I see the job ahead for the remainder of this century to be fairly clearly outlined, requiring much research and hard work, and well within the capacity of the American society.

REFERENCES

Block, James H. (ed.)
1974 Schools, Society, and Mastery Learning. New York: Holt, Rinehart and Winston.
Bloom, Benjamin S.
1976 Human Characteristics and School Learning. New York: McGraw-Hill.
Carroll, J. B.
1963 "A model of school learning." Teachers College record 64:723-733.
Coleman, James S.
1966 Equality of Educational Opportunity. Washington, D.C.: Government Printing Office.
Jackson, Jesse L.
1976 "Give the people a vision." New York Times Magazine (April 18).
Katz, Michael
1971 Class, Bureaucracy, and the Schools: The Illusion of Educational Change in America. New York: Praeger.
Lash, Trude W. and Heidi Sigal
1976 State of the Child: New York City. New York: Foundation for Child Development.
Louis, Arthur M.
1975 "The worst American city." Harpers (January).
Mayor's Advisory Panel on Decentralization of the New York City Schools
1967 Reconnection for Learning: A Community School System for New York City. New York: Ford Foundation.
Orfield, Gary
1976 "Is Coleman right?" Social Policy 6(No. 4): 24-29.
Tyack, David
1974 The One Best System: The History of American Urban Education. Cambridge, Massachusetts: Harvard University Press.
Wolf, Richard
1966 "The measurement of environments." in Testing Problems in Perspective, Anne Anastasi (ed.) Washington D.C.: American Council on Education.

PROFESSIONALIZATION AND THE PROFESSORIATE

LIONEL S. LEWIS
The State University of
New York at Buffalo

MICHAEL N. RYAN
Niagara County
Community College

This paper examines how the professoriate has attempted, with only moderate success, to fashion an identity. Academics define themselves as professionals and, like countless other occupations, have for many years sought to have this characterization publicly recognized in order to attain commensurate power and rewards. They have mostly depended on the professional association, which in turn rests heavily on information, education, and persuasion to further its claim. However, some weaknesses in this approach are evident. The paper concludes with the suggestion that the professoriate's increasing dependence on labor unions to defend its autonomy may not have any significant effect on the structure of institutions of higher learning, but may only erode the core principle of merit.

A new militancy is said to characterize American academics: in response to the "depression" in higher education, the professoriate is becoming more conscious of its economic interests, and has actively begun to challenge those, principally administrators, who would threaten professional prerogatives. Consider, for example, the growing number of faculty who are joining labor unions. According to Kemerer and Baldridge (1975:1), in 1966 there were 11 campuses with faculty bargaining units; in 1970, the figure was 160, and by mid-1975, it was 430.

Is collective bargaining as a new force on American campuses a harbinger of significant changes in the course of higher education? Is there evidence that faculty are prepared to transcend or abandon their self-image and ideology to alter not merely the structure of one or another committee, but the core of the educational process, e.g., what is taught, how things are taught? This seems unlikely.

Those who will need to know how the professoriate will react to conditions in the 1980's and beyond, may learn from a close look at how the professoriate has attempted over the years to fashion one important aspect of its self-definition, that of being professional. This paper focuses on the endeavors over a fifty-nine-year period of the professoriate to formulate an ideology that would affirm its professional status. The path has been circuitous, and its success has been mixed and uncertain. Some of the time, the ideology that claims professional status seems to have taken on a life of its own, at the expense of concrete benefits to the professoriate. Most of the time, it seems to have clouded the professoriate's perception of its real status and interests. Yet, the approach taken by academics is fairly consistent with what one would expect given what is known about the process of professionalization and the working conditions of professors.

According to Eliot Freidson (1973:22):

> Professionalization might be defined as a process by which an organized occupation, usually but not always by virtue of making a claim to special esoteric competence and to concern for the quality of its work and its benefits to society, obtains the exclusive right to perform a particular kind of work, control training for and access to it, and control the right of determining and evaluating the way the work is performed.

Everett Hughes (1963:655-56) has suggested that service and trust are, in fact, the sum and substance of professional performance—more central than technical competence emphasized by Parsons (1937). The principles of service and of the possession of esoteric knowledge thus seem at the heart of the professional's claim for autonomy. These observations are consistent with what Bennett and Hokenstad (1973:28) see "to be the *core* essentials of the ideal type [profession] : a knowledge base, a service ideal, and autonomy (trust)" or Wilensky's (1964: 137) "traditional model of professionalism which emphasizes autonomous expertise and the service ideal." The extent of an occupation's autonomy is the very quality that determines its location along the professional-employee continuum.

Haug and Sussman (1973:89-91) believe professionalization, like unionization, is a process "by which members of an occupation seek to achieve collective upward mobility" by improving their work conditions and rewards without engaging "in a power contest," as labor unions do. Instead "the association undertakes to protect and expand the profession's knowledge base, enforce standards of learning, entry and performance, and engage in similar activities. . . " (1973:91). Yet, as Perrucci (1973:122) has noted, "a basic *resource* that is necessary for any occupational group seeking to transform itself into a profession is *power*." Haug and Sussman (1973:92) have also observed that when professions are pursued in organizational settings, because "the role of the professional association and of the union overlap in the context of bureaucratic controls," they like all other employees must adopt some of the features of unionization.

THE AMERICAN ASSOCIATION OF UNIVERSITY PROFESSORS

American academics have sought professional status since they ceased viewing themselves as schoolmasters sometime near the end of the nineteenth century. Laurence R. Veysey (1965:355-56) notes that their aspirations gained momentum in the first fifteen years of the twentieth century when, in growing numbers, professors made "the claim for exemption from interference on the ground that they were 'professional experts'. . . . The plea for a 'professional' definition of academic goals . . . culminated in the establishment of the American Association of University Professors in 1915."

The founding of the American Association of University Professors (AAUP) represented the first attempt on a national scale to unite the professoriate and to elevate its status. Since then this organization has been central in promoting the ends of the professoriate. This effort has focused on activities characteristic of all professional associations, which are formed for the precise purpose of protecting and advancing the prerogatives of the individual members of an occupation (Greenwood, 1957:51; Vollmer and Mills, 1966:153). "The American Association of University Professors has other purposes than increasing the bargaining power of members," Wilson (1942:119) has noted, "but this [the protection and advancement of in-group status] is its most important objective. . . . "

The Presidential Addresses

In order to identify the scope and nature of the professoriate's claim for professional status, a content analysis of each of the bi-annual convention addresses of AAUP presidents was completed. These addresses, usually delivered near the end of the incumbent's term, are not taken as literal representations of the state of all or most academics at any particular time, but they do reveal recurring themes, patterns, or trends from which inferences may be drawn.

While the AAUP is at the core of this analysis, this organization is not seen as the sole influence in the process of the professionalization of the professoriate. Rather, it is a visible, organized voice expressing concerns fairly consistent with those of many college and university faculty. Recognizing that no single group or organization always expresses the sentiments of such a diverse occupation, no other formal body of academics, until recently, has emerged with an ideology in conflict with it.

The speeches of thirty-two AAUP presidents covering the years from the organization's founding in 1915 to 1974 are analyzed. Figure 1 shows the presidents whose speeches are contained within this study and the years of their tenure in office.

Relevant statements were identified and coded according to their subject matter. A count summarized the number of speeches where references to a specific phenomenon appeared and the total number of times the topic was addressed in all of the speeches. The coding system contained six major categories:

FIGURE 1

Presidential Addresses

Tenure	President	Year of Publication	AAUP Bulletin Volume	Pages
1915–1916	John Dewey	1915	1	9–13
1916–1917	John H. Wigmore	1916	2 (No. 1)	8–10
			2 (No. 5)	9–52
1917–1918	Frank Thilly	1917	3	11–24
1918–1919	J. M. Coulter	1918	4 (No. 7)	11–12
			4 (No. 1)	3
1919–1920	Arthur O. Lovejoy	1919	5	10–40
1920–1921	Edward Capps*			
1921–1922	Edwin R. A. Seligman	1922	8	6–26
1922–1924	Joseph Villiers Denney	1924	10	18–28
1924–1926	A. O. Leuschner	1926	12	90–99
1926–1928	W. T. Semple	1928	14	162–166
1928–1930	Henry Crew	1928	14	167–168
		1930	16	103–111
1930–1932	W. B. Munro	1932	18	6–17
1932–1934	Walter Wheeler Cook	1934	20	84–96
1934–1936	S. A. Mitchell	1936	22	93–97
1936–1938	A. J. Carlson	1938	24	9–18
1938–1940	Mark H. Ingraham	1940	26	13–34
1940–1942	Frederick S. Deibler	1942	28	32–45
1942–1944	William T. Laprade	1944	30	176–195
1944–1946	Quincy Wright	1947	33	43–54
1946–1948	Edward C. Kirkland	1948	34	15–26
1948–1950	Ralph H. Lutz	1950	36	18–32
1950–1952	Richard H. Shryock	1952	38	32–70
1952–1954	Fred B. Millett	1954	40	47–60
1954–1956	William E. Britton	1956	42	256–267
1956–1958	Helen C. White	1958	44	392–400
1958–1960	Bentley Glass	1960	46	149–155
1960–1962	Ralph F. Fuchs	1962	48	104–109
1962–1964	Fritz Machlup	1964	50	112–124
1964–1966	David Fellman	1966	52	105–110
1966–1968	Clark Byse	1968	54	143–148
1968–1970	Ralph S. Brown, Jr.	1970	56	118–122
1970–1972	Sanford H. Kadish	1972	58	120–125
1972–1974	Walter Adams	1974	60	119–125

*Capps' death, while in office, necessitated the appointment of Vernon L. Kellogg as Acting President, and he did not formally address Association members at the annual meeting.

1. Status–Remarks about professional models, or ideal types, to serve as a frame of reference for measuring progress toward professionalization.
2. Functions–Specific objectives of the Association.
3. Justifications–Any statement offering a rationale for seeking professional status, and its concomitant autonomy. Comments defending the objectives of the AAUP were also assigned to this group.
4. Tactics–Suggested methods that might be employed to attain the objectives of professionalization. These comments relate both to strategy and public posture.
5. Movement from Employee to Professional Status–Statements indicating the professoriate's location along the employee-professional continuum.
6. Obstacles to Success–Remarks that reflect or define the difficulties encountered in attempting to achieve the Association's objectives, e.g., statements considered symptomatic of the struggle to achieve autonomy in a bureaucratic setting.

While codification and tabulation are customarily associated with exacting empiricism, the figures generated by the content analysis should not be reified. Coding the content of speeches required the use of judgment when segments could not be neatly fitted into a coding system. In addition, some of the broader issues raised were placed into more than one category since a number of topics were discussed within a paragraph or series of sentences.

ACADEMICS AS INDEPENDENT PROFESSIONALS

The speeches reveal that physicians and lawyers, because they enjoy the kind of professional autonomy the professoriate desires, serve as models. But many are aware that the employee status of academics imposes formidable problems. As Richard H. Shryock (1952: 54) notes:

All would probably agree . . . that the quasi-employee status of academic men . . . lowers their general prestige. In contrast, the professional independence of physicians and lawyers may contribute something to their social standing.

Yet, this does not preclude Ralph F. Fuchs (1962:107) from arguing in the 1960's that the employed and self-employed can share the same honored status.

Working in a bureaucratic setting requires some modification of this professional model. The answer apparently has been found in the relative independence of faculty in certain European universities, particularly in Germany and England. Physicians and lawyers set the standard for measuring degree of autonomy while the conditions enjoyed by some European faculty represent an accommodation to the bureaucratic system. European faculties were on the mind of A. O. Leuschner in 1926 (94):

Many presidents have been chosen from the ranks of professors. After all, the title of this officer . . . does not matter much, but it is of great importance that his functions should permit of faculty cooperation in university government in accordance with the successful traditions of the Old World.

In 1938 (12), A. J. Carlson still thought

those who are afraid of permitting or encouraging an increasing democracy in university organization and university life should take a look at some of the well-known universities in Europe.

The evidence suggests the intention of establishing an academic guild.

From the outset, the AAUP is seen as eventually playing a role comparable to that of the American Medical Association and the American Bar Association. Frank Thilly in 1917 (11) restates a position outlined at the "Call for the Meeting for Organization of a National Association of University Professors," issued in 1914, by suggesting that a society, comparable to the American Bar Association and the American Medical Association in kindred professions, could be of substantial service to the ends for which universities exist. . . .

In 1922 (6), Edwin R. A. Seligman repeats:

> it has . . . been made abundantly clear that our Association must be regarded not as a trade union, but rather as an association comparable to the American Bar Association, or the American Medical Association.

Ten of the thirty-two speeches contain references to either doctors and lawyers, their professional organizations, or to European faculty. The issue is everpresent, found in speeches from 1917, 1918, 1922, 1926, 1930, 1938, 1952, 1962, 1966, and 1974, with a total of twenty-one such comments.

FUNCTIONS

From the perspective of these presidential addresses the AAUP has four basic functions: (1) unification; (2) establishing autonomy; (3) establishing standards; (4) improving job security. Table 1 specifies these functions, shows the number of speeches in which each is mentioned and the total number of references to it.

TABLE 1

Functions

Topic	Number of Speeches Topic Appears at Least Once	Total References (All Speeches)
1. Unify occupation and provide it with a collective voice	17	36
2. Free occupation from external control/interference	21	38
3. Establish/maintain occupational ethics/standards	14	21
4. Improve economic status/job security	9	20

In 1915 (11), John Dewey referred to the first of these four functions in warning that

> the Association must remain a national Association, concerned with common and fundamental interests. . . .

Some years later, Henry Crew (1930:103), looking back on the motives of the founding members of the Association, notes that:

> They came together in the belief that by joining forces they could raise the standard of the teaching profession, could increase its consciousness of power, and could create a vital interest in our common purpose.

Like the American Medical Association and the American Bar Association, the AAUP hoped eventually to speak for an entire occupation.

Table 1 illustrates that establishing the autonomy of the occupation has been of primary interest, although this is rarely explicit. The contention by William T. Laprade (1944:186) is fairly typical:

> A university is a great and indispensable organ of the higher life of a civilized community, in the work of which the trustees have an essential and highly honorable place, but in which the faculties hold an independent place, with quite equal responsibilities. . . .

While noticeably less prevalent than statements reflecting a desire to be free from external control, the establishment and maintenance of ethics and standards seems an essential corollary; it would be difficult to argue for freedom from outside interference without demonstrating a concern for internal control. John H. Wigmore (1916:32) optimistically reports:

> Now for the first time, since the formation of this Association, has the profession an organ of expression and a means of sanction for its professional ethical consensus.

In 1970 (121), Ralph S. Brown, Jr., suggests that

> another facet of responsibility is the promulgation and enforcement of standards of professional ethics. . . . It is a delicate and prickly business for us to purport to sit in judgment on the occasional derelictions of our colleagues. But if one of the conditions for the continued autonomy of a profession is its capacity for self-discipline, we had better get on with it.

It is probably symptomatic of a deeper malaise that after more than fifty years the Association is, apparently, yet to establish the machinery necessary for enforcing standards or ethics. As an AAUP self-survey ("Report of the self-survey committee of the AAUP," 1965:161) noted, "the Association . . . has no . . . tradition of procedures directed against its members who are guilty of violations of good academic practice." While the claims of other professionals to internal control are obviously overstated, a list of censured professors, including those who have moonlighted and are still working as intelligence operatives, as well as those who in other ways have clearly abrogated the trust placed in them by gross acts of incompetence or exploitation, is yet to be published.

Finally, the Association seeks to improve the economic status and job security of faculty members. The fact that this function is not mentioned as frequently as the other three may indicate an assumption that once the Association fulfills its other functions economic factors will naturally fall into place. Arthur O. Lovejoy in 1919 (12) highmindedly suggests that

> the question of professional salaries . . . no longer concerns merely the private interests of teachers; it has come to be—I choose the words with careful consideration—among the most critical and most pregnant questions of general social policy.

The general prosperity of the post World War II period left academics relatively untouched, and led Helen C. White, in 1958 (400), to argue as follows:

> I think we should face the economic aspects of our professional life more candidly and more systematically and effectively than we have in the past.

JUSTIFICATIONS

Invariably, the appeal for professional status is sustained by the claims of sublime service and the possession of esoteric knowledge. No occupation seeks autonomy ostensibly for its own aggrandizement. The AAUP is no exception; as evident from Table 2, the justification of service is much more prevalent than the one of esoteric knowledge.

TABLE 2

Justifications

Topic	Number of Speeches Topic Appears at Least Once	Total References (All Speeches)
1. Sublime service	19	43
2. Esoteric knowledge	6	8

J. M. Coulter, in 1918 (3), presses the issues of public service in arguing "that this great teaching and investigating organization is our most valuable national asset. . . . " In 1932 (6), W. B. Munro notes:

the association has held firmly to its original purpose, which is to promote the general welfare of higher education rather than to safeguard the special interests of its own members.

William T. Laprade (1944:186) echoes these sentiments: "Scholars and teachers and the institutions in which they do their work are intended to serve the public. . . . " The unselfish devotion to sublime service thus takes precedence over personal privilege for academics, as it does for all who would like their assertions that they are professionals publicly acknowledged.

Although claims for autonomy, based on the argument that only members of the occupation are able to judge the work of their peers, are not made frequently, they appear enough times to make them worth mentioning. Edward C. Kirkland (1948:23) suggests:

> publication is practically the only means by which the professor is brought to the judgment of his peers. To be sure, undergraduates form opinions about him. But such standards are immature.

Similarly, Bentley Glass (1960:152), speaking about the availability of financial aid from governmental agencies, asserts that

> it is gratifying that the government agencies consult the scientists themselves in making awards. No scientist would prefer to be judged other than by his own peers.

It is difficult to guess why more references to this topic do not arise. Perhaps the speeches are intended for public consumption, making it strategically advantageous to emphasize service. An explanation that also deserves serious attention is that employment in bureaucracies, supervised by administrators who have a pretty good idea of a professional's activities and functions, reduces the mystique of esoteric knowledge.

TACTICS

Adopting means appropriate to both the mission of the organization and its operating milieu is of critical importance; how nearly ideals and objectives are achieved is dependent upon the tactics employed. As Table 3 shows, the speeches indicate the American professoriate has rested its hopes for success in attaining the status of professionals upon the efficacy of five basic tactics: (1) reason and debate; (2) cooperation; (3) defense of academic freedom; (4) emphasis on individual responsibility; (5) involvement in governance.

John H. Wigmore (1916:14) was the first to identify the use of rational argumentation and publicity.

> Immediate Utopia cannot be hoped for. We must patiently proceed to formulate our own views of the needs of our own time, and must then endeavor to impress these views on the community at large. Our function is to build up a sound public opinion.

TABLE 3
Tactics

Topic	Number of Speeches Topic Appears at Least Once	Total References (All Speeches)
1. Reason, debate, publicity, moral rectitude	20	34
2. Cooperation with representatives of the bureaucratic system	16	39
3. Defense of the individual in academic freedom tenure cases	17	46
4. Emphasis on need for individuals to assume responsibility for their actions	18	51
5. Involvement in institutional governance	14	36

W. T. Semple (1928:163) argues that a professional sanctuary may be realized through "the recourse to reason and argumentation." And David Fellman, nearly forty years later, in 1966 (106), says:

> Our principal weapon is moral influence; our principal method is to appeal to the opinions of the public. In the hard-core cases where our efforts at mediation and conciliation have failed, we resort to our ultimate weapon, which is to pronounce public anathema in the name of the academic community.

Implicit here is the assumption that reasonable and honorable academics can resolve their differences with reasonable and honorable administrators and trustees. This process, if successful, is aided by the support of an interested and sympathetic general public.

The speeches also indicate that tension between academics and administrators can be reduced by fostering a spirit of cooperation. In 1922 (24), Edwin R. A. Seligman optimistically reports that

> we may look forward in the not distant future either to a virtual inclusion of most of the administrative authorities in our membership or at least to a situation where we can count upon the sympathetic cooperation of those who at one time were active in our own management and deliberation. . . . Mutual understanding, good-will and wholehearted cooperation will do more to bring us together and to solve our outstanding problems than dozens of independent reports and reams of separate discussions. . . .

The speeches give no indication that administrators and trustees share the cooperative spirit embodied in Henry Crew's (1928:167) optimism:

> This organization was conceived in a spirit of good sportsmanship. Cooperation is written large in the first article of our Constitution. The Charter members . . . clearly recognized the need for more conference and less regimentation in university control.

It seems reasonable to assume that this posture was intended to bridge the gap created by the power differential between the professoriate and administrators. Apparently, there was the implication and hope, until 1952 when no further mention is made of what Frederick S. Deibler (1942:39) called "cooperative attitudes," that power would be voluntarily shared.

The speeches confirm the result of the Association's self-study ("Report of the self-survey committee of the AAUP," 1965:141) which notes that a considerable amount of resources and energy have been devoted to the defense of violations of academic freedom and tenure. In the context of this analysis, the defense of beleagured faculty is viewed as another method of establishing the autonomy essential to professional status. This approach does not mean these activities serve no other useful purpose. However, it is obvious that internal control is weakened if members of the occupation can be summarily dismissed. Unlike the emphasis on cooperation, this issue is raised constantly throughout the fifty-nine years. In 1917 (23), Frank Thilly admits that

> the academic freedom investigations have . . . constituted a large part of our activities. It is not true, however, . . . that too much emphasis has been laid upon this phase of our work; but it is true that not enough emphasis has been laid upon other phases. . . .

For as S. A. Mitchell speaking in 1936 (94) argues

> the Association has many other important functions to perform, some of them of the very greatest value in educational life, but as long as there is life, I fear there will always be autocratic presidents and incompetent and slothful professors. . . .

Mark H. Ingraham, in 1940 (21), defending the existence of tenure, assigns responsibility for substantiating dereliction to the bureaucratic system.

> Attaining tenure represents a shift in the burden of proof. . . . After attainment it is

still possible to separate the undersirable person from his position, but the burden of establishing the fact that he is undesirable rests on the administration.

More recently, Ralph S. Brown, Jr. (1970:121) states:

> if we can uphold our interests in academic freedom, and academic responsibility, and shared authority, I can see . . . a prospect of honorable respect and rewards for our profession.

In this passage, the relationship between the defense of academic freedom and tenure and the striving for professional status seems clear. Academic objectives cannot be fully attained until interference by individuals, or groups, outside the profession is minimized or, in the best of all possible worlds, eliminated.

The emphasis placed in the speeches on the responsibilities of members of the occupation appears to represent an attempt to persuade outsiders it is safe to grant the desired autonomy since academics can still be counted on to behave responsibly. In 1917 (18), Frank Thilly pleads:

> I would earnestly urge those who have the good name of our universities at heart to exercise such restraint upon their feelings as is becoming in the custodians of higher education from which the people have a right to expect tolerance and fairness.

In 1948 (16), Edward C. Kirkland muses that

> the events and circumstances of the last two years have grouped themselves around two convenient themes—the persistent erosion of faculty salaries under the attack of a rising cost of living and threatened, if not materialized, investigations and purges of radicals and communists. . . . Both types are so immediate and important as to be worthy of discussion and address. But I am sanguine enough to believe that both are passing phenomena; that it is more fruitful on this occasion to discuss a more enduring problem of the profession: professional responsibility.

Becoming involved in institutional governance is the final tactic identified in the addresses—a tactic reflecting both the influence of European faculty and the problem of establishing occupational autonomy within a bureaucratic setting. An alternative to the creation of a separate power base is a sharing of the power concentrated in the hands of administrators and trustees. This approach represents an attempt to maximize the autonomy of the occupation by integrating it into the institutional power structure. Presumably, the intention is to create an arrangement somewhat comparable to that existing in hospitals where physicians sit on governing boards. Early on, Arthur O. Lovejoy (1919:39) argues

> that the body of scholars composing the faculty of any university or college should, either directly or through its chosen representatives, have a definitely recognized and an important part in the shaping of all the policies of the institution, except with respect to technical financial questions. . . .

Joseph Villiers Denney (1924:23) expands upon, and adds specificity to, the position by suggesting that state boards of regents follow the Cornell model by including faculty representatives as members. More faculty control, Ralph F. Fuchs (1962:107) argues, would mean fewer intramural problems: "Many of the strains in our institutions tend, I think, to diminish when faculty authority is clearly bestowed. . . . " It is curious that the mechanics involved in bringing about the hoped for reforms in governance are not mentioned; the assertion that they in themselves are desirable appears sufficient for the initiation of this kind of institutional realignment.

EMPLOYEE TO PROFESSIONAL: A DIFFICULT PASSAGE

If the approach taken by the AAUP is viable, we would expect the addresses to contain indications of some shift in the professoriate's status along the employee-professional continuum. While the early speeches ought to contain references to issues associated with employee status, later speeches should reflect conditions associated more with professional status. Inferences drawn from the content analysis do not, however, support the notion that the professoriate has been moving steadily toward the professional end of the continuum. While the occupation has altered the "schoolmaster" image of an earlier era, there is no evidence to suggest that it has the momentum to carry it to full professional status. The confusion, or ambivalence, created by the impasse appears in the following areas:

1. Difficulty in establishing the location of the professoriate along the employee-professional continuum: while it is generally assumed that academics are, by and large, fully professional, there seems to be a need to defend repeatedly this contention.
2. Since the status of the professoriate is problematic, it is similarly unclear whether the professional association or the trade union is the most appropriate organization to further its interests. Invariably the argument is made for the professional association, although there is a need to reaffirm continually this position against those critics, real or imagined, who would select the trade union.
3. There are ambiguities relative to the internal structure of the AAUP: it has not been satisfactorily resolved whether professional interests are best served by a centralized type of organization with decision making at the national level or through the encouragement of activities at the local, or chapter, level.
4. There is a need to restate, almost as a ritual of reassurance, the objectives and ideals of the Association.

Frank Thilly (1917:20), for one, has difficulty deciding whether faculty should be supervised employees or autonomous professionals.

A thoroughly conscientious man will carefully question himself whether he has really been conscientious enough in examining his judgments and whether he is justified in promulgating ideas which may be dangerous to the public welfare. While we cannot leave the decision of the correctness of his behavior . . . entirely to his own individual conscience, we are surely not prepared to leave it to any group of persons who would deny him the right of a fair defense against specific charges.

Note that the emphasis is on the "right of a fair defense," and not on the right of the professional to reach his own conclusions. On the other hand, Frederick S. Deibler (1942:37-38), after observing that faculty "have been forced more and more into the status of employees," contends:

To relegate the faculty to the status of employee is tantamount to dwarfing much of the driving force which contributes to the success of an institution. Within his own sphere of learning, the faculty member is more like an entrepreneur than an employee.

More recently, Sanford H. Kadish (1972:122), offers a variation on this theme.

Their status as employees, as well as professionals, places them, like any industrial or

TABLE 4

Indicators of the Difficult Passage

Topic	Number of Speeches Topic Appears at Least Once	Total References (All Speeches)
1. Ambiguity of status	15	34
2. Ambivalence about unionism	15	27
3. Ambivalence regarding structure of organization	18	49
4. Ritual clarification of organizational purpose	12	17

business employee, under the economic control of those who employ him. . . . But professors are the essence of the university enterprise, as well as its employees.

Since autonomy is one of the crucial distinguishing features of the professional, it is difficult to be autonomous and an employee at the same time. It is the incompatibility of these two roles, of course, that creates a dilemma for the professoriate.

Although some uncertainty exists about where to locate the professoriate on the professional-non-professional continuum, AAUP officials have no doubt that the professional association rather than the labor union can best serve it. Thus, the defense of the general ideology of the professional association is continuous. W. T. Semple (1928:162) supports the professional association.

It was really odd to perceive at times how quickly and how vigorously I have responded to the suggestion . . . on the part indeed of some of our best friends among administrative officers that the American Association of University Professors is a "professors' union."

David Fellman (1966:106) more emphatically declares:

Of course we defend the right of professors to join a trade union if they so desire, and we are strongly opposed to the imposition upon them of reprisals of any sort for so doing. Nevertheless, our Association is not a trade union, it is not part of the trade union movement, and it does not seek that identification with organized labor which trade union status would imply.

Such a strong affirmation of the AAUP's posture is taken as a response to mounting pressure from alternative kinds of organizations. Sanford H. Kadish (1972:122) again defends the professional association.

Take the economic strike . . . which some unions seeking professional representation urge as the standard policy to resolve bargaining impasses, after the industrial model. . . . [T]he strike proceeds by deliberately harming the educational mission, although temporarily, in order to promote the personal employee interest, in contradiction to the service ideal of subordinating personal interest to the advancement of the purposes of the university.

This statement provides an indication of how the Association's assumptions may inhibit its chances for success. In order to move along the continuum toward professional status, members of the occupation must look after their own interests since administrators are simply not likely to place "the personal employee interest" ahead of institutional needs. The failure to perceive the relation between power and autonomy results in continued uncertainty about the best vehicle for the achievement of professional status.

The addresses also reflect a lack of consensus over the internal organization of the AAUP. On the one hand, centralization would be required in order to exert a unifying force, to present a united front, and to challenge the power of administrators and trustees. On the other hand, a partnership of equals, diffused power, and occupational diversity require autonomous local chapters. As Table 4 shows, the Association has been unable to reconcile these competing claims. Joseph Villiers Denney (1924:25) attempts to limit the role of local chapters ("On local questions no chapter may assume support from the national association unless the latter has already adopted a principle that clearly governs in the specific case."), while Walter Wheeler Cook (1934:93) stresses their importance ("If the purposes of the Association are to be accomplished, it is clear that it can be done only with the aid of active local groups.")–although he mitigates his stand with the characteristic professional qualifications against all extreme positions (1934:95).

Periodic clarifications of the professional association's basic purposes and functions is yet another predictable development of the ambiguities discussed so far. To be sure, these explanations are often prompted by confusion among members of the occupation as well as outsiders. Yet, it is doubtful whether spokesmen for the American Medical Association and the American Bar Association, or the Teamsters Union for that matter, would feel the need to reiterate even as a matter of course their *raison d'être*. The lack of certainty about the status of academics and the type of organization to best represent their interests, coupled with the organizational dilemmas discussed above, make it difficult to define the mission of the AAUP.

In 1922 (7), seven years after the founding the the AAUP, Edwin R. A. Seligman laments this lack of clear definition. In succeeding decades, the issue is again addressed by, among others, Walter Wheeler Cook (1934:84) and William T. Laprade (1944:191). If members of the occupation are unfamiliar "with the work of the Association," (Laprade, 1944:191) how much less an impression must it have made, one must ask, on administrators and trustees? This equivocalness may explain why the AAUP has had limited success in attaining its dual goals of unifying the occupation and providing it with a collective voice.

OBSTACLES TO SUCCESS

There are distinct themes, commonly found somewhere near the end of each speech, suggesting why the tactics employed by academics to achieve full professional status may not always be appropriate, and why the approach of the AAUP has not been more successful. The content analysis revealed two fundamental problems, the consequence of questionable assumptions, in the posture adopted by the Association:

1. A tendency to emphasize the individual, or personality, characteristics of representatives of the bureaucratic system rather than focusing on the structure of, and distribution of, power within that system.
2. The commitment to an accomodating role when reacting to the intrusion by outside forces into the affairs of the occupation.

Table 5 shows the relative frequency of these symptomatic problems.

TABLE 5

Obstacles to Success

Topic	Number of Speeches Topic Appears at Least Once	Total References (All Speeches)
1. Emphasis on individual characteristics	20	42
2. Commitment to accommodating role	29	159

Focusing on individual qualities of administrators rather than on structural characteristics of colleges and universities represents a common but serious error, as this assumption that "better people" will improve the position of the professoriate probably accomplishes little more than to reinforce any existing state of affairs, John H. Wigmore (1916:18) is the first to personalize.

> In my own opinion not so much depends upon the governmental structures as upon the spirit of the institution. . . . And this will ultimately go back to the personality at the head of all.

A. J. Carlson (1938:12) expands on this theme:

> The better men and women in executive positions in the university . . . have usually had an uncommon amount of common sense, good leadership, and some sense of justice. . . .

This seems to bring the problem down to men and women rather than to organization and laws.

Frederick S. Deibler echoes these sentiments in 1942 (38) when he observes that "the mechanism of government is of less importance than the spirit which operates the mechanism." Most recently, Walter Adams (1974:124) has observed that "what we need, alas, is not a PPBS [program-planning-budgeting-systems] deus ex machina, but a new brand of academic leadership—administrators capable of analytic thought and endowed with civilized values." There is nothing to suggest that these spokesmen have seriously considered the distribution of power in institutions of higher learning, and whether or not the balance of power between faculty and administrators can be altered by focusing on personalities.

An even more prominent theme revolves around the reluctance of AAUP presidents to suggest anything resembling an assertive or activist position. The addresses repeatedly skirt the question of power and show little interest in active conflict to aid the professoriate's efforts to attain professional status. Rather, the speeches reflect an accommodating and mostly passive posture. As A. O. Leuschner (1926:91) sees it, an activist approach would be imprudent.

No educational association has the power or intent to impose its will on the educational public, not even on its own members. It stands in an advisory relation to all concerned. In general, principles adopted in the form of resolutions are intended as carefully considered recommendations.

Even without an explanation of how an organization is to proceed if its recommendations are ignored, Henry Crew (1930:105) can exult

if Herbert Spencer's definition of progress as an increasing adaptation to environment is correct, we may, I believe, modestly claim to have been progressive without being radical and conservative without being reactionary.

There are, of course, creditable reasons why the professoriate should react rather than act. William T. Laprade (1944:189) explains:

The necessity that scholars and teachers have the cooperation of executives and administrators and in some degree of the trustees of institutions in which they work if freedom and tenure are to be maintained should preserve the Association from the temptation to become a pressure group, primarily concerned with the personal interests of its members.

However, there is some doubt that the occupation can achieve its objectives without becoming a pressure group; and it is unclear what the interests of the AAUP should be if not those of the members of the occupation. In 1972 (123), Sanford H. Kadish again affirms the thesis that has become a self-defeating predicament for the professoriate: academics must demonstrate that they are worthy of full professional status by always putting the interests of others before their own.

Since our classic claims to autonomy from the outside and to academic freedom have rested in large part on the concept of a university as a neutral and nonpartisan haven for intellectuality, such super-citizen activist roles for the university and the faculty reduce the authority of our claim. . . . [W]e lose the only persuasive argument we have for our extraordinary claim to support without control: a haven for research and teaching is one thing; a special lobby is another.

It is doubtful that a "haven" can be created without a somewhat more sophisticated approach to the problem of power than is reflected in these thirty-two presidential addresses.

CONCLUDING REMARKS

Taken as a whole, these spokesmen seem to be responding: to the attacks on academic freedom in the 1920's, to the consequences of the economic depression of the 1930's, to the censorship accompanying both World Wars, to the renewed attacks on freedom of speech during the McCarthy era, to the attacks by student activists in the 1960's, and, finally, to the effects of the financial retrenchment of the 1970's. In the course followed to further its interests, the professoriate has relied more on the professionalization than the unionization model. Since academics are not independent practioners, however, this appraoch— though the process has been followed true to form—has been less than totally successful. The high road, so to speak, taken by those who make the professional claim can only be taken if they seize and utilize power effectively to advance their ends.

There is a growing awareness by the professoriate that the approach to professionalization adopted by the AAUP has been somewhat ineffective. In their recent and comprehensive study of the impact of collective bargaining on academic governance, Kemerer and Baldridge (1975:47-48) contend that professional associations have limited access to internal campus affairs, a lack of legal status, and an inability in times of economic uncertainty to apply potent sanctions, and are therefore restricted as to what they can do. This is not a revelation on their part, for they cite (1975:30) a 1973 AAUP document recognizing that a more activist stance might be necessary to achieve its ends:

> The implementation of Association-supported principles, reliant upon professional traditions and upon moral suasion, can be effectively supplemented by a collective bargaining agreement and given the force of law.

The AAUP was late in accepting collective bargaining, having waited until 1973 to commit its resources to compete with more traditional organizations, such as the American Federation of Teachers and the National Education Association, to represent the professoriate in an expanding capacity as a union. As a consequence, it is far behind (Semas, 1976:5) in organizing colleges and universities, particularly those that offer a two-year degree. It is, of course, too early to assess the impact of this late movement to unionization as a device to achieve full professional status. Although Kemerer and Baldridge (1975:7) find that *"faculty unions may help to raise standards in institutions where professional practices, peer judgments, and faculty rights have had little foothold,"* their final conclusion (1975:12) that *"most disturbingly, unionization challenges one of the most cherished principles of the academic profession—merit judgments based on peer evaluation,"* gives one reason to pause. The professoriate, thus, is faced with what seems an unresolvable dilemma: if it is to attain finally the status and rewards necessary to manage its professional responsibilities successfully, it needs more power. However, the mechanism easily at hand to better its position, collective bargaining, seems to erode the valued *sine non qua* which gives the academic enterprise its vitality—the principle of merit (Lewis, 1975). Our data offer no clues on how the professoriate might resolve this final quandary.

This analysis does, however, suggest that American academics are not likely to assume roles comparable to those of some European faculty. This forecast stems from the fact that to date, unions (like the professional associations) are not seeking basic structural changes in institutions of higher learning. The principal difference between the two organizational forms seems that unions attempt to offset the power vested with administrators and trustees by creating a counterweight dependent upon unified faculty action. As noted earlier, the professional association has sought to share this power through cooperation. In neither case are questions raised about the existing institutional hierarchy, or the differential distribution of power within it. It is likely that administrators, trustees, and increasingly legislators will continue to make those broad policy decisions determining the basic nature of higher education in the United States.

The fact that we were unable to discern any variation in the basic ideology of the professoriate over the period of nearly sixty years, also suggests there will not be a precipitous outcry for radical change. Academics have seemed mostly preoccupied with trying to delineate the parameters of their autonomy, and many apparently perceive the union as merely another vehicle to achieve this end. A new-wrought social organization hardly seems to be uppermost in people's minds or a subject for serious discussion—nor does the creation of a community where idle curiosity is prized and the pursuit of ideas is an all-absorbing activity.

The speeches, themselves, reflect a certain self-satisfaction on the part of the AAUP leadership. And, why not, given the nature of the *men* (elitist oriented, mirrors of the conventional wisdom) who make it to the top of the AAUP? Unless procedures are introduced to elect officers who represent the previously neglected elements in the professoriate (women, minorities, radicals, the younger members), the AAUP will not interest these other academics in any significant number. The pattern of elections might even suggest to the neglected segments of the professoriate that the AAUP itself has been a party to discrimination. The general style, such as the continued use of male pronouns throughout the addresses, might make some wonder if the organization is truly committed to universal membership. Further, the obvious disjunction between the prestige of the professoriate's position and its actual institutional power (Cavan, 1970), raises questions about judgement and even practical common sense in the higher reaches of the AAUP. Why are not these gross disparities between self-accorded prestige ratings and actual power reflected in their addresses? Finally, some might wonder how committed these spokesmen for the professoriate are to the education of the public, given the relative unimportance of the issue compared to others in these thirty-two addresses. It is unlikely that reforms in the educational system will be initiated by this complacent body. Here, as in other occupations, the cry for professionalization seems rather narrowly self-interested.

REFERENCES

Bennett, W. S., Jr. and M. C. Hokenstad, Jr.
    1973 "Full time people workers and conceptions of the 'professional.' " Pp. 21-45 in P. Halmos (ed.), Professionalisation and Social Change. The Sociological Review Monograph 20.
Cavan, S.
    1970 "Aristocratic workers." Pp. 170-80 in A. K. Daniels, R. Kahn-Hut, and Associates, Academics on the Line. San Francisco: Jossey-Bass.
Freidson, E.
    1973 "Professions and the occupational principle." Pp. 19-38 in E. Freidson (ed.), The Professions and Their Prospects. Beverly Hills, California: Sage.
Greenwood, Ernest
    1957 "Attributes of a profession." Social Work 2:45-55.
Haug, M. R. and M. B. Sussman
    1973 "Professionalization and unionism." Pp. 89-104 in E. Freidson (ed.), The Professions and Their Prospects. Beverly Hills, California: Sage.
Hughes, Everett C.
    1963 "Professions." Daedalus 92:655-68.
Kemerer, Frank R. and J. Victor Baldridge
    1975 Unions on Campus. San Francisco: Jossey-Bass.
Lewis, Lionel S.
    1975 Scaling the Ivory Tower: Merit and Its Limits in Academic Careers. Baltimore: The Johns Hopkins University Press.
Parsons, Talcott
    1939 "The professions and social structure." Social Forces 17:457-67.
Perrucci, R.
    1973 "Engineering." Pp. 119-33 in E. Freidson (ed.), The Professions and Their Prospects. Beverly Hills, California: Sage.

"Report of the self-survey committee of the AAUP"
    1965 AAUP Bulletin 51:99-209.
Semas, Philip W.
    1976 "Faculty unions add 60 campuses in 1975-76 academic year." Chronicle of Higher Education
          (May 31) XII:5.
Veysey, Laurence R.
    1965 The Emergence of the American University. Chicago: University of Chicago Press.
Vollmer, Howard M. and Donald L. Mills (eds.)
    1966 Professionalization. Englewood Cliffs, New Jersey: Prentice-Hall.
Wilensky, Harold L.
    1964 "The professionalization of everyone?" American Journal of Sociology 70:137-58.
Wilson, Logan
    1942 The Academic Man. New York: Oxford.

FACULTY TEACHING GOALS, 1968-1973*

GERALD M. PLATT
The University of Massachusetts, Amherst

TALCOTT PARSONS
Harvard University

RITA KIRSHSTEIN
The University of Virginia

The findings reported in this paper are taken from two national surveys of faculty conducted in 1968 and 1973. A comparison of these findings indicates that there has been no change in degree of emphasis upon and content of teaching among faculty during this period despite pressures upon them to change their attitudes toward undergraduate teaching. This lack of change is explained in terms of a dominant teaching orientation which is an outgrowth of a compromise between professional value commitments and institutional work obligations.

There have been numerous characterizations of the goals or aims of American higher education. For example, some social analysts have suggested that American higher education does not have its own values; at best higher education is oriented toward the development of persons who will reproduce the existing society (Touraine, 1974; Bowles and Gintis, 1976). Others have suggested that the values of higher education have become those of professionals, thus distorting the uniqueness of undergraduate teaching and education and making it simply a reflection of graduate studies (Jencks and Riseman, 1968). Still others have suggested that higher education is a conveyor belt for the industrial society, its aim to produce trained workers (Kerr, 1963). And still others suggest that the powerful Boards of Trustees and Administrations dominate the educational environments of higher education moving them in one direction or another depending upon their interests (Hartnett, 1968).

All of these analyses speak upon behalf of the faculty who in their day-to-day work implement educational curriculum. Such analyses frequently are accomplished without reference to faculty's own interests and without reference to faculty's conceptions of their own roles. These analyses therefore make one or another of the following assumptions: that faculty are unaware of what they are attempting to accomplish in their teaching; that faculty are handmaidens to forces beyond their interests or control, lacking their own values and norms of behavior; that there are unintended consequences to the faculty-student relationship which are revealed exclusively to the analyst of higher education and unrelated to faculty's intentions; and that the system of undergraduate education is undifferentiated and unidimensional in its intentions and consequences. Our theoretical and empirical analyses do not accept these conceptions of undergraduate teaching aims nor do we agree with the assumption which undergirds them.

There have been other studies of higher educational goals which are less inferential, but also less influential than the works noted. Using content analysis, these studies analyzed statements from college administrators and other university personnel and descriptions found in college catalogues to describe empirically the aims of colleges and universities

---

*We would like to acknowledge the support of the National Science Foundation Grants, GS 1479 and GS 2425 and the Carnegie Corporation. We would also like to acknowledge the help of the American Council on Education and to thank Alan Bayer, Jeanne Royer and Victor Lidz for their help too.

172

(Koos and Crawford, 1921; Palley, 1968; Binstock, 1970). But these studies also remain several steps removed from the faculty's own conception of their teaching goals.

A recent study of college professors in six institutions attempted to examine faculty views on educational goals for undergraduates and to relate these goals to actual teaching practices and to attitudes toward change in higher education (Wilson, Gaff, Dienst, Woodland and Bavry, 1975). Additionally, previous to this study there were intensive investigations of teaching orientations in particular departments and in specific colleges (Gamson, 1966; Vreeland and Bidwell, 1966; Reid and Bates, 1971; and Zelan 1974). However, all of these works included only a small number of faculty and colleges and they tended to focus upon specific departments. Any conclusions regarding teaching goals and their persistence in the American academic system inferred from these investigations are tenuous.

Thus, not enough attention has been given to the expressed teaching goals held by faculty throughout the higher educational system; this study attempts to rectify this oversight. The foci of this work are: to specify the degree and distribution of explicitly held teaching goals throughout higher education; to spell out the content of these goals; and to assess their persistence and change over a five year period. Subsequent to this analysis we will discuss the theoretical and practical implications of these findings for the higher educational system.

UNDERGRADUATE TEACHING GOALS: THE SURVEYS OF 1968 AND 1973

In 1968 we surveyed 3045 faculty regarding a number of issues concerning their working and professional lives. These faculty were located in 115 universities and four-year colleges throughout the United States. They were in all the major disciplines including a number of faculty in undergraduate vocational and technical disciplines such as pre-engineering, business administration, and so on.

This sample was a proportionate one and properly weighted; the responses represent the self-reported attitudes, opinions and behaviors of approximately 12,000 faculty at all four-year liberal arts colleges and universities in the nation. One item on the questionnaire asked of the faculty, "In your undergraduate teaching, do you attempt to direct your students toward any particular goals?" A "yes" or "no" check response was given to this item. However, if the respondent answered "yes" he or she was asked to, "Please state one or two of the most important goals." A coding system was constructed using the responses to the latter question, and the faculties' answers were categorized according to this scheme.

In 1973, using the goal categories in the coding system and some additional categories from another investigator, the American Council on Education developed a closed-ended response question regarding teaching goals which was included in their questionnaire circulated to a national sample of faculty at 301 higher educational institutions. This question had two parts; only the first of these is of interest to our work. It asked, "How important is each of the following as your personal goal or aim in your teaching of undergraduate students . . . ?" This question was followed by sixteen possible goals to which the respondent could check, "essential, very important, somewhat important, or not important, irrelevant." The following analysis builds upon the answers to these questions to obtain insights into the professed teaching goals of working faculty in 1968 and 1973. In the analysis, we will briefly employ a scale which groups together similar types of institutions. Our Scale of Institutional Differentiation (SID) arrays institutions along a continuum from those which score high on size, quality and research-orientation measures to those which rank low on such indices.[1]

---

[1] The scale of institutional differentiation combines a measure of faculty size with an assessment of orientation toward research and an institutional quality index; each factor contributes relatively equally

TABLE 1

The Percent of Faculty Who Have Undergraduate Teaching Goals, 1968-1973
Scale of Institutional Differentiation (SID)

	Higest Level (1)	2	Middle Level (3)	4	Lowest Level (5)	Total
1968	63.0	76.4	84.3	88.7	85.3	12,376
1973	86.7	87.2	97.3	92.5	97.5	12,302

In the 1973 sample there are forty institutions coincident with those surveyed in 1968. These forty colleges and universities have been arrayed along the Scale of Institutional Differentiation also. While within cell comparisons between 1968 and 1973 are valid, the forty institutions are not representative of the universe of colleges and universities since this subsample of institutions is predominated by highly differentiated schools. Therefore, marginals reported herein are taken from responses of faculty at all colleges and universities as these are given in Alan E. Bayer's, *Teaching Faculty in Academe: 1972-1973*, which is an initial report on the ACE survey (Bayer, 1973; also see Liebert and Bayer, 1975).

TO HAVE OR NOT TO HAVE TEACHING GOALS

Since faculty who professed to have goals in undergraduate teaching in 1968 indicated this with a simple "yes" to the direct question, determining their number is an easy matter. However, this task was not as simple for the 1973 sample; they were not asked a "yes-no" question regarding goals. The most conservative way of estimating the percent who have and do not have undergraduate teaching goals is to assume that faculty persons who considered all sixteen goals either "not important or irrelevant" or who did not respond at all did not have any undergraduate teaching goals. This number then was the faculty considered to have said they had "no undergraduate teaching goals" while those faculty who checked even one of the sixteen goals as "somewhat important" to them are considered as having said "yes" to holding goals.

Given the different methods by which having goals was assessed in the two time period, it is impossible to compare the figures in absolute terms. However, it is possible to compare trends by using the Scale of Institutional Differentiation (SID) for the two periods. The result is that holding teaching goals is negatively related to institutional differentiation in both 1968 and 1973. Table 1 below indicates the percent of faculty in 1968 who checked yes to having teaching goals, and in 1973, faculty who reported that at least one goal was somewhat important to them in their undergraduate teaching.

Naturally the figures for 1973 are inflated and therefore we cannot assume that faculty at all higher educational institutions were more involved in undergraduate teaching in 1973 than they were in 1968. At best we can assume that there is a stability in having under-

---

to the scale scores. Size was defined by the number of full-time faculty and their equivalent part-time faculty, and not by the size of the student body. A measure of faculty size was used because it was faculty and not students who were the focus of our interest. Research orientation was measured by (1) the proportion of graduate students among all arts and science students (2) amount of grant funds per faculty member, and (3) number of periodicals taken by the university library per faculty member. Quality was measured by (1) general and educational monies per student, (2) percentage of staff members holding Ph.D.'s and (3) the student-teacher ratio. Essentially this scale is based upon Alexander Astin's factor analysis model which he published in 1962. Examples of schools in each of the SID levels are as follows: SID 1: Harvard, Princeton, University of California at Los Angeles; SID 2: Ohio State, City College of New York, Duke University; SID 3: Vassar, University of Cincinnati, Bowdoin; SID 4: Kalamazoo College, Bennington, South Carolina State College; SID 5: Calvin College, Eastern Baptist, Paine College.

graduate teaching goals between the two periods and that the relationship manifest in 1968 was again replicated in 1973; to repeat, the lower the differentiation of the institution the more likely the faculty member will have undergraduate teaching goals.

THE RANK ORDERING OF TEACHING GOALS

The rate at which faculty agree with, or suggest they find a particular goal important to them in their teaching is also inflated for the 1973 sample. It is a methodological truism that if respondents are given substantive categories with which they can agree, the response rate will be much greater than if the respondents are asked to write down their own thoughts on the same issue. In short, rates of agreement to closed-ended items will be higher than to responses to open-ended questions on the same substantive issues. Thus, in 1968 the most frequently suggested goal, that is the most frequently written in teaching goal to the second part of the question, was to "encourage mastery of the subject;" that is, "to master the subject matter in the course, to develop competence in the field, understanding the course material, including mastery of the basic principles in the field and special methodological techniques." This goal received 28.0 percent of the mentions among the suggested goals. By contrast, in 1973, 91.4 percent of the faculty thought that "to master knowledge in a discipline" was either "essential" or "very important" as a "personal goal or aim in . . . teaching of undergraduate students." However, using these figures to rank the goals, we find that in 1968, "mastery of the subject" was first in importance to faculty while in 1973 it was the second most important undergraduate teaching goal.

In 1968, 82 percent of the respondents checked "yes" to having goals but only 60 percent of these recorded the content of their goals. Some faculty suggested more than one goal and thus it was decided to calculate the frequency of mentioned goals against the total goals noted. The teaching goals in 1968 were therefore ordered as follows.

The ranked position of "mastery of the subject matter," (28.0%) for 1968 has already been noted. This goal was followed by, "appreciation of the subject matter," (24.6%), the distinction between the first and second ranked goals being a thorough and technical knowledge of the subject implied in the former, in contrast to a layman's acquaintance with the subject matter connoted in the latter. The third ranked goal was, "to develop the students' character, to build self reliance, independence, personal virtues, to encourage or help in the students' adjustment," (21.9%). The fourth most frequently mentioned goal among the goals was, "to encourage clear thinking and openmindedness, to encourage considered judgments, clarity and precision in thought, writing, reading, and so on," (20.5%). "Creativity" was the fifth ranked goal; that is, "to encourage creative and innovative thought," (10.0%). "Scholarly thinking," was the sixth ranked aim of faculty, or that is, faculty tried in their teaching, "to encourage scholarly thinking and reasoned analysis, to develop an understanding of the scientific method, how inferences are drawn from data, conclusions derived from considerations of findings, and so on," (8.6%).

In 1968 when "relevance" was a central concern on college campuses, only a small proportion of the faculty considered it worthy as an aim; "making the subject relevant" was the seventh most often mentioned teaching goal. By "making the subject relevant" faculty meant, "making the subject relevant to the student's personal life, social life, making the subject relevant to other subjects, and to modern day existence," (7.5%). The eighth most frequently mentioned goal was, "preparation for graduate school" and this implied, "advanced training in the respondent's discipline, teaching the subject so that the student could get into graduate school," (7.2%). The most frequently mentioned job preparation goal was "preparation to become a teacher" (6.7%) which was the ninth most often suggested undergraduate teaching goal. The tenth was "citizenship" and frequently what faculty suggested along these lines was "to develop responsible citizens, to encourage social responsibility, political awareness and responsibility, concern for world affairs, and so on," (5.7%).

No other goal received a rating of five percent of the total goals mentioned. The eleventh ranked goal, "curiosity (to stimulate the desire to learn, incentives to further study, to encourage additional study not related to graduate work)" received 3.8 percent of the goal responses. "Reasoning, understanding as opposed to rote learning" was the twelfth ranked goal but received only a 3.3 percent response. "Developing capabilities in general, developing the student to his or her fullest abilities," was ranked thirteenth (2.9%); "job preparation in general," fourteenth (2.5%); "commitment to pursue research," fifteenth (1.7%); "developing religious beliefs," sixteenth (1.6%); "job preparation, professional occupations," seventeenth (1.4%); "job preparation, semi-professional occupations," ranked eighteenth (1.2%); and the nineteenth ranked goal was "job preparation for academic work" with a .7 percent.

Because some of the goals noted had essentially the same intention in undergraduate teaching, as well, the frequencies with which some of the goals were mentioned were exceptionally small, and because the coding error among coders was 7 percent, wherever plausible and possible, goal categories were collapsed. Under these circumstances the coding error was considerably reduced; the collapsed list of ranked goals for 1968 is presented below.

TABLE 2

Ranked Order of Undergraduate Teaching Goals, 1968

Goals	Percent of Mentioned Goals	Rank
Mastery and appreciation of subject	52.6	1
Clear thinking, scholarly thinking, reasoning	34.0	2
Develop character and capabilities	24.8	3
Preparation for job—all occupations	12.5	4
Creativity	10.0	5
Making the subject relevant	7.5	6
Preparation for graduate study	7.2	7
Citizenship	5.7	8
Curiosity	3.8	9
Commitment to pursue research	1.7	10
Developing religious beliefs	1.6	11

Discussion of the meaning of this rank order of goals will be postponed until we present the ordering for 1973. A comparison of goals between 1968 and 1973 is possible and will be pursued even though there are two obstacles to their congruence. The methodology of ascertaining adherence to undergraduate teaching goals has already been discussed. Another difficulty with this analysis is that we did not have control over the exact number and precise wording of goal items in the ACE questionnaire. An excellent example of the latter problem is found in the wording of the goal regarding attempts to develop students' character through teaching. In the 1973 ACE questionnaire, the word "moral" was used to modify character in a goal item which read, "to develop moral character." The word "moral" obviously has a negative connotation to faculty which they tended to eschew. This avoidance is evidenced both in the rate and pattern of positive responses to this goal when it is compared to: the importance of "character building" in 1968; and the response patterns to the other goals in 1973. The former problem concerning inclusion of goal items is evidenced by the absence of a "relevance" goal in the 1973 list to which faculty could respond.

Keeping such shortcomings in mind, we will present the 1973 rank order of goals and then compare it with the 1968 order. Faculty respondents in 1973 considered the sixteen goals "essential" or "very important" to their teaching in the following degree.

TABLE 3

Ranked Order of Undergraduate Teaching Goals, 1973

Goals	Percent of Faculty Who Hold Goal	Rank
To develop the ability to think clearly	95.4	1
To master knowledge in a discipline	91.4	2
To increase the desire and ability to undertake self-directed learning	89.4	3
To develop creative capacities	78.0	4
To prepare students for employment after college	60.7	5
To develop responsible citizens	57.4	6
To provide tools for the critical evaluation of society	57.3	7
To convey a basic appreciation of the liberal arts	55.1	8
To achieve deeper levels of students' self-understanding	54.9	9
To prepare students for graduate or advanced education	53.8	10
To provide the local community with skilled human resources	46.0	11
To develop moral character	44.6	12
To develop the ability to pursue research	43.4	13
To provide for students emotional development	38.2	14
To prepare students for family living	20.1	15
To develop religious beliefs or convictions	9.3	16

In general, there is a considerable stability in undergraduate teaching goal priorities for faculty between 1968 and 1973. Four of the five top ranked goals in 1968 are among the first five ranked goals in 1973; that is, mastery of subject matter, clear thinking, creativity, preparation for employment are included in the first five ranked goals in both periods. Developing character dropped from the first five ranked goals to the lowly position of twelfth ranked goal in 1973. But this extreme loss in position is attributable to the inadvertent use of the word "moral" to modify character. In 1973, self-directed learning took the place of building character at the third ranked position. Self-directed learning may be likened to curiosity as this was coded in 1968, and therefore this goal received a considerable increase in salience between the two time periods. And while preparation for employment remained among the five most important goals in 1973, it slipped from fourth to fifth position.

There is no way to compare the importance of relevancy in teaching between 1968 and 1973. Preparation for advanced or graduate training remained constant in a position about two-thirds down the list of goals in 1968 and in 1973. Citizenship also remained constant in importance to faculty at about mid-point in rank ordering for both periods. However, commitment to pursue research fared badly in both surveys; it was close to the bottom of the list in both 1968 and 1973. Finally, religious beliefs or convictions as a goal in the classroom was least important to faculty in both periods.

Although there is considerable stability, there are also slight shifts in rankings which tell an interesting story. For example, between 1968 and 1973, the ability to think clearly moved up ahead of mastering the subject matter. While both are goals addressed to cognitive learning, the connotations in the former are in the direction of the development of autonomous cognitive capacities, while the latter to a greater degree implies the student having cognitive control over a set body of material. Furthermore, when developing character moved out of the five top goals it was not replaced with a goal that might be tantamount to character building, such as developing the students' emotions, but was replaced with self-directed learning, another goal which implies the teaching of autonomous cognitive capacities to students.

Again, in contrasting '68 with '73, we find that developing creative capacities (a third goal which implied cognitive autonomy) also shifted upward in rank order while concerns with practical goals, that is for example, preparing students for employment after college, shifted slightly downward. There are additional shifts in goals to be sure, but if we use the first five ranked goals to act as bellwether for the direction of change, it appears that between '68 and '73 if anything, there was an intensification of the expression of cognitive teaching goals in undergraduate teaching. *However, because of the methodological and substantive incompatibilities between the two studies such a conclusion would be, at best, precarious.*

Therefore, as already noted, we can conclude that the frequency with which faculty hold undergraduate teaching goals and their distribution related to levels of institutional differentiation, have remained constant over the five year period. Similarly the rank ordering of substantive content of teaching goals has also remained relatively constant between 1968 and 1973. In short, when faculty hold teaching goals they stress cognitive learning over all others they might possibly emphasize.

THE THEORETICAL AND PRACTICAL IMPLICATIONS OF THE FINDINGS

Although the methodological differences in the studies constitute an important obstacle to precise comparisons between 1968 and 1973 the paucity of systematic research on faculty teaching goals and the total absence of longitudinal studies on this topic (Liebert and Bayer, 1975: 197) encourages us to explore the meanings of these findings for higher education even in the face of methodological shortcomings. The years between 1968 and 1973 were especially stormy ones for higher education and critical for its faculty. This was a period in which faculty were being urged and pressured by trustees, administrators and students (some even by their own consciences) to devote more time to undergraduate teaching, to give more emphasis to moral, aesthetic, expressive and practical values in their classrooms, to devote more energy to developing students' personalities and to making courses more relevant to the lives of their students (Grant and Riesman, 1975).

Thus, the persistence in degree, distribution and content of teaching goals in the higher educational system comes as somewhat of a surprise. It says that undergraduate teaching in its importance to faculty as this is stressed across the system of institutions and in terms of what they consider important to teach (even in the face of some legitimate pressures for change) have remained more constant than altered. The simplest explanations of these findings could be made in terms of faculty intransigence and conservatism. Lipset and Ladd have pointed to faculty political liberality and academic conservatism (1974). Thus, lack of change despite internal and external pressures might be taken as further evidence for faculty conservatism. But such an analysis is too facile and it does not accord well with information from other sources regarding changes in higher education.

Newspapers and popular literature have remarked upon the several forms of faculty response to the pressures of the 60's. There is evidence of a grade inflation. There have been reports of increased availability of faculty to students and of administrative reward for outstanding teaching. A large number of universities and colleges have developed alternate curricula and degree requirements have been loosened on many campuses. Some of these efforts have been essayed in good faith, presenting an apparent paradox: how can such change exist side-by-side with the data reported on teaching goals?

We feel the resolution resides in deeper level commitments plumbed by the questions regarding personal goals or aims in teaching undergraduate students. These findings drawn from faculty in the total array of higher educational institutions and not solely from the top research oriented universities, have touched upon shared commitments at the core of academic values.

We have referred to these core academic values as cognitive rationality (Parsons and Platt, 1973). By cognitive rationality we mean a differentiated value system which, in this century, became institutionalized in the American higher education system. It is a value pattern mandating rational action, in Weber's sense of the term, in the comprehension and solution of intellectual problems. It is a flexible value integrated with several forms of intellectual activity but especially institutionalized in the academic world in the forms of scholarship and research (Ben-David, 1973). Despite this priority, it is a shared value pattern, without regard to the actual presence, absence or extent of research or graduate education at particular higher educational institutions. Thus, this value acts as an integrative mechanism tying the system together in terms of shared evaluation standards for faculty activities.

More specifically, the findings suggest that undergraduate teaching goals such as "mastery and appreciation of the subject or discipline," "clear thinking," "scholarly thinking," "reasoning," interest and desire for self-directed learning," "developing creative capacities," are manifest solutions indexing faculty commitment to the core academic values. Further, in light of the *specific content of the goals items* stressed in 1968 and 1973 we would like to summarize this manifest solution as an undergraduate teaching orientation—an orientation stressing the development of intellectual autonomous and cognitively competent students. Finally, in light of *the degrees of stress* placed upon these items, in contrast to all others, we would like to suggest that this is a widespread normative (although not exclusive) teaching orientation shared by faculty throughout the system of higher educational institutions.

If we are correct in these interpretations then such an orientation is not a direct expression of the core values but rather is a compromise integrating value commitments with institutional obligations. Were this not a compromise solution we would have expected faculty to have placed much greater stress upon teaching undergraduates "to pursue research" and "to prepare them for advanced or graduate training." We are suggesting therefore, that this is an undergraduate teaching orientation which simultaneously integrates professional and institutional demands for performance within the faculty role. Faculty employing such a perspective can orient their behavior to several reference groups simultaneously minimizing potential role strain.

This formulation helps us advance our conception of the faculty role. Previously we had suggested that academic values are interpreted in behavioral performances oriented either toward disciplinary and professional standards or expressed in terms of institutional demands, a kind of Merton-Gouldner cosmopolitan-local dichotomy (Parsons and Platt, 1968). However, we now find this formulation too simple. The cognitive rationality value pattern appears to have myriad behavioral forms of expression not readily segregated into professional and institutional domains; human actors are too complex to act in so simple a dichotomous manner. In their consciousness regarding their values and their social circumstances, faculty in undergraduate teaching have come to a more complex resolution of this one component of their occupational performance. They have remained true to their own values, yet have not turned undergraduate education into professional or vocational environments. They have developed a dominant undergraduate teaching orientation sustaining their professional identities in their daily work by stressing cognitive values but in terms appropriate to their working conditions.

If, however, faculty have remained true to their value commitments it raises again the question regarding educational changes reported in the popular literature. We can better understand these changes in relation to the persistence of teaching goals if we view such innovation as peripheral to the academic value core. These have been structural alterations which did not threaten the persistence of academic values or the normative teaching orientation. For example, all of the commissions and committees on higher education urging changes in higher education suggested accomplishing these without sacrificing academic excellence; the expression, educational innovation without the sacrifice of academic excellence, became commonplace. Thus, faculty have viewed these as acceptable structural innovations insofar as they did not undermine academic values.[2]

If academic core values and their manifest undergraduate resolution have a sanctity in practical terms, what changes are possible in higher educational teaching? Some economists, employing complex models have suggested that faculty *degree of involvement with,* and *quality of* teaching could be improved with increased pecuniary return to teaching (Hansen and Kelley, 1973; Becker, 1975). But these economic analyses have little to say about the content of teaching and how this might be changed.

The latter is the more sociological issue discussed here. We do not consider the cognitive rationality pattern as existing *sui generis* but rather as a differentiated part of the Western rational tradition of which economic, legal, etc. rationalities are also part. Thus, practical considerations of change in the content of teaching, especially modifying the cognitive rationality stress as it has been integrated in undergraduate teaching, would necessitate changes in the Western value system, or a differentiation of this value standard from the higher educational system or the isolation of specific institutions of higher education from the rest of the system. We feel the former two solutions are highly unlikely in this present historical moment of American society and that the latter solutions where it has been tried, for example as in the experiments at Old Westbury or Monteith Colleges have not fared well. Such experiments in higher education have not been able to free themselves from the larger cultural values and the dominant orientational mode of higher education. In the end, their innovative educational experiments gave way to the values of cognitive learning (Riesman, Gusfield, and Gamson, 1971).

REFERENCES

Astin, Alexander W.
    1962 "An empirical characterization of higher educational institutions." Journal of Educational
        Psychology 53: 244-232.
Bayer, Alan E.
    1973 Teaching Faculty in Academe: 1972-1973. Washington D.C.: American Council on Education.
Becker, William E., Jr.
    1975 "The university professor as a utility maximizer and producer of learning, research and income."
        The Journal of Human Resources 10:107-115.

---

[2] This is somewhat of an overstatement of the situation. For example, the grade inflation was quite threatening to academic values because it meant losing controls by which academic values could be reinforced with undergraduate students. However, recent reports indicate that there has been a slight reversal and that inflated grading has begun to decline (Jacobson, 1976). Widespread curricula changes within institutions, especially giving credit for non-academic activities, would also be a serious threat to academic values. But these programs where they occurred tended to be limited in terms of the amount of credit that could be earned in such activities and frequently such programs were physically isolated on the campus as if to prevent them from contaminating the academic curriculum.

Ben-David, Joseph
1971   The Scientist's Role in Society, A Comparative Study. Englewood Cliffs, New Jersey: Prentice-Hall.
Binstock, Jeanne S.
1970   Design from Disunity: The Tasks and Methods of American Colleges. Doctoral Dissertation. Brandeis University.
Bowles, Samuel and Herbert Gintis
1976   Schooling in Capitalist America. New York: The Free Press.
Gamson, Z.F.
1966   "Utilitarian and Normative orientations toward education." Sociology of Education 39: 46-76.
Grant, Gerald and David Riesman
1975   "An ecology of academic reform." Daedulus Winter: 166-191.
Hansen, W. Lee and Allen C. Kelley
1973   "Political economy of course evaluation." Journal of Economic Education 5: 10-21.
Hartnett, Rodney T.
1968   College and University Trustees: Their Backgrounds, Roles, and Educational Attitudes. Princeton, New Jersey: Educational Testing Service.
Jacobson, Robert L.
1976   "Undergraduate averages dip for the first time in a decade." The Chronicle of Higher Education 13: 1.
Jencks, Christopher and David Riesman
1968   The Academic Revolution. New York: Doubleday.
Kerr, Clark
1963   The Uses of the University. Cambridge: Harvard University Press.
Koos, L. and C. Crawford
1921   "College aims past and present." School and Society 14: 499-513.
Liebert, Roland J. and Alan E. Bayer
1975   "Goals in teaching undergraduates: Professional and client-Centeredness." The American Sociologist 10:195-205.
Lipset, Seymour M. and Everett C. Ladd, Jr.
1971   "The divided professoriate." Change 3: 54-60.
Palley, David
1968   The Aims of American Colleges and Universities. Honor's Thesis. Harvard University.
Parsons, Talcott and Gerald M. Platt
1968   The American Academic Profession: A Pilot Study. National Science Foundation, mimeographed.
1973   The American University. Cambridge: Harvard University Press.
Reid S.T. and A. P. Bates
1971   "Undergraduate sociology programs in accredited colleges and universities." American Sociologist 6: 165--175.
Riesman, David, Joseph Gusfield and Zelda Gamson
1971   Academic Values and Mass Education. New York: Anchor Books, Doubleday.
Touraine, Alain
1974   The Academic System in American Society. New York: McGraw-Hill.
Vreeland, R.S. and C.E. Bidwell
1966   "Classifying university departments: An approach to an analysis of their effects upon undergraduates' values and attitudes." Sociology of Education 39: 237-254.
Wilson, Robert C., Jerry G. Gaff, Evelyn R. Dienst, Lynn Woodland and James L. Bavry
1975   College Professors and Their Impact on Students. New York: Wiley.
Zelan, Joseph
1974   "Undergraduates in Sociology." The American Sociologist 9: 9-17.

SOME CHARACTERISTICS OF FACULTY UNION MEMBERSHIPS[1]
AND THEIR IMPLICATIONS

A. LEWIS RHODES
Florida State University

Some aspects of policy formation as an outcome of aggregation from diverse collective bargaining agreements are identified. Data from a nationwide sample of 7,325 full-time teaching faculty were used to show differences between membership or nonmembership in either AAUP, AFT, or NEA organizations by site and type of college or university, the career situation, the research orientation, and general conservatism. The implications of these differences for possible outcomes of social policy are considered.

Friends and foes of faculty unions agree that they have become a permanent and growing feature of higher education in the United States. Some may find it curious that this social change in the lives of scholars has commanded so little attention in the major journals of this discipline.[2] Either as social scientists or as members of the academic community, sociologists have reason to ask: "What will public policy be regarding faculty unions and how will it affect my work?"

The eventual policy will be the cumulative result of agreements between faculty organizations and administrators, made in past and future decades. These agreements are political; they will be influenced by the values, opinions, and powers of faculties, administrators, governing boards, students, and various publics vis-à-vis various structural and historical constraints. It is beyond the scope of this research to identify and interrelate all the social forces behind the creation of a stable policy. Rather, I will limit my task in three ways. First, only some of the many issues which seem likely points of policy formation will be selected. Second, *some* structural and social psychological characteristics which seem to diffrentiate between membership and nonmembership in the three largest faculty bargaining agencies are identified. There is no direct information on administrators or processes of interaction with the faculty, although such information is obviously desirable.[3] Third, the implications of information on the faculty for the chosen issues will be examined in the light of information from this and other research.

The issues. The issues which public policy must address regarding faculty unionization are a subdivision of a set of issues concerning the mission of higher education in America and its sources of support. The expansion of functions, student enrollments, faculties, and the incredible increase of professional administrators are well-known features of the post-World War II academic scene. The growth of faculty unionization can be partially understood in the light of theory regarding interrelationship between structures of complex organization

[1] Support for computer analysis came from the RANN program of the National Science Foundation (grant SSH72-03432-A02). Grateful acknowledgment is made to the American Council on Education, University of California at Los Angeles and to Alexander W. Asten for providing the data and to Alan Bayer for suggestions. The interpretations are solely the responsibility of the author.

[2] Neither the American Journal of Sociology, The American Sociological Review nor Social Forces has an entry on this topic during the past three years. Sociology of Education has nothing at the nationwide level and only two studies of faculty attitudes at single campuses (Nixon, 1975 and Feuille and Blandin, 1976). Ladd and Lipset (1973,1975) are exceptions.

[3] Data on administrators were not available to this researcher at this time. For a good example of how AFT became the bargaining agent for nine universities in Florida, see James Fendrich's account of the collective bargaining campaign (1976).

and generation of collective behavior. A succinct application of such theory to explain student protest was accomplished by M. Brown and A. Golden (1973). They remark,

> Points of confrontation are usually reached when collectivities, through their practical activities, encounter items not consistently accounted for by their collective constructions of the situation and are forced to recognize competing constructions (1973: 202).

It seems plausible that faculty confrontations associated with the unionization process occur when traditional conceptions of faculty statuses and roles (entertained by the faculty in the course of their various pursuits) collide both with "real" structural changes in status *and* with conceptions of status held by college administrators, and either state governments or private boards of control. The traditional social construction of the faculty themselves is that of academia as an autonomous community of nonpolitical, nonbureaucratic colleagues, bound by a common search for truth (as recognized by standards of scholarship implying mutual tolerance and respect for hard work and expertise) and facilitated by a small administration headed by former colleagues. This self-conception has been overwhelmed by administrations changing from a supportive to a dominating role and by a further shift of control to more remote state and federal agencies and/or private industry (the latter is particularly important for private universities). The subordination of the faculty to external interests was hastened by emphasis on research activity as validating the status of individual faculty members and their university. The rapid expansion of research and graduate programs during the 1960's generated rising expectations which were abruptly met by the "academic depression" of the 1970's. Further tension was generated by slow implementation of equality of opportunities for minority groups after the depression had set in. These and other pressures seem sufficient to satisfy the preconditions for collective action by faculty members, including confrontation with administrators and state or private agents of control (as described by Brown and Golden, 1973:202-282 and Fendrich, 1976). Such confrontation, past and present, centers on the following general issues:

1. What are professors supposed to do?
2. What should be the conditions of their employment?
3. How will what they do be evaluated and rewarded, and by whom?
4. How will this affect the quality of teaching and research?

These simple questions mask a host of specific issues: the competition between production and dissemination of knowledge (should there be increasing specialization by individuals and/or institutions?); the limitation of academic freedom, tenure, teaching loads, seniority, definition of merit and means of evaluation (by peers, administrators, students?), and creating standards for appeal of evaluations and actions by administrators. No universal resolution of these issues seems likely but, case by case, a public policy will emerge from cumulative bargaining. The shape of that policy will be influenced by the adversaries in these political struggles. Some knowledge about the types of unions, their memberships, and the general context of such memberships permits speculation about the shape of public policy to come.

The Structure of union membership. Here I summarize a report on correlates of membership in the American Association of University Professors (AAUP), the National Education Association (NEA), and/or the American Federation of Teachers (AFT).[4] That study examined relationships between membership in each of these organizations and the profes-

---

[4] See Lewis Rhodes, "Union Support and Status Security," presented at the annual meeting of the American Educational Research Association, Washington, D.C., April, 1975. Copies of this paper which includes tables resulting from the multiple classification analysis (not shown here) may be obtained by writing the author.

sors's organizational setting, his or her career situation, research orientation and degree of conservatism by an ex-post-facto analysis of data on 7,325 full-time teaching faculty in the United States for the academic year 1972-1973. The organizational setting of individuals in the sample was defined by region,[5] public or private control, and type (two-year, four-year, or PhD-granting campuses). Career characteristics were limited to rank, tenure, and highest degree. Orientation was determined by the quality of the college where the highest degree was obtained,[6] teaching field (collapsed into three categories relatively homogeneous regarding orientation and union membership: the humanities and social sciences, versus education, versus the remaining fields), and attitudes toward research. Two attitude scales were formed, one to indicate research orientation and the other to indicate conservatism.[7] Multivariate analysis was employed to assess interplay between organizational setting, career situation, research orientation, conservatism and membership in each of the three faculty organizations. Although the income of the faculty member seemed the most obvious correlate of union membership, the relationship was in fact unimportant. Race and sex of subject were excluded from this discussion for the same reason.

Table 1 shows the simple percentage of faculty belonging to each of three organizations for every category of each of the indicators of site, career, research orientation and conservatism. Region, type and control of institution make appreciable differences in the case of each of the three organizations. Furthermore, the effects of region, type, and control are not additive.[8] Indicators of career situation tend to be additive: tenured full professors with PhD's from highly rated graduate schools are more likely to belong to AAUP, especially if they teach humanities or one of the social sciences. Conversely, NEA membership is largely drawn from non-PhD's at the rank of instructor or lecturer, recruited from unranked graduate schools and concentrated in the field of education. However, the membership is more likely to be tenured than not. AFT contains a mixed group: concentrated in the lower ranks and slightly less likely to have a doctorate, the members are more likely to be drawn from a ranked graduate school and are somewhat more likely to teach in either the humanities or social sciences.

Research orientation doesn't differentiate much between members and nonmembers of unions, except that AAUP members are more likely to be research oriented. Both AAUP and AFT draw more members from the less conservative faculty, while NEA tends to draw members from the more conservative faculty.

Characteristics denoting the type and location of the institution in which professors teach seems to outweigh other considerations in accounting for membership. There are striking differences in the non-additive effects of region, type of college, and public or private con-

---

[5] There are four regions: "Atlantic" includes Eastern seaboard states through Maryland; "Midwest" includes Northern states from Ohio as far west as Nebraska and as far south as Kansas and Missouri; "South" includes Kentucky, West Virginia and states to the south and west as far as Arkansas and Louisiana; and "West" includes Oklahoma, Texas, mountain and Pacific states.

[6] Quality of graduate program was coded according to the rating by Roose and Anderson (1970). Smaller graduate programs not rated by Roose and Anderson are designated as "no rating" in the present study.

[7] Two pools of items were selected from the questionnaire, one of which appeared to have face validity as indicating research orientation; the other appeared to indicate conservatism. Factor analyses (principal-factor solution) were performed on each item pool and factors were rotated according to varimax criteria. After items with unsatisfactory loadings were eliminated, the remaining items loading on these factors were standardized, weighted by factor scores and summated for each scale. A sample item on the research is, " . . . to develop the ability to pursue research" in teaching students is "essential" or "very important." Sample items on the conservatism scale include, "I consider myself to be politically conservative" (agree) and "Claims of discrimination against women are exaggerated" (agree).

[8] Leo Goodman's method of testing for higher-order interactions involving nominal or ordinal variables were used (see Davis, 1974 for a review).

TABLE 1

Teaching Faculty in Higher Educational Institutions of the United States,
1972–73: Percent Belonging to AAUP, AFT, and NEA by Region, Type of College
Control, Degree, Quality of Degree, Teaching Field,
Research Orientation, Rank, Tenure, and Conservatism

Characteristic of College or Faculty Member	AAUP	AFT	NEA
Region			
Atlantic	32.8	9.2	20.3
Midwest	28.2	6.7	18.0
South	27.6	.6	19.0
West	17 9	5.5	15.9
Type of College			
University	26.7	2.0	11.2
4-Year	31.7	8.9	17.9
2-Year	15.6	14.1	40.7
Control			
Public	22.5	9.4	24.7
Private	34.6	1.6	14.0
Quality of Highest Degree			
College not rated	23.0	6.3	26.1
Low rating	28.3	6.0	18.5
High rating	33.9	8.1	11.2
Teaching Field			
Physical sciences, business, engineering	22.3	4.9	17.6
Education	22.7	6.4	56.6
Humanities and social sciences	36.0	9.6	14.3
Research Orientation			
Low	24.9	6.8	21.5
High	29.2	6.2	20.2
Highest Degree			
No doctorate	20.2	6.8	30.5
PhD	32.7	6.2	15.2
Rank			
Instructor or lecturer	15.3	10.9	28.4
Assistant or associate professor	29.5	5.7	19.2
Full professor	35.1	4.6	17.8
Tenure			
No	19.4	5.5	16.4
Yes	30.4	8.8	23.1
Conservatism			
Low	32.5	8.1	16.2
High	20.0	4.8	26.0

trol.[9] Cross-classification by these aspects of site reveals heavy concentration of each type of organization in differing contexts. AAUP membership is particularly concentrated in *private* four-year colleges, especially those in the Atlantic states, but also to a lesser extent in the South and West. Over-representation in the public sector is confined to four-year colleges in the Midwest; elsewhere it tends to be under-represented. NEA is uniformly under-represented in PhD-granting universities and over-represented in the two-year public institutions everywhere except in the South. Only in the Atlantic states is it over-represented in four-year public schools. AFT is under-represented everywhere except for public four-year colleges in the Atlantic states and the West and in two-year public schools in the Midwest.

These site-type-control differences are largely independent of career setting, research orientation, or conservatism. Membership in AAUP would be greater in two-year colleges

---

[9] Lack of space prevented inclusion of these tables. Copies of the tables may be obtained from the author at Department of Sociology, F.S.U., Tallahassee, Fl.

except for the conservatism of their faculties. Reduced NEA membership in private universities is partly due to under-representation of persons in the education field at such places. AFT membership is a consequence of site and type of school except that orientation and conservatism have a suppressant effect on facilities of Atlantic two-year colleges.

In sum, the context effects of location and type of school appear to be the major determinants of what type of organization, if any, a professor will join; his or her options are defined and set by the character of the college and its socio-political environment.

Implications of the findings for public policy. The percentage of some 2,600 institutions of higher education whose faculties have chosen bargaining agents has increased from twelve to eighteen percent (from 314 to 461, with fifty-nine places rejecting union bargaining agents—thirty-six of these were private four-year colleges; Tice, 1973: 180, and *Chronicle of Higher Education:* 1976) over the three years since the data were gathered for this study. It seems likely that unionization will increase as rapidly as enabling legislation is passed. Faculty unionization has followed the pattern set by unionization in general: diffusion from the most-urbanized, most-industrialized states to the less urbanized and industrialized states.

Growth was not even: AFT grew the most rapidly, NEA was next and AAUP was the slowest. NEA added the largest number of campuses in the past year, but these gains were largely confined to two-year colleges. AFT gained most in Florida, New York, and Illinois, particularly among public four-year colleges and universities. AAUP did well at private four-year colleges. These trends suggest that neither the growth nor the effects of unionization will be uniform by type of school or geographic location. The most prestigious universities (especially the private ones) may be the last to unionize, given the research entrepreneurship, autonomy, and economic advantage of their senior faculties. If unionization comes, AAUP seems to be the most likely agent for such places, given its current success at several of the stronger universities (e.g., Rutgers and Temple). My data suggest that AAUP has greater appeal for full professors whose own PhD's are from these same prestigious universities. AFT is experiencing success in some large multiversity systems (New York and Florida). NEA's strength resides in the large body of junior-college or community college teachers who have less than a doctorate, who are less often research-oriented, and who are more often teachers in the field of education.

The variation by type of school and faculty member in affiliating with or rejecting these several types of bargaining agents suggests that higher education in America may become more functionally specialized than it is now. Research entrepreneurs ("stars") now located at soon-to-be-unionized multiversities may flee to nonunionized universities or to private research firms, taking their grants with them. If that happens, the consequences will be severe, since as much as a seventh of the total funding of public universities comes from federal and state funded research (Grant and Lind, 1973:105).

Conditions of employment should become more standard according to either AAUP, AFT, or NEA traditions. Collectively, professors in middle- and lower-prestige universities may be able to arrest the continuing erosion of professional autonomy by administrators and state bureaucracies if they are successful in generating sufficient public concern and support for bargaining efforts. These and other implications may be arranged in the order of the four policy issues set fourth at the beginning of this article:

1. What are professors supposed to do? The data and trends reported here suggest that there will be increased division of labor by type and location of institution. Within state-wide systems, it is likely that there will be greater standardization of duties (e.g., examinations, teaching loads, time for scholarship such as sabbaticals). Unless public policy provides for innovative or eccentric approaches through actions of the unions themselves or of other

interested parties, the standardization now imposed externally by state bureaucracies will increase.

2. What should be the conditions of employment? Assuming that political activity of unions is more systematic, and therefore more successful, in competing for state or private funding, conditions should improve for the community colleges and for all but the most-favored sectors of the multiversities. Negotiation will produce public policies that guarantee academic freedom and tenure in practice rather than in theory through carefully specified appeal or grievance procedures. This offers no new advantage to the most prestigious universities which already enjoy such guarantees.

3. How will professors be evaluated, and by whom? Some charge that student evaluation has led to grade inflation and emphasis on entertainment rather than communicating knowledge. Evaluation by standardized testing is another alternative (Murphy and Cohen, 1974). Whether unionization will reinforce peer evaluation (already enjoyed by faculty at prestigious institutions) or emphasis on seniority remains to be seen. It seems likely that research activity will receive greater rewards in universities emphasizing the orientation of AAUP members in our data.

4. How will this affect teaching and research? Union bargaining could be a vehicle for resisting further bureaucracy in classroom procedures. This could benefit students. Public policy is needed to guarantee that universities remain (or become—in some cases) free market places for ideas. Unions could be instrumental in generating public support. If research activity and hence graduate education, becomes more concentrated, such a trend would be counter to a public policy of equality of opportunity. Professors and students outside research centers would be more isolated. Either the equality policy may be revised or an alternative may be explored (such as a "year at MIT" instead of "a year abroad").

REFERENCES

Brown, Michael and Amy Golden
  1973   Collective Behavior. Pacific Palisades, Ca.: Goodyear.
Chronicle of Higher Education
  1976   "Fact file." 12(May, 31) p. 4.
Davis, James A.
  1974   "Hierarchial models for significance tests in multivariate contingency tables: an exigisis of Goodman's recent papers." in H. L. Costner (ed.) Sociological Methdology 1973-74. San Francisco: Josey-Bass.
Fendrich, James M.
  1976   "Unions help faculty who help themselves." Paper presented to the annual meeting of the American Sociological Association. New York, August.
Feuille, Peter and James Blandin
  1976   "University faculty and attitudinal militancy toward the employment relationship." Sociology of Education. 49(April)139-145.
Grant, W. Vance and C. George Lind
  1973   Digest of Educational Statistics. Washington, D.C.: National Center for Educational Statistics.
Ladd, Everett Carl, Jr. and Seymour Martin Lipset
  1973   Professors, Unions and American Higher Education. Washington, D.C.: American Enterprise Institute for Policy Research.
  1975   The Divided Academy. New York: W. W. Norton.
Murphy, Jerome T. and David K. Cohen
  1974   "Accountibility in education—the Michigan experience." The Public Interest. 36:53-81.
Nixon, Howard L., II
  1975   "Faculty support of traditional labor tactics on campus." Sociology of Education. 48:276-286.
Roose, Kenneth and Charles Anderson
  1970   A Rating of Graduate Programs. Washington, D.C.: American Council on Education.
Suntrup, Edward L. and Mavio F. Bognanno
  1976   Survey of recent books on unionism in higher education. Contemporary Sociology. 5:17-19.
Tice, Terrence N.
  1973   Faculty Bargaining in the Seventies. Ann Arbor: Institute of Continuing Legal Education.

LEVEL AND RATE OF DESEGREGATION AND WHITE ENROLLMENT DECLINE IN A BIG CITY SCHOOL DISTRICT

DANIEL U. LEVINE
and
JEANIE KEENY MEYER

Review of the literature on "white flight" from desegregated schools indicated that recent controversies have been partly resolved through agreement that this is most likely to occur in city districts with high proportions
of minority students surrounded by largely white suburbs. Enrollment
data from 1956 to 1974 for the Kansas City, Missouri Public Schools were
examined to test this hypothesis. The findings were consistent with the
conclusion that white enrollment decline tended to accelerate in schools
with a relatively high percentage of black students (above about 30%)
and/or a recent rapid increase in the percentage of black students.

INTRODUCTION

During the past few years a major research controversy has arisen on the issue of whether
or not desegregation accelerates the enrollment decline of whites from central city public
school districts. Until 1975, only a few studies dealt with this issue. Among these were
studies in which Giles, Cataldo, and Gatlin (1974) reported data which led them to conclude
that there is no clear "tipping point" or "threshold" at an hypothesized thirty percent
minority level, beyond which schools tend to resegregate more rapidly. These studies, however, were conducted in Florida, which has county-wide school districts surrounded by
districts also undergoing desegregation; for this reason the conclusions might not be applicable in states outside the South, generally lacking state-wide desegregation efforts inhibiting
white flight by shutting off avenues of escape from systematic desegregation plans.

In the spring of 1975, Coleman (1975), reported on the preliminary results of a study he
and his colleagues conducted, using data on the degree to which white and black students
attended segregated schools between 1968 and 1973. To focus on the issue of whether
segregation in relatively large districts (25,000 or more students) was perpetuated o: increased
through "segregating responses on the part of whites" to desegregation, Coleman and his
colleagues conducted a separate analysis on the seventy largest central city school districts
in the United States. Using regression analysis, they concluded that among the twenty
largest districts, there was an increase of seventeen percent in the proportion of whites
leaving districts in which the percentage of black students was fifty percent and the increase
in black proportion was five percent in the preceding two years, as compared with hypothetical estimates for whites leaving districts with no black students and no increase in
proportion black.

The release of this preliminary report and the widespread publicity it received precipitated
considerable discussion in professional publications and the popular press. Professional
reactions were mostly critical of the methods Coleman and his colleagues used in their
study and the conclusions drawn; critics did not believe they substantiated the existence of
a so-called "white flight" phenomenon over and beyond natural changes occurring in urban
areas from such causes as deterioration of housing stock.

For example, Coleman's conclusions were disputed by Farley (1975), who collected data
on forty Southern and seventy-five Northern or Western city school districts enrolling
sixty percent of the nation's black elementary students and twenty percent of the nation's
white elementary students. Utilizing a measure of segregation based on how much schools

in these districts were similar or dissimilar to the respective district percentages, Farley studied changes in enrollment between 1967 and 1972 and concluded that neither in the South or North "is there a significant relationship between school integration and white flight."

After examining patterns in a number of cities which actively implemented integration plans, however, Farley further concluded that his data were

> . . . consistent with the hypothesis that whites fear integrated schools with large black enrollments and withdraw their children from public schools prior to integration. They also are consistent with many other hypotheses. Cities with a high proportion black may have particularly unfavorable tax bases, may be losing employment, may be viewed by whites as dangerous or may have an especially old stock of housing. . . . when public schools are desegregated or when they become predominantly black, some white parents –perhaps many–hasten their move away from the central city. However, whites [also] are moving out of central cities for many other reasons.

Jackson (1975) identified several "methodological limitations" in Coleman's approach, then reanalyzed the data, and added additional data dealing separately with the nineteen largest school districts and fifty next largest districts. These analyses suggested "rather different findings and conclusions" from those of Coleman:

> . . . First, in the 69 largest school districts the rate of white public school enrollment declines between 1970-72 were generally greater in districts with a higher proportion of blacks. Second, in the 19 largest districts (all in large cities) the declines in white enrollment over this period were also generally higher in districts with greater increases between 1968-1970 in the extent to which the average white pupil had black schoolmates, and this relation holds even after controlling for a number of other factors. Third, in the 19 largest districts, declines in white public school enrollment are *not* consistently related to changes between 1968-1970 in the degree of segregation within the districts . . . Fourth, in the 50 next largest districts declines in white public school enrollment are not related to either changes in the degree of racial proximity or changes in the degree of desegregation, at least not after controlling for the *district's* proportion of blacks [original italics].

One of the most virulent criticisms of Coleman's methods and conclusions originated with Rossell (1975), who, after reporting the results of her own analysis of desegregation and enrollment trends in seventy large and medium sized northern school districts, concluded that

> This study . . . shows with clear, verifiable data, that there is little or no white flight as a result of school desegregation . . . Coleman has pulled off one of the great swindles of public policy research.

Rossell's data dealt with school racial composition over a ten year period from 1963 to 1973. Her data-gathering and analytic methods incorporated several advances over previous studies, including collection of data directly from persons in the cities in the sample, utilization of longitudinal data covering a longer time span, construction of a useful quantitative measure of the proportion of black and white students reassigned for the purposes of school integration and statistics for the analysis of time-series trends. In addition, Rossell presented considerable raw data so that readers could check her analysis and draw their own conclusions.

As with other studies examining relationships between school integration and white enrollment decline, Rossell's research still presents problems involving the definition of desegregation, the types of school districts which should be included in a single analysis (e.g. central city only or city and suburban), and the proper unit for analysis (e.g. school level, district level, metropolitan level). Such issues are critical because they determine whether one ends by comparing entities which may be very different with respect to "white flight," as when heavily-minority central city districts ringed by predominantly white suburban districts are compared with county-level districts adjacent to districts already having substantial desegregation. Logically, the likelihood of white withdrawal from the public schools following desegregation is much greater in the former than in the latter case.

Rossell attempted to minimize such differentials in constituting her sample but did not entirely succeed because of the need to maintain a relatively large sample size in order to carry out multivariate analysis. In addition, her study takes little account of the possibility that imminent large-scale desegregation such as might follow a court order may stimulate as much or more white withdrawal before desegregation as after. Hence her method of time series analysis may be misleading for cities like San Francisco, where the rate of white withdrawal increased to 4.1 percent two years before a major desegregation plan was implemented and then fell off to three percent after desegregation.

Still another major critique of Coleman's conclusions has been prepared by Green and Pettigrew (1975), who painstakingly reviewed the development of his analysis at four points in time and concluded that "there has been a confusion between his limited research and his sweeping views against court-ordered desegregation." More specifically, Green and Pettigrew reanalyzed Coleman's data and also introduced data of their own before reaching the following conclusions concerning the relationship between desegregation and white enrollment decline in the public schools:

1. There has been an enormous, long-term trend of whites leaving the central cities for the suburbs and blacks coming into the largest central cities.

2. There is agreement among the studies that there is little or no effect of desegregation on the "white flight" of students in medium- and smaller-sized cities.

3. There is also agreement that there is little or no effect of desegregation on the "white flight" of students in metropolitan-wide districts.

4. Desegregation required by federal court orders has not had different effects on "white flight" from other desegregation of equal magnitude.

5. The loss of white and black students from large urban school systems is significantly related to the proportion of black students in the systems.

6. Extensive school desegregation in the largest, non-metropolitan school districts, particularly in the South, may hasten the "white flight" of students in the first year of the process; but at least part of this effect may be compensated for in later years.

More recently, Wegman (1976) reviewed the research dealing with change in school racial composition following desegregation and reached tentative conclusions generally in agreement with those of Green and Pettigrew:

White flight may or may not occur. . . . The degree of white flight to be expected when there is governmental intervention to desegregate schools may vary depending on the proportion of minority students who are being assigned to a given school, and the social class gap between the minority and white students.

Both these conditions,—high minority proportion and large social class gap between minority and white students,—tend to be more characteristic of big city school districts than of small city or suburban school districts.

In addition, Wegman also identified a number of additional variables which appear to play a part in determining whether white enrollment decline accelerates following desegregation. For example, his review of the literature suggested that non-entrance of whites (i.e. failure to enroll students in local public schools) often may be more important than withdrawal of currently-enrolled children, depending on the type and rate at which racial transition occurs in neighborhood housing. Similarly, his analysis suggested that court-ordered desegregation may have differing effects on white enrollment than does desegregation attributable to neighborhood change, and that the pace and level of desegregation may affect decisions to withdraw from or not enroll children in the public schools. These findings suggest that it often is misleading to draw conclusions from samples not accounting for building- or neighborhood- level conditions and changes in school composition.

To a degree, the differences of opinion among researchers studying white withdrawal and school desegregation now have been reduced to a minimum following the most recent re-analysis Coleman and his colleagues conducted on their own data. Responding to the criticisms of Jackson and other critics, Coleman (1976), reported that the results of his latest analysis

> . . . show that the effect of desegregation on white loss is dramatically different for a city that has largely black schools and largely white suburbs. . . . and for a city that has a small proportion of blacks and no sharp racial differences between city and suburbs. . . . The former condition characterizes the larger, older, Northern and Eastern cities, while the latter more nearly characterizes new cities in the West, and Southern cities with county-wide school districts. . . .

In short, for at least some of the participants in the controversy on desegregation research occurring during the past two years, there is now explicit agreement that accelerated white withdrawal connected with school desegregation is most likely to occur in large Northern districts with a relatively high proportion of minority students surrounded by predominantly white suburban districts.

One of the major lessons emerging from the controversy among researchers concerning "white flight" is that school districts with greatly differing characteristics in social class and racial composition, city-suburban differentiation, regional location, type and extent of desegregation action, and other important characteristics should not be lumped together in trying to determine whether desegregation accelerates the withdrawal or decrease in enrollment of white students in the schools. Respecting this conclusion, it would be useful to have more case studies of enrollment patterns in individual school districts. Such studies allow for longitudinal analysis at the individual school building level to determine whether the converging views of researchers using district-level data are confirmed by events at the level at which the phenomena in question actually occur. The purpose of the present study is to provide such an analysis for the Kansas City, Missouri Public School District, a relatively large central city school district in the lower Midwest.

METHODS AND RESULTS

The Kansas City, Missouri, Public School District is a central city district increasing in percentage of minority students for most of the past twenty years. The number of white students declined from 32,412 in 1956 to 21,405 in 1976, while the number of black students increased from 10,076 to 33,001.

Located in a metropolitan area with a 1970 population of 1,253,916, the district serves only part of Kansas City, Missouri, which also includes all or part of twelve other school districts. However, most of the minority population of the city is included within the Kansas City School District. As of 1972-1973, the percentage of minority students in the district was fifty-four percent, as compared with eight percent for the public school population of the remainder of the metropolitan area.

Although data on the percentage of minority students inside and outside the district in 1950 and 1960 are not available, it is clear that compared with surrounding districts, the Kansas City School District has had a relatively high proportion of minority students throughout this period, during which time many of its schools have changed from predominantly white, to desegregated, to predominantly black. In addition, the median 1970 family income within the district ($8803) already was considerably lower than that of the metropolitan area as a whole ($10,568).

To determine whether white enrollment decline in the district has been associated with level and rate of desegregation at the school building level, data were examined for all the seventy-five schools serving as elementary schools during all or most of the period between 1956 and 1975.

Note that nearly all of the desegregation which occurred in the Kansas City School District during the period under study was "natural"; i.e. there was no court-ordered desegregation plan and only a few schools were briefly desegregated in a limited fashion through busing in order to relieve over-crowding or to help obtain federal grants available to desegregated school districts.

Note also that certain schools may be categorized as having experienced an acceleration of white enrollment decline more than once in this analysis, as in the case of a school where white enrollment decline might change from ten percent in one four-year period to twenty and then thirty percent in the following two four-year periods.

1. *Relationship between percentage of black enrollment and increase in black enrollment percentage in subsequent years.* It is frequently hypothesized that urban schools with a relatively high percentage of minority students (e.g. thirty to fifty percent) are more likely to become resegregated (predominantly black) than are schools where minority students constitute a smaller proportion of the student body. Other things being equal, white parents may tend to withdraw their children more readily from schools they perceive are likely to become predominantly non-white than from schools perceived as having potential for stable integration. This tendency might be particularly evident if members of an incoming minority group were lower in socio-economic status or if, as sometimes happens, some white parents merely assumed that incoming minority students were likely to be socioeconomically disadvantaged.

To investigate the relationship between percentage of black students and subsequent racial change in the Kansas City, Missouri, Public Schools, changes in percentage of black students were compared over two year periods for three groups of schools which for selected years between 1956 and 1974 had the following proportions of black students: A) 15 to 29%; B) 30-45%; and C) 46 to 60%.

As shown by the data in Table 1, schools with a proportion of black students between fifteen and twenty-nine percent have had a much smaller increase in percentage of black during the subsequent two year period than have schools with between thirty and sixty percent black students. Although the numbers in the comparison groups for any one year are too small to draw firm conclusions; overall, the average increase in the percentage of black students in the subsequent two year period among schools with a percentage of black students between fifteen and twenty-nine was 10.5% (485 ÷ 46); the comparable increases for schools between thirty and forty-five percent black and between forty-six and sixty percent black were 18.2% (436 ÷ 24) and 28.2% (310 ÷ 11), respectively. These findings suggest that Kansas City schools with a percentage of black students between fifteen and twenty-nine were more likely to remain stably integrated, at least for the following two year period, than were schools with a higher percentage of black enrollment.

It should be mentioned that the group of Kansas City schools which had between fifteen and twenty-nine percent black students probably has included a higher proportion of schools where black students were bused in to relieve overcrowding elsewhere, than did schools in the other two groups. To the extent that the groups might have differed in this way, our findings may be partly due to school board policies and practicalities limiting transportation

TABLE 1

*Comparisons of Increases in Percentages of Black Students
Over Two Year Periods for Kansas City Elementary Schools With Differing
Percentages of Black Students* in Selected Years Between 1956 and 1972*

*A) Schools 15 to 29 Percent Black in Designated Year
B) Schools 30 to 45 Percent Black in Designated Year
C) Schools 46 to 60 Percent Black in Designated Year

Year for Comparison Groups	Subsequent Time Period for Comparison and Average Percentage of Increase in Black Students
1958	*1958–1960* A (N = 3) 8.3% B (N = 1) 2% C (N = 1) 38%
1960	*1960–1962* A (N = 5) 16.3% B (N = 3) 21% C (N = 1) 39%
1962	*1962–1964* A (N = 7) 14.3% B (N = 2) 3.2% C (N = 3) 22.5%
1964	*1964–1966* A (N = 3) 13.7% B (N = 4) 8.2% C (N = 2) 21.8%
1966	*1966–1968* A (N = 6) 5.8% B (N = 2) 27.1% C (N = 1) 36.4%
1968	*1968–1970* A (N = 6) 7.7% B (N = 2) 14.8% C (N = 1) 36.4%
1970	*1970–1972* A (N = 5) 7.7% B (N = 4) 29.8% C (N = 1) 29.9%
1971	*1971–1973* A (N = 7) 13.3% B (N = 4) 17.1% C (N = 1) 19.3%
1972	*1972–1974* A (N = 4) 6.2% B (N = 2) 30.0% C (N = 0) —

into the schools in question, and to the likelihood that neighborhoods where these schools are located probably were not undergoing as rapid racial turnover as was true among schools with thirty to sixty percent black enrollment. On the other hand, schools with a black enrollment between forty-five and sixty percent has less "room" to increase substantially in black enrollment in subsequent years than did schools between fifteen and thirty percent black. Taken together, our findings appear to confirm the hypothesis that schools reaching an hypothetical "threshold" in percentage of minority students are more likely to become

TABLE 2

Comparison of Increases in Percentages of Black Students Over Two Year Periods for Kansas City Elementary Schools in Which the Increase in Percentage of Black Students in the Preceding One or Two Year Period Was:
A) One to Ten Percent and B) More Than Ten Percent *

*A) Schools in Which the Increase in Black Students in Designated Time Period Was Between One and Ten Percent
B) Schools in Which the Increase in Black Students in Designated Time Period Was More Than Ten Percent

Time Period for Choice of Comparison Groups	Subsequent Time Period for Comparison and Average Percentage of Increase in Black Students
1956–1958	*1958–1960* A (N = 8) 9.0% B (N = 6) 20.8%
1958–1960	*1960–1962* A (N = 9) 9.6% B (N = 6) 27.3%
1960–1962	*1962–1964* A (N = 8) 7.9% B (N = 8) 17.3%
1962–1964	*1964–1966* A (N = 11) 9.6% B (N = 7) 14.1%
1964–1966	*1966–1968* A (N = 10) 8.9% B (N = 8) 13.5%
1966–1968	*1968–1970* A (N = 9) 6.6% B (N = 8) 18.2%
1968–1970	*1971–1973* A (N = 13) 5.9% B (N = 16) 11.1%
1970–1971	*1971–1973* A (N = 11) 8.8% B (N = 6) 19.1%
1971–1972	*1972–1974* A (N = 11) 4.4% B (N = 3) 11.2%

predominantly minority than schools with a smaller proportion of minority students. This threshold probably varies in accordance with a number of local conditions such as perceptions of neighborhood services, previous history in a community, social class mixture in school and community, and quality of educational leadership and programming in local schools. For this reason we made no attempt to identify any precise tipping point in the Kansas City, Missouri Public Schools. It does appear, however, that once Kansas City schools have reached a percentage of thirty to sixty percent black, they have tended to become nearly all black in pupil composition during subsequent years.

2. *Relationship between percentage of increase in black enrollment and increase in black enrollment percentage in subsequent years.* It frequently is hypothesized that a rapid increase in the percentage of black students enrolled in a school is more likely to stimulate withdrawal among whites than would a less rapid or more gradual increase. To examine this possibility,

we calculated the percentage of increase in black enrollment for Kansas City elementary schools for various one and two year periods between 1956 and 1972, and then compared the subsequent increase in the following two-year period for two groups of schools: those in which the percentage of black students increased from one to ten percent, and those in which the percentage of black students increased by more than ten percent.

As shown in Table 2, schools where the percentage of black students increased by more than ten percent during the time periods examined between 1956 and 1972 had a much higher increase in percentage of black students during the subsequent two year period than did schools where black enrollment increased from one to ten percent. On six of the nine comparisons, the increase in percent black among the former group (more than ten percent) was at least double that among the latter group (one to ten percent). For the schools with an increase in black enrollment of more than ten percent, the average increase in black enroll-ment during the following two year period was 16.25% (1105 ÷ 68); for schools where the percentage of black enrollment increased from one to ten percent, the comparable average increase was 7.8% (698 ÷ 90). These results indicate that schools experiencing a substantial and relatively rapid increase in percentage black (i.e. ten percent or more during a one or two year period) also had a much larger subsequent increase in percentage black and, by implication, a much larger decrease in white students, than did schools in which desegrega-tion occurred less rapidly and precipitously.

To examine the relationships further between percent black at several levels of desegrega-tion and subsequent racial composition, we identified four levels of desegregation (the three levels shown in Table 1 plus schools sixty-one to eighty percent black) for selected years between 1960 and 1970 and then examined the percent of black enrollment in these schools four to six years later.

As shown in Table 3, schools at various levels of desegregation generally tended to become resegregated in the following four or six year period.[1] However, beginning in the 1966 comparison, schools with a percentage of black students between fifteen and twenty-nine tended to remain stably desegregated and did not have a much higher proportion of black students, on the average, four to six years later.

This pattern may indicate that there is a good chance to maintain desegregation in Kansas City schools as long as the percentage of minority students is not much over thirty percent. It may also be true, however that schools between thirty and forty-five percent black can also maintain a good racial balance—schools in this range in the 1966, 1968, and 1970 periods became predominantly black in subsequent years, but there were only eleven schools in these categories and one cannot draw confident conclusions from so small a sample.

3. *Changes in the number of white students in schools with differing percentages of black students.* One additional way to examine the possibility that decline in the enrollment of white students is associated with level of desegregation is to consider the actual number of white students in schools at differing levels of desegregation and determine the degree to which white enrollment may be rising or falling. This approach has the advantage of being independent of general enrollment changes which may be occurring and which might obscure the relationship between desegregation and white withdrawal.

To examine this possibility we computed a ratio based on the number of white students in 1974 divided by the number of white students in 1968 for elementary schools with the following percentages of black students in 1968: fifteen to twenty-nine; thirty to forty-five;

---

[1] The numbers shown in Table 3 reflect the fact that more KCSD elementary schools became desegre-gated and resegregated in the latter 1960's than in the early 1970's, primarily because schools on the Southeast Side were undergoing rapid racial change in the latter period.

TABLE 3

*Comparisons of Percentage of Black Students Four to Six Years Following Selected Years and Levels of Desegregation Among Kansas City Elementary Schools**

*A) Schools 15 to 29 Black in Designated Year
B)   "   30 to 45   "   "   "   "
C)   "   46 to 60   "   "   "   "
D)   "   61 to 80   "   "   "   "

Year for Comparison Groups	Subsequent Time Period for Comparison and Average Percent of Black Students for Comparison Groups**
1960	*1966* A (N = 5) 54.6% B (N = 3) 66.7% C (N = 1) 97.9% D (N = 0) —
1962	*1966* A (N = 5) 45.5% B (N = 2) 40.1% C (N = 3) 83.9% D (N = 0) —
1964	*1970* A (N = 4) 51.2% B (N = 4) 41.3% C (N = 2) 92.8% D (N = 1) 97.5%
1966	*1970* A (N = 9) 24.3% B (N = 4) 56.2% C (N = 2) 57.0% D (N = 2) 92.8%
1968	*1974* A (N = 10) 29.8% B (N = 4) 60.0% C (N = 1) 97.1% D (N = 4) 95.5%
1970	*1974* A (N = 8) 31.9% B (N = 3) 76.4% C (N = 1) 95.0% D (N = 2) 99.9%

**Numbers of schools in the categories differ between Table 1 and Table 3 due to missing data for some schools in some years. Group D was not included in the Table 1 analysis because there was too little room for a percentage increase to allow for meaningful analysis.

forty-six to sixty; and sixty-one to eighty. A high ratio represents a case in which the number of whites in 1974 was nearly as high as in 1968, and a low ratio represents a case in which there were fewer whites in 1974 than in 1968.

As shown in Table 4, the number of white students in 1974 as compared with 1968 was substantially higher (1974-1968 ratio = .45) at the ten schools in which black students constituted between fifteen and twenty-nine percent of the enrollment in 1968 than at the nine schools where black students constituted between thrity and eighty percent of the enrollment. This finding suggests that white enrollment declined in the latter schools at a much more rapid rate than was true at the schools where black students constituted less than thirty percent of the enrollment.

TABLE 4

Ratio of White Students in 1874 to White Students in 1968 for
. Schools with Differing Percentages of Black Students in 1968

Percentage of Black Students	Number of Schools	Number of White Students	Ratio of White Students 1964/1968
15–29	(10)	(4331)	.45
30–45	(4)	(1240)	.27
46–60	(1)	(428)	.03
61–80	(4)	(948)	.08

4. *Statistical correlation between changes in racial composition in two year periods.* Another way to examine the question of whether increases in black enrollment in one time period are associated with still higher increases in subsequent time periods is by computing the correlation between changes in racial composition at differing times.

To assess the relations between changes in elementary school racial composition during different time periods, we computed the correlation between increases in percentage of black enrollment for adjacent two year periods between 1956 and 1974. If schools increasing in percentage black enrollment during one time period also increase during the following time period, the correlation between these increases will be positive and significantly different from zero. Simple correlations between increases in percentage of black students in Kansas City elementary schools for the two year periods are shown in the second column of Table 5. To reduce confounding effects from schools with few or no black students during the 1960's, only thirty-three schools with at least two percent black enrollment in 1964 were included in this analysis.

The correlations in column two of Table 5 indicate that increases in percentage black in one two year period generally were associated with increases in the following two year period. They do not, however, indicate whether increases in earlier periods were associated with still larger increases in later periods. If the latter were the case, logging the scores should improve the correlations, because the logged scores would help to take account of curvilinearity in the relationships.

Actual plots for the two year periods between 1956 and 1974 were examined and several were found which suggested that many schools which increased in percentage black in one

TABLE 5

Correlations Between Increases in Percentage of Black Students
for Selected Two Year Periods Between 1956 and 1974

Time Period Examined	Correlation	p	Correlations Between Scores Transformed to Logarithms	p
1956 to 1958 with 1958 to 1960	.60	<.001	.57	<.001
1958 to 1960 with 1960 to 1962	.63	<.001	.70	<.001
1960 to 1962 with 1962 to 1964	.42	<.015	.63	<.001
1962 to 1964 with 1964 to 1966	.08	<.625	.46	<.007
1964 to 1966 with 1966 to 1968	.47	<.006	.62	<.001
1966 to 1968 with 1968 to 1970	−.08	<.638	.19	<.300
1968 to 1970 with 1970 to 1972	.00	<.976	.47	<.006
1970 to 1972 with 1972 to 1974	−.12	<.49	.14	<.450

period either had a sharp rise in the percentage black during the following period or continued to increase about the same amount as in the preceding period. In many cases, schools in this latter category were approaching one hundred percent black and had no more "room" to increase. Correlations among the logged data for the two year periods are shown in the fourth column of Table 5. Several of the correlations increased dramatically, particularly where they were not already quite high for data of this kind. Thus the data in Table 5 suggest that Kansas City schools frequently experienced an acceleration in the increase in their black enrollment percentage once they already had begun to increase in this characteristic during the 1956-1974 time period.

SUMMARY AND CONCLUSIONS

A review of the literature on white enrollment decline in desegregated schools indicated that the controversy that recently became so intense among researchers in this area has been at least partly resolved through agreement that such decline is most likely to occur in big city school districts with a relatively high proportion of minority students surrounded by largely white smaller districts. In addition, the literature underlines the difficulties of analyses mixing school districts which differ greatly in characteristics such as neighborhood housing patterns, thus suggesting the desirability of conducting longitudinal case studies of change in racial composition at the building level in individual districts.

The study reported on data from 1956 to 1974 on enrollment trends in the Kansas City, Missouri Public School District, a relatively large midwestern district surrounded by predominantly white smaller districts and undergoing decline in the proportion of white students for most of the period since 1956. If it is true that white enrollment decline is most likely to be accelerated by desegregation in districts of this type, longitudinal data on enrollment and racial composition in the Kansas City schools should clarify this phenomena.

Enrollment data were examined to determine whether level and rate of desegregation have been associated with decline in white enrollment in the district. Data on percentage of black students indicated that schools between fifteen and twenty-nine percent black increased eleven percent in percentage black during the subsequent two years, as compared with increases of eighteen and twenty-eight percent, respectively, for schools thirty to forty-five percent black and schools forty-six to sixty percent black. Analogously, schools which increased one to ten percent in proportion black during various one and two-year periods between 1956 and 1972 increased eight percent in proportion black during the following two years, as compared with sixteen percent for schools which increased more than ten percent in percentage black during the preceding period. Similarly, schools which had black percentages between fifteen and twenty-nine percent in 1966, 1968, and 1970 tended to remain desegregated, while schools with a higher percentage of black students became almost totally resegregated during the following four to six years. Examination of data on the ratio of white students in 1974 to 1968 indicated that the number of white students fell much faster during this period in schools thirty to eighty percent black than in schools fifteen to twenty-nine percent black. Finally, correlation data and scatterplots indicated that a number of schools experienced an accelerating increase in percentage of black students during the eighteen year period between 1956 and 1974.

Although most of these concern the percentage of white and black students and thus do not directly address the issue of whether white enrollment declines attendant to desegregation occurred in absolute terms, the findings were consistent with the conclusion that white enrollment decline has accelerated in schools with a relatively high percentage of black students (above about thirty percent) and/or a recent rapid increase in the percentage of black students. These findings suggest that policymakers should be cautious in determining the level and rate of desegregation to be obtained in the near future in big city school districts like Kansas City, if one of their goals is to avoid accelerating declines in white enrollment which have helped resegregate many big city schools during the past twenty years.

REFERENCES

Coleman, James. S.
  1975 "Recent trends in school integration," *Educational Researcher* 4:3-12.
  1976 "Coleman on Jackson and Coleman," *Educational Researcher* 5:3-4.
Farley, Reynolds
  1975 "School integration and white flight," University of Michigan Population Studies Center.
Giles, Michael W., Everett F. Cataldo, and Douglas Gatlin
  1974 "The impact of busing on white flight," *Social Science Quarterly*, 55:493-501.
Green, Robert L. and Thomas F. Pettigrew
  1975 "Public school desegregation and white flight: a reply to Professor Coleman." Paper prepared for United States Civil Rights Commission, Washington, D. C.
Jackson, Gregg
  1975 "Reanalysis of Coleman's 'recent trends in school integration,' " *Educational Researcher*, 4:21-25.
Rossell, Christine H.
  1975 "The political and social impact of school desegregation policy: a preliminary report." Paper presented at the annual meeting of the American Political Science Association, San Francisco.
Wegman, Robert G.
  1976 "White flight: some hypotheses." Paper presented at the annual meeting of the American Educational Research Association, San Francisco.